Questions in Dataviz

This book takes the reader through the process of learning and creating data visualisation, following a unique journey with questions every step of the way, ultimately discussing how and when to bend and break the "rules" to come up with creative, unique, and sometimes unconventional ideas. Each easy-to-follow chapter poses one key question and provides a selection of discussion points and relevant data visualisation examples throughout.

Structured in three parts: Section I poses questions around some fundamental data visualisation principles, while Section II introduces more advanced questions, challenging perceived best practices and suggesting when rules are open to interpretation or there to be broken. The questions in Section III introduce further themes leading on to specific ideas and visualisation projects in more detail.

Questions in Dataviz: A Design-Driven Process for Data Visualisation will appeal to any reader with an interest in creative or unconventional data visualisation and will be especially useful for those at a beginner or intermediate level looking for inspiration and alternative ways to deploy their data visualisation skills outside of conventional business charts.

T0384449

AK Peters Visualization Series

This series aims to capture new developments and summarize what is known over the whole spectrum of visualization by publishing a broad range of text-books, reference works, and handbooks. It will contain books from all subfields of visualization, including visual analytics, information visualization, and scientific visualization. The scope will largely follow the calls of the major conferences such as VIS: techniques, algorithms, theoretical foundations and models, quantitative and qualitative evaluation, design studies, and applications.

SERIES EDITORS:

Tamara Munzner, *University of British Columbia, Vancouver, Canada*
Alberto Cairo *University of Miami, USA*

RECENT TITLES:

Visualization Analysis and Design
Tamara Munzner

Information Theory Tools for Visualization
Min Chen, Miquel Feixas, Ivan Viola, Anton Bardera, Han-Wei Shen, and Mateu Sbert

Data-Driven Storytelling
Nathalie Henry Riche, Christophe Hurter, Nicholas Diakopoulos, and Sheelagh Carpendale

Interactive Visual Data Analysis
Christian Tominski and Heidrun Schumann

Data Sketches
Nadieh Bremer and Shirley Wu

Visualizing with Text
Richard Brath

Mobile Data Visualization
Bongshin Lee, Raimund Dachselt, Petra Isenberg, and Eun Kyoung Choe

Questions in Dataviz
A Design-Driven Process for Data Visualisation
Neil Richards

For more information about this series please visit: https://www.routledge.com/AK-Peters-Visualization-Series/book-series/CRCVIS

Questions in Dataviz

A Design-Driven Process for Data Visualisation

Neil Richards

CRC Press
Taylor & Francis Group
Boca Raton London New York

CRC Press is an imprint of the
Taylor & Francis Group, an **informa** business

AN A K PETERS BOOK

First edition published 2023
by CRC Press
6000 Broken Sound Parkway NW, Suite 300, Boca Raton, FL 33487-2742

and by CRC Press
2 Park Square, Milton Park, Abingdon, Oxon, OX14 4RN

Library of Congress Cataloging in Publication Data
Names: Richards, Neil (Data visualization expert), author.
Title: Questions in dataviz : a design-driven process for data
visualisation / Neil Richards.
Description: First edition. | Boca Raton : AK Peters/CRC Press, 2023. |
Series: AK Peters visualization series
Identifiers: LCCN 2022019497 (print) | LCCN 2022019498 (ebook) |
ISBN 9781032146201 (hardback) | ISBN 9781032139449 (paperback) |
ISBN 9781003240211 (ebook)
Subjects: LCSH: Information visualization.
Classification: LCC QA76.9.I52 R53 2023 (print) | LCC QA76.9.I52 (ebook) |
DDC 001.4/226—dc23/eng/20220810
LC record available at https://lccn.loc.gov/2022019497
LC ebook record available at https://lccn.loc.gov/2022019498

ISBN: 978-1-032-14620-1 (hbk)
ISBN: 978-1-032-13944-9 (pbk)
ISBN: 978-1-003-24021-1 (ebk)

DOI: 10.1201/9781003240211

Typeset in Minion Pro
by codeMantra

Contents

Section II Challenging Questions

Section III Idea Questions

Preface

I worked for over 20 years in a Market Research data processing career.

Now I've started with what might be the most soul-destroying sentence I write in this whole book, so if you've made it past that first sentence, I hope you stay! I did enjoy those days, to a point, even though were many of them – the meticulous and logical process of collecting data, processing data and handing over vast printed decks of numbers to internal clients suited my analytical and introverted nature. And the limited programming knowledge needed to write online surveys was just about my technical level.

But I would never see the results of my labours. I never knew how survey results were interpreted or reacted upon, or even whether they were genuinely understood. I just saw a load of numbers printed in black on a lot of paper. A mathematician by trade I might have been, but even I didn't get inspired by that, the numbers told no story and held no attention. My limited interest in what I did for a living ended each day the second I logged off or left the office.

But then a few things happened around about the year 2015. First, I began to be more aware of data visualisation in the media world around me. I'd seen really engaging charts online or in print in the

Guardian, or National Geographic, or the BBC. I bought books aimed at the public such as David McCandless's *Information is Beautiful* – I loved the fact that more striking versions of these kinds of visually engaging yet data-filled charts were made for coffee table reading for a layperson like me. I began to realise that it was OK to be interested in this kind of thing, that there was a whole scientific and creative field that existed around it. As a consumer, data visualisation really appealed to me – it was a visual medium I could really understand.

Towards the end of the year, the small consultancy where I was working started looking at a software tool called Tableau, and I got hold of a trial version. We were interested in seeing results in a visual manner, not just as numbers on a printed deck or in an Excel spreadsheet. Tableau ticked the box as a Business Intelligence (BI) tool with great data visualisation capabilities, and that's why we made tentative exploratory steps in its direction.

But this book isn't about any one specific tool or methodology. This book is about a journey into data visualisation. And still in late 2015, my job abruptly came to an end. The Tableau experiment at work had not been a success but it had opened my eyes. What if people like me, with readily available Business Intelligence tools, could create these kinds of charts and visualisations that make it into the books I like to read and websites I like to visit? And although it didn't apply to my own situation, the question could equally apply to those with other coding tools and libraries readily available who had the ability and willingness to code – could they also create these kinds of charts and visualisations?

Is this how I could escape Market Research and get into a whole different field that was both analytical and creative? A way of creating pictures and not numbers? That could be a really exciting shift from my comfort zone as a mathematics graduate. What if I could get paid for it, and, even better, what if we could do it for fun? Could I be a creator of data visualisation as well as an interested consumer? I was asking a lot of questions and I'd barely started!

In my next role, I was delighted to be able to use Tableau, this time in a social research field, and move my skills away from the number crunching non-visual background of my past experience. But, as is often the case, my tasks at my new company were many and varied, meaning that my chances to visualise data, though good, were relatively limited. I knew I could improve my new data visualisation skills purely by taking opportunities to visualise data at work when they came up, but I'd found a whole new field to get excited about. I wanted to learn faster.

I bought books and read them. I invested time in Twitter to follow experts and immerse myself in the field. I listened to podcasts, followed blogs and learned new techniques. I found community initiatives online, and I participated every week and shared my visualisations, whatever the quality (and believe me, my first attempts were very rudimentary!).

I started at rock bottom in terms of experience and skill, while constantly looking for new ideas and improvements. I joined user groups and attended whatever events I could attend where data visualisation experts were talking or presenting, from local talks to larger-scale conferences.

By this point, data visualisation had become both a genuine professional interest and an escapist hobby. Every talk I heard and person I met drew me further into the field. I felt fortunate that I was in this situation – it was certainly the first time I'd thought of my work and hobby as being in any way related, using the same skills and the same software tools for both, albeit in different ways.

This dichotomy meant that first of all, I could use BI tools to make charts at work to "help clients see and understand their data". This was such a more fulfilling way to work for me than it had been in the past, knowing that I didn't just hand over pages and pages of numbers with little idea of how they were used or interpreted.

But second, I could enjoy myself. I could be creative and make visualisations in my personal time that nobody would ever expect to hand over to a business client. I could use data as a creative medium to produce visualisations that, in my own eyes, were creative, artistic, fascinating, intriguing or just plain fun. I could do the same thing in a colourful, or geometric, or abstract, or unorthodox manner, as other practitioners could do with a bar chart.

I'd found an outlet for creativity which I hadn't found since I gave up playing the piano 30 years ago. Of course, the teenage me, like so many of us, got bored of piano, never practiced and reached a threshold beyond which he never improved. But the more mature me, or at least the older version of me with a more mature boredom threshold, was practising my data visualisation regularly, and, like any good music teacher will tell you will happen, I improved gradually with every session.

It's this duality of data visualisation that has had me hooked and taken me on a journey from the early days of 2015/2016 to where I am now, writing this book in late 2021. In my early days, I sought out talks from Tableau's "Zen Masters", a title awarded by Tableau to those most active in the user community who are at the top of their craft in mastery, teaching and collaboration, restricted to only a small number of users worldwide.

And now I've been honoured and fortunate to have since been awarded the title myself (now renamed to Tableau Visionary) four times at the time of writing - it's a title I use to promote not the technical "how to" aspects of one particular tool, but the joy to be found in creativity, unorthodoxy, new design ideas, stretching boundaries and rules and visualising data for personal enjoyment.

One of the benefits of the pleasure and recognition I gained through my journey into data visualisation is a genuine desire to give back and reciprocate. My journey started with attending talks, following blogs and reading books. And now I love nothing more than talking, teaching and presenting around my experiences and design ideas at events and conferences.

Having gained so much from other blogs, I soon started a blog called *Questions in Dataviz* (questionsindataviz.com) where I showcased and documented my journey in a series of blog posts. This book is the formal version of my blog and the final part of that puzzle – ultimately a book for people with an outlook like me who are looking for creative thought processes and ideas to take their visualisations to another creative level.

This book details many of the things I have learned, explored, experimented with, queried and created along my data visualisation journey. It's the journey of someone who has learned and tried to put into practice data visualisation best practices, but who has then wanted to emulate the creativity, data art and imagination of data visualisation practitioners he has encountered on the way. A non-artist who has found a creative outlet using data, and who continues to look for ideas and influences in every new project he creates.

Walk with me along the way, encountering the principles, questions and ideas I've encountered, and encounter them in a series of chapters posing questions at every point. The journey might not be exactly linear in terms of how I progressed through my learning so far, but it aims to be a logical progression through a selection of principles, suggestions and ideas that I have encountered, and lays them out for you to follow a similar pathway.

You won't have had the same journey as me, since we all have our own unique career paths. And so, you may not have faced the same questions as me in your data visualisation pathway. You have probably started in your data visualisation journey and faced some of these questions posed in the book, and perhaps you are at your creative crossroads now, wondering how you can find the opportunity to be more creative, or how to find inspiration for some new ideas.

If at least some part of this resonates with you, then I hope you will enjoy this book and be similarly inspired to emulate those you admire in the field, to look for inspirations far and wide, to apply your own unique ideas and perspectives and most importantly to enjoy the process and have fun along the way.

Author

Neil Richards is a data visualisation specialist and enthusiast with over 25 years of experience in the data industry. Through his regular personal creative data visualisation projects, he has been awarded the title of Tableau Visionary (formerly Tableau Zen Master) a total of four times and is a regular speaker at data visualisation conferences and user groups. Formerly Knowledge Director for the Data Visualization Society, he also sits on the board of data visualisation non-profit Viz for Social Good. Neil works as a Lead Business Intelligence Analyst at JLL and has a BSc in Mathematics and a BA in Environmental Studies. He lives in Derbyshire in the United Kingdom.

Introduction

For me, there are no answers, only questions, and I am grateful that the questions go on and on. I don't look for an answer because I don't think there is one. I'm very glad to be the bearer of a question.

P.L. Travers

What are best principles?

Data visualisation has a number of best practices but very few rules. A good visualisation, or a good chart, is often then considered "good" by consensus. The designer may have got their message across expertly with just the right level of clarity and conciseness, an aesthetic design and a muted colour palette that conforms perfectly to accessibility considerations. But even then, how often do you see a chart considered good being critiqued by those with a different opinion? Those with preferences for different colours, chart types or aesthetic styles, or who would prefer to see a different story told from within the same dataset? Or simply those who think the subject holds no interest to them?

Most would agree that the simplest of datasets in the hands of ten of the field's most respected experts would be visualised in ten different ways, all of which would confirm to each designer's personal style and visualisation preferences. Yes, all ten would likely be considered much better than something a beginner or intermediate practitioner might create, but all ten, while conforming to best practices, would look different enough to each other to be identifiable as unique.

This book is not about defining rules, principles or best practices in the field so much as discussing them, questioning them and being aware of when you might want to bend or even contradict them. It won't tell you the best things to do, neither will it tell you the things to avoid. It's not called "Answers in Dataviz", for good reason!

In fact, many of the questions posed in each chapter won't be given a definitive answer. They may have one answer, based on my own opinion, circumstance or experience. Or they may go completely unanswered, leaving the relevant elements completely open to interpretation. In some cases, you may well come up with your own answers which contradict mine. I'd be surprised if you didn't and would encourage you to do so.

But, and I'm aware I'm phrasing this in the form of a question, why so many questions?

With so many entry routes into the field of data visualisation, often people will learn the software or the tool first. In formal training terms, or self-learning terms, it might be that that's all you learn before you get straight into action creating your own output. We might find that a tool makes it easy to apply different colours to every one of our bars in a bar chart, to generate arbitrary packed bubble charts with just a few mouse clicks and drags or to create pie charts with 24 segments adding up to 143%. But that doesn't mean these are the charts we **should** create …

Asking questions allows us to critique and improve

The very first chart I produced, within minutes of data being loaded into a charting tool for me, looked something like this. Why did I choose to visualise it like this? Because it was easy to do so quickly, and it caught my eye – I knew no principles, guides or rules at this stage (Figure I.1).

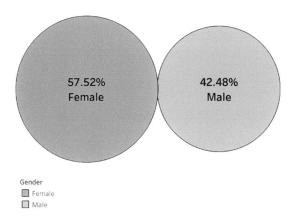

FIGURE I.1   My first data visualisation.

There might not be anything truly incorrect or deceitful about the chart (we're not truncating axes on a bar chart, for example), but a few simple questions can act as both discussion and critique. There may be no definitive best way to show this simple data, but most of us would improve on it. Some questions that come to mind might be:

- What's the title of this chart – what do the numbers represent?
- Can we really discern amounts and differences using circles accurately?
- Do we need different colours for the circles as they are labelled anyway?
- Given that we've chosen colours, are blue and pink for male/female really appropriate?
- Why have we included a colour legend which isn't necessary?
- Shouldn't we use the term "Sex", rather than "Gender"?
- Do we really need to have two decimal places on the percentages?

This list of questions and potential improvements is far from exhaustive, but it didn't take long to come up with a few right off the bat. It certainly wouldn't take long for someone with a little more experience to improve significantly on the above, using these questions, and potentially others, as a basis.

Just minutes into my data visualisation journey, with no training and a freshly installed chart tool, I didn't know what questions to ask. But as I gained experience, learned from established wisdom, and gained confidence in challenging my own instincts, it's likely that visualising the same data, even for a quick snapshot summary, would relate in something very different with a few months' worth of experience down the line.

Asking questions allows us to develop our own philosophy

In his introduction to the 2020 book *Data Visualization in Society*, Alberto Cairo writes that the best philosophical writing "doesn't aspire to settle matters outright, but to inspire further reflection" adding "the variety of topics and approaches of the chapters in this book is astounding, but what most have in common is an open ending: they are links in a chain of reasoning – a dialogue".

My own style of data visualisation relies heavily on inspiration from many current practitioners who will be attributed and showcased during the course of this book. But it also comes from many of those acknowledged to be historical pioneers in the field. The following three stand out not just because of their output, but because of their unique questioning mindset that allowed their work to stand the test of time and inspire others such as myself many decades into the future.

Florence Nightingale

Florence Nightingale is arguably best known in the United Kingdom as the founder of modern nursing. But her Wikipedia tagline describes her as an "English Statistician" and indeed is well known as an important figure in data visualisation. As I write, my daughter is studying nursing at university, and Nightingale's family home growing up in Derbyshire is less than 8 miles from me at home. With so many connections to me, my profession and my family, it's no wonder she is an inspiration to me.

Being labelled just a statistician would be underselling Nightingale – she was the first woman fellow of the Royal Statistical Society. In terms of data visualisation, she is best known for her diagrams from the Crimean War, known as coxcomb diagrams or, indeed, the Nightingale Rose diagrams. Below is an image of her diagram of the causes of mortality, photographed in situ in the Science Museum in London.

Circulated in 1858 and published earlier in 1859, Tim Harford describes the coxcomb thus in his book *How to Make the World Add Up*: "What it isn't is a dry presentation of statistical truth. It tells a story" (Figure I.2).

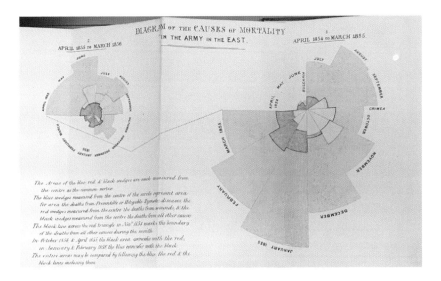

FIGURE I.2 *Diagram of the causes of mortality – Florence Nightingale.*

Now we know that data visualisation was in its infancy when this was produced, certainly compared to today's standards, and it's safe to say that we hadn't seen coxcomb charts like this before. Even now, almost 200 years later, many people, including those reading the book right now, will still not be familiar with the coxcomb chart, how to read it or even be aware of the term itself. And that's no criticism of today's audience, rather a statement on how unconventional Nightingale's chart choice was, even in the context of today's practices.

Nightingale would have known that this was unorthodox, it was a striking chart type that would need explaining to her intended audience, which was generally an audience of men in positions of authority. But she would have been aware of this and known that it was a concession worth accepting to achieve impact.

And of course, Nightingale would have been looking for impact for the right reasons – not to gain attention for her skills and creativity, but to press home the vital story her charts were designed to tell. By dividing the death toll in the British Army into two periods, she deliberately draws attention to the periods before and after sanitation improvements at the Scutari hospital where she was posted in Crimea, creating a sharp break, making the importance of improved sanitation jump off the page.

She was on a mission to persuade those in positions of influence to introduce similar sanitation across Britain and the Empire, to such an extent that "the visual rhetoric helped people to reach a conclusion that happened to be correct". Acts of Parliament followed in the UK in the 1870s, and death rates in the UK began to fall.

Furthermore, Florence Nightingale didn't invent the coxcomb chart without prior data visualisation knowledge. As RJ Andrews stated in his article "Florence Nightingale was a Design Hero" published in the Data Visualisation Society's online journal (also known as *Nightingale*), "Florence Nightingale made lots of bar charts. No one cares about them! Her roses gripped 1858 readers and they still hold our attention today".

So, we can assume that she would have known that although to display the data in bar chart form would have been perfectly valid, something else was needed to get her point across and ultimately to save lives. Did she question whether displaying numbers in wedge shapes scaled by area was an acceptable alternative to the norm? I like to think so – and the resultant chart, with the resultant impact it caused, is why we celebrate her as a data visualisation pioneer over a century and a half later.

Charles Joseph Minard

A second historical influence was the work of Charles Joseph Minard. Minard's work, especially the chart depicting Napoleon's March on Moscow, is often heralded for its excellence. First published in 1869, Edward Tufte, himself one of the most well-known and influential data visualisation authors, has described it as "Possibly the best statistical graphic ever drawn." (Figure I.3).

The chart depicts the journey west to east with the width of the trail proportional to the size of the army. Incidentally, contrary to

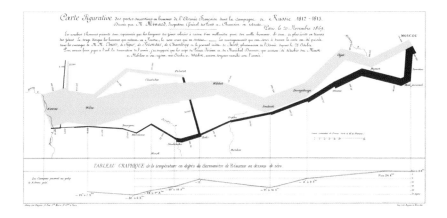

FIGURE I.3   Napoleon's March on Moscow – Charles Joseph Minard.

popular misconception, the west-most point of the trail is in what is now modern-day Lithuania, not Paris. With tan representing the journey east and black representing the journey back east, it tells the story of a gruelling campaign in sub-zero temperatures where, on finding Moscow almost deserted, just a fraction of the initial number of men returned.

However, Minard himself acknowledges that it is inaccurate. Locations are approximate, routes are simplified and the visual representation is exaggerated, all, arguably, allowing for easier understanding and greater impact. Minard regularly uses such tricks to simplify his visualisations.

In her book "The Minard System", Sandra Rendgen catalogues the full portfolio of Minard's work, much of which visualises flow of trade and commerce, and there are many examples of geographic over-simplification. We see vastly widened Straits of Gibraltar, maps of Europe which obliterate countries such as Denmark or Wales to allow for placement of trade routes and incredibly rudimentary versions of the United States, for example.

Minard's work strikes a chord with me for two reasons. First, he must have questioned the need for absolute analytical and geographical accuracy in order to make his point clearly and aesthetically. He knew that his audience was not the general public, but engineers like himself, and local politicians, so perhaps he trusted the level of education of his readers to accept his cartographical shortcuts in the name of visual impact.

The second reason I empathise with Minard as an influence for me and my outlook on data visualisation is that I can only wonder what kind of rigorous data analysis Minard needed to produce as one of France's premier engineers throughout a long and distinguished career in France. But most of his published work, including the March on Moscow map, was produced well into retirement.

To my mind, when Minard was considering how to visualise Napoleon's route to and from Moscow, he questioned the principles he used throughout his career, decided how he could query and bend these principles in order to come up with a striking and aesthetically pleasing visualisation, and, what's more, he did this as a hobby, a personal project. He identified the pleasure that could be derived from expressing himself with creative non-standard data visualisations that bent the rules he knew about and had stuck rigidly to in his day job for so many years.

Amazingly, especially given life expectancies in the 19th century, the March on Rome was produced when Minard was 88 years old. It's never too late to visualise data!

W.E.B. Du Bois

I didn't learn about W.E.B. Du Bois until a couple of years into my data visualisation journey. His work will be heavily featured in a later chapter (see Chapter 3.4 on Data Portraits). But Du Bois is another example of a historical visualisation practitioner whose work inspired me from the moment I came across his work.

W.E.B. Du Bois was a Black American scholar who was commissioned to showcase an exhibition at the Exhibition Universelle in Paris in 1900, in order to demonstrate the progress made by American Negroes since emancipation. Along with students and alumni from Atlanta University, he used the opportunity to exhibit over 60 data visualisations.

But as Whitney Battle-Batiste and Britt Rusert asserted in "Visualising Black America", there was

> nothing auspicious about the space assigned to the Negro Exhibit, nestled as it was in the right corner of a room of the Pavilion of Social Economy. To garner attention from this unenviable location, this exhibit would need to radiate its own sparkle and originality.

One such exhibit is shown below. A common critique to any non-standard visualisation is "it could've been a bar chart". There's no doubt that this fits this particular category. But in this case, the bar for country and village living would have needed to be over ninety times the length of the bar for those living in cities from 5,000 and 10,000 and significantly longer than all of the other bars put together.

Du Bois chose the memorable depiction of small angled coloured bars for the non-rural dwellers, with rural dwellers in red spiral form. There's no doubt that it would have bent and broken almost every rule or guideline of the time and would continue to do so now (Figure I.4).

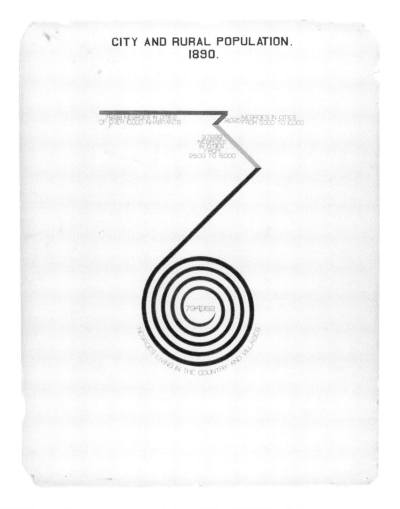

FIGURE I.4   *City and rural population 1890 – W.E.B Du Bois.*

A number of questions must have led to the decision to create this and so many other unorthodox visualisations. How could he create something impactful that would "radiate its own sparkle and originality"? How could he fit all the required measures on one page? How could he draw attention to individual charts within a portfolio of 60 on display to the general public? Could he justify combining elements of line chart, bar chart and spiral chart all in one?

Without considering these questions en route it's likely he would never have got to the final output, which in turn became part of a legacy not only of fantastic and unusual charts, but of a successful exhibition visualising important social issues to the general public far in advance of the age of mass media.

Questions in Dataviz

For all three of the above influences, it's not so much the people and their data visualisation work that influenced me, but each of their philosophies on data visualisation that inspired me. What questions did they ask themselves in order to come to the decision to break the mould? What made them challenge the status quo? It's doubtful that any of them expected or wanted to be considered a pioneer in the field over a century later, but it's fair to imagine that they did know that a new approach was needed in order to make the impact they wanted with their visualisations there and then.

And we know that each of them will have had significant experience in their data and statistics-related fields prior to their most renowned creations. All three will have learned principles, asked themselves questions whether to comply with or circumnavigate some of the established principles of the time and created their own unique ideas as a result of these questions they posed along the way. They have inspired me to approach creative data visualisation in my own personal way and have left their mark with unique and creative data visualisations which have stood the test of time through their uniqueness and unorthodoxy.

The blog of *Questions in Dataviz* (questionsindataviz.com) came about as I documented my early to mid-career learnings in a series of blog posts which have grown to an extent further than I would have imagined, and which, in turn, have inspired this book. In the blog, every post was inspired by a question, and so this book remains faithful to the format of the blog by posing every topic and discussion in the form of a question.

The next series of chapters comprises a number of challenges to perceived principles and best practices. You might find them phrased in a different way to how you will have learned – perhaps even contradicting the perceived normal thinking. Or they might ask questions which aren't usually considered at all. I hope that the examples and discussions I introduce will lead you to think around perceived wisdom.

Section I – First Questions: This section lays out some, but by no means all, of the data visualisation principles you will encounter early in your career. I have already mentioned that there are very few rules in data visualisation, but there are many principles that it's usually advisable to adhere to. Unless you have had a thorough grounding in principles before you attempt your very first chart, you may encounter some of these significantly after you get started, and you may not be yet familiar with all of the concepts discussed.

It's not an exhaustive list but takes you through the period of discovering and learning some important principles. If you have a certain level of experience, you may not need to cover these chapters in detail. But you may encounter some suggestions that once you have gained confidence, you might have some answers of your own …

Section II – Challenging Questions: This section introduces some questions that are more of a challenge than those discussed in Section I. This could be for a number of reasons: perhaps the questions are more unusual and introduce a discussion not usually discussed within analytical data visualisation or conventional training paths, for example, *2.2. Why do we visualise using triangles?*

Some of the questions may pose a challenge to acknowledged principles and perceived best practices, for example, *2.3 Does it matter if shapes overlap?* The questions might even directly challenge answers and assertions we have reached in Section I, such as *2.5. What is design-driven data?*

All questions in this section have arisen as I have wanted to try new ideas, or been presented with interesting challenges that conflict with some of the principles we have been taught in Section I. As for answers – once again, that's usually up to you.

Section III – Idea Questions: This is a section full of creative ideas that have arisen as I have challenged myself to explore within the field. These are a finite section of ideas that have led to unique and individual projects specifically for me, building on the questioning mindset from Sections I and II and my resultant fledgeling data visualisation philosophy, and usually influenced by ideas and projects from existing data visualisation practitioners.

A unique "grab bag" of creative ideas which all came from rules and principles I enjoyed questioning, considering, bending and in some cases breaking. You may never need the ideas from this section – consider it a finite sub set of several examples that indicate the formation of new ideas.

These chapters show where inspiration has specifically taken me, and I hope that they lead you in turn to your own inspirational ideas and data visualisation projects.

Conclusion

Again, this book is therefore not an exclusive list of things you need to know or consider to become a more skilled and creative practitioner in the data visualisation field. Far from it, it is a journey that leads to a select but significant group of my own unique ideas. I hope you will enjoy the journey through the process that led to some of my ideas, and while doing so, be inspired to think of your own, or find your own inspirations.

The field of data visualisation is growing. I almost stated here that it is infinite, but it occurs to me that "is the field of data visualisation infinite?" would make a great question for another chapter, on another occasion. One thing I would certainly agree is that if it is finite, it is definitely growing at pace. And it grows with every new chart, every new data art piece, every new visualisation, every article, paper or blog post and every new practitioner or designer entering the field. With every new addition, new questions are asked, and the field continues to flourish.

Once again, Alberto Cairo sums up my thoughts in his introduction to "Data Visualisation in Society":

> Does any of these chapters inspire you? Do you agree or disagree with it? Reason why. Argue. Establish a conversation with it. Write and publish, and be open to further responses and critiques. That's how philosophy begins.

Taking this further, the combination of the questions you ask and the answers you settle on will allow you to develop your own unique data visualisation philosophy. It's this that will allow you to become your own unique part of the ever-growing and infinite data visualisation field.

FIRST QUESTIONS

Chapter **1.1**

Should the data drive the visualisation?

Obviously, the answer to this is "yes", at least inasmuch as it can't be the other way round. [...] You can't just decide on a visualisation without thoroughly knowing your data and its suitability for the job.

Neil Richards

The challenge

This chapter shares a title with one of the first topics in my blog in June 2016, which I opened with the line quoted above. At this point in time, I considered it a pretty hard and fast answer. I'd seen a fantastic, detailed scatterplot in The Upshot – a data visualisation themed subsite of the *New York Times*.

The chart in question is shown below, with the choice of colour to determine race really showing how the voting intentions of Black and White Americans were so different in 2012, across all US states and the full range of other demographic breakdowns such as sex, age and education. I really liked this chart and wondered, though it was early in my career, could I recreate this chart with different data? What if I looked at UK voting patterns at the last General

DOI: 10.1201/9781003240211-2

3

Election, which had been in 2015. Could I use such a striking visual to identify similar patterns? (Figure 1.1.1).

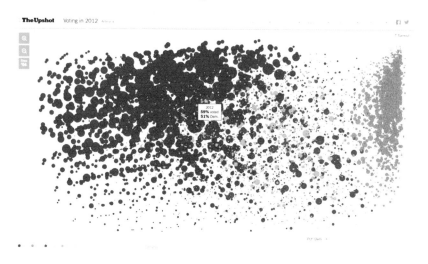

FIGURE 1.1.1   Voting in 2012- https://www.nytimes.com/interactive/2016/06/10/ upshot/voting-habits.html.

A first cursory thought might have suggested that it would be possible in some way, but the biggest difference between US voting data and UK data was already insurmountable. The US is a two-party voting system which leads to the election of 435 senators across 50 states depending on votes cast at a state level, all of whom are Republican or Democrat. Whichever story we decide to tell with the data, it's a story featuring just two protagonists. For accuracy, I should acknowledge there are alternative candidates to the Republican/Democrats, but the two main candidates received over 94% of the votes.

In the UK, the top two political parties received a little over 67% in total between them, meaning that a third of the population voted for an alternative candidate. The winning candidates become Members of Parliament (MPs) who are elected to represent 650 seats in parliament. And wide differences in regional voting mean that ultimately eleven political parties gained enough votes for representation in parliament (twelve if you count the independent Speaker of the House of Commons).

Clearly, we don't have an equivalent situation here in the UK. In the USA, our data is split into two categories in terms of voting. "Voted

Democrat" represent, you guessed it, those who voted Democrat. And crucially, the second category of "Did not vote Democrat" is a pretty good proxy for those who voted Republican, given the low third-party figures in every state. Could we make a similar analysis for "Voted Conservative" and "Did not vote Conservative" in the UK?

Unfortunately not – there isn't the same equivalence in terms of the effect that particular vote had, or whether the particular demographic that didn't vote Conservative voted Labour, or voted any of the other available parties, all of which will have their own particular ethos and therefore potentially very different demographic profiles. For that reason, a simple one-dimensional x-axis just won't work.

The alternative and its limitations

It's probably already time to rule out a chart like the Upshot scatterplot. But there are more reasons we really might struggle to replicate this. The US voting data comes with full intersectionality in its data. With two gender categories, 50 states, 4 races, 5 categories for educational attainment and 4 for age, the full intersectionality between them all allows for a total of 8000 blobs, all of which can be seen in the Upshot version (and if you can't see them all, they are at least all available to be seen once filtering is applied).

The UK exit poll data had nowhere near this amount of intersectionality. I was able to divide my data into 11 regions, with two ethnicity values (white versus all non-white), seven age categories and two gender categories, giving 308 categories in total ($11 \times 2 \times 7 \times 2$). This worked okay up to a point, but given the exit survey sample size, only gave an average of ten or so voters in each category.

And if the average was ten in each category, then, by definition, a large number of categories had a lot fewer voters than that. Many categories were empty, or had odd looking results, e.g. 100% Labour, or 0% turnout. Even those that looked to have reasonable results will have had huge margins of error if they only represented by a single-figure number of respondents.

This really left me with two options – either to go for a much-changed version unrecognisable from my original intention, and with many limitations, or to abandon the initial plan completely. I did create and publish a chart, seen below, but felt it was important to acknowledge its limitations and publish my thought processes alongside it, in the form of the blog post that has in turn influenced this chapter.

It's not something that could have been produced for a client or public-facing article, not because of the final overall "look", but because of the large number of outliers. In reality – it's these outliers that give it the pleasing triangular shape because circles with low sample size take unrealistic positions on the edges of the graph. It told us nothing about the UK results, but it taught me how to create triangular charts with three axes and posed a useful discussion (Figure 1.1.2).

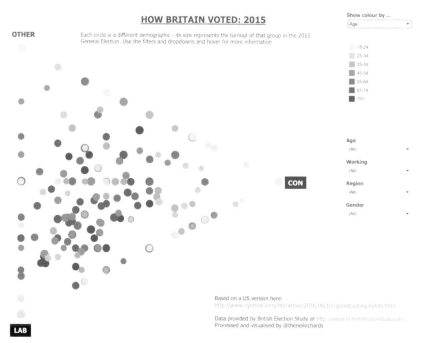

FIGURE 1.1.2   *Three-party system leads to very different visualisations.*

It's important to add that in writing this book I'm posing many questions, some of which were encountered pretty early on in my data visualisation experience. For that reason, I won't always show visualisations here that are representative of my experience level as I write this now in 2021. The above chart was produced within my first year of using any visualisation tool, and as a result, even if I

decided to produce the exact same chart now, I'm sure there are better and more polished design decisions I would make.

But the sooner in your data visualisation career that you have a
grasp of the kind of questions you may encounter, the sooner you
can answer or challenge them, even if the visualisations that these
questions affect at this point are likely to be less skilled and a little
more rough around the edges.

A few years later, I was fortunate to have the opportunity to ask
Shirley Wu, a leading data visualisation freelancer and author, what
she thought on the question of whether design or data should come
first, during an online book review of her Data Sketches project. She
had the following to say on the subject:

> I learned very early on (pre-Data Sketches) to never design
> before I have the data, and even after I get the data, to not
> design until I have a good understanding of the dataset.
> This is a really important rule for me, especially for client
> projects, because I can spend all the time thinking up the
> coolest designs, but I might find that as soon as I put data
> into it, the design doesn't work.

Back to my initial dilemma – given that a pre-conceived idea may
lead us to a sub-optimal chart, or a chart somewhat different to first
intentions (or both), what should we do if we already have our dataset and are looking for visualisation ideas? There are many resources
to determine ideal chart choices for any given data structure.

Resources for choosing charts

If you know your dimensions, your continuous variables, your
numeric measures, your discrete variables and generally have a good
feel for your data's structure in terms of its granularity or its number
of records, then you may be able to make that design decision, and
what's more there are several excellent resources that might help you.

The *Financial Times'* Visual Vocabulary is a great start to give you
some ideas of what to show and how to show it – easily findable and
downloadable in print form. Equally excellent alternatives to this
would be to check out Jon Schwabish's Graphic Continuum (available via the policyviz.com website) or Andy Kirk's book "Visualising
Data" which has a detailed central section cataloguing each chart

type. All three will give examples and advice on which options to consider, and by contrast, which options to rule out.

I would heartily recommend that any data visualisation practitioner, whether beginner or expert, has access to at least one of these excellent resources as an aide-memoire to which type of charts they might want to be considering for a given dataset, and which type of charts just wouldn't work.

When giving a talk to the London Tableau User Group in 2017, Alan Smith, who was leading the *Financial Times* data journalism team, arguably some of the best data journalists in the business, stated that they have a copy of the Visual Vocabulary prominently displayed in the office – definitely a strong endorsement (Figure 1.1.3).

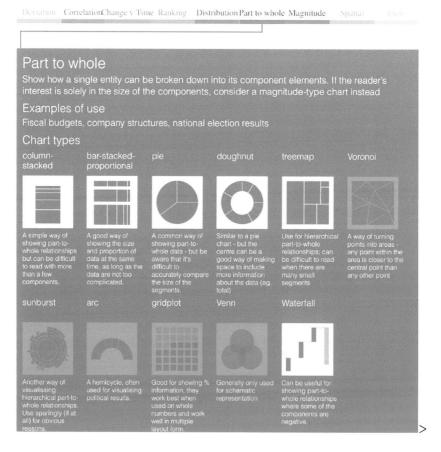

FIGURE 1.1.3   *Visual vocabulary online interactive version (part) – part to whole:*
https://ft-interactive.github.io/visual-vocabulary/.

Conclusion

In this book, I'm posing so many questions because I want to encourage creative and non-standard thinking. The important thing is that nothing will tell you the one, single, correct chart to use for any given dataset, but experience, guidance and best principles will rule out the wrong ones. And even at that point, you may well make the decision to overrule those principles or have your own reason for producing something non-standard. In other words, you'll have a reason for choosing the "wrong" one.

After all, a personal creative project at least gets a free pass on the "especially for client projects" clause as mentioned by Shirley Wu above. But here, all these decisions are generally taken once the data has been obtained, processed, examined and explored. And the key thing is that your data and its structure will almost certainly rule out some wrong or unworkable options.

Given the data, it then becomes your choice to determine which route you want to take, focusing on analytics, aesthetics, impact – if you're really lucky you'll hit the sweet spot and manage all three, if that's your intention. And as you're learning your trade, there's an advantage in going down the path of an unorthodox visualisation type that you haven't tried before: the advantage of learning, discovery and gaining technical skills.

The trade-off may be between the chart type being less than ideal and the valuable lessons learned while learning these new skills – but next time these skills may be more useful for a more appropriate use case for something similar. And you won't have found this out if you hadn't made that initial decision. Once you have your data, then you can choose a myriad of design directions.

Chapter 1.2

What's in a colour?

I found I could say things with color and shapes that I couldn't say any other way.

Georgia O'Keefe

Colour blunder

Many years ago, in the early two-thousands, I was working in an office in a team leader role where I had a team of eight people reporting to me. Some of the responsibilities were quite daunting but one task was particularly trivial. The new desk calendars for the year 2001 (I may have the year wrong but that's not important to the story) had arrived and I had to distribute them to the members of my team. This was in the time where a lot of appointments were still made and deadlines were recorded in good old-fashioned diaries and calendars.

The calendars were a collection of standard issue red, black, or blue, but, in all honesty, I never even noticed that they were different colours, until, with just one calendar left, I approached the last member of my team. Brian was older than me, quite intimidating,

DOI: 10.1201/9781003240211-3

not least because he was comfortably the tallest person in the office at about two meters tall and could be very stubborn.

I liked him a lot and felt I generally had a good working relationship with him, but he was, without doubt, the most challenging person to deal with in the team and could be quite daunting if you got on the wrong side of him. In fact, Brian isn't his real name – I suppose the very fact that I'm using a different name means I must still be a little intimidated by him now!

As I approached his desk, there was a hush in the office. I got the feeling that the rest of the team were watching me, expecting trouble or confrontation. This new young team leader (me) was about to make a rookie mistake – he'd be eaten alive, but why? What could possibly go wrong? What had my team noticed that I was oblivious to?

I handed him the shiny new red calendar. He handed it back, with a shake of the head and just one firm word, uttered softly but firmly in his familiar Liverpudlian brogue. "No."

I was somewhat intimidated and not sure what to make of this. Rather than question his refusal to take the calendar, I backed down and went back to my desk to nervous laughter and sighs of relief from the rest of my team. It troubled me for a while, until finally when Brian next left his desk for a short break, another team member came up to me and explained.

"I can't believe you tried to give Brian a red calendar."

"Why not, what's wrong with a red calendar?"

"Haven't you noticed, he refuses to have anything red?"

"No … why on earth is that?"

"He supports Everton!"

At this point I should explain – the English city of Liverpool has two large, rival football teams: Liverpool FC and Everton. Liverpool FC play in red and are strongly associated with that colour, whereas Everton play in blue. A devoted Everton fan like Brian wants no reminders of his bitter city rivals, which means he owns, uses or wants absolutely nothing which is red. *Definitely* not a red calendar.

This was to be one of my first lessons learned on the importance of colours and their associations. When Brian returned to his desk, wearing his blue shirt, he sat back at his seat which I soon noticed was surrounded by entirely non-red objects. I wouldn't make that mistake again! (Figures 1.2.1 and 1.2.2).

FIGURE 1.2.1   *Liverpool Football Club.*

FIGURE 1.2.2   *Everton Football Club.*

Tribal colour associations

Fast forward to about 2015 when I had one of my first ever onsite client presentations. I was presenting very simple data visualisations on the progress of a project in three north-western English cities: Liverpool, Manchester and Blackpool. It was just a very simple bar chart and summary figure for each city, followed by one page combining and contrasting the data.

I decided I needed one colour for each city. Flash back to Brian – I can't use red for Liverpool, I'll upset Everton fans. I can't use blue for Liverpool either, this could get tricky. What else can't I use? Manchester also has two clubs, one associated with red (Manchester United) and one associated with sky blue (Manchester City). It looks like I'm best off avoiding red and blue completely. Blackpool have only one team, and they play in orange. I think I'm safe to associate Blackpool with orange since it has a strong association with the town and wouldn't be associated with any rivals. But I went very "safe" with Liverpool and Manchester, eventually choosing purple and green, respectively. Two colours that hac no associations with any of the three cities that I was aware of.

I'd probably over-thought this a lot. I'd reached a colour palette of orange, green and purple, and the main considerations behind my thought process had not been aesthetics, branding or clarity, but paranoia over English football culture. Ultimately, I doubt anyone who attended my presentation knew the thought processes I'd been through. But it had reaffirmed my learnings that colours can be tricky!

Colours can be associated with sports teams, political parties or deep-rooted ideologies. And some of these associations can be very strong – I would certainly be very careful using green or orange in Northern Ireland, for example, due to their association with Catholicism and Protestantism, respectively. As an aside, I mentioned above that I chose purple and green for Liverpool and Manchester. I even bore this in mind above when considering Liverpool's high Irish Catholic and Protestant population and therefore deciding to use another neutral colour (purple) for Liverpool.

Red and blue have traditional political connotations in the UK, just like they do in the USA, though the association of these colours to Republican and Democratic parties is much more recent. However, the multi-party system in the UK means that yellow, orange, green, purple and other colours can also be seen to have connotations, at least when in the context of political visualisations.

Further culture associations

Aside from the kind of connotations described above (which could probably all be categorised as "tribal" connotations), data visualisation must consider the use of colour in many other different contexts. Some of these contexts that come to mind are:

- **Discernability:** are you using too many colours for the reader to easily discern the different colour categories, or are you using colours that are not easy enough to distinguish?

- **Accessibility:** are you using colours (e.g. red/green in combination) that are not accessible to those with visual impairments or issues of colour vision deficiency?

- **Aesthetics:** are your colours overbearing or distracting from the essential message of the visualisation, do they look distasteful, distracting or just plain bad?

- **Cultural Considerations:** do your colours have additional associations that would confuse or distract your readers or imply associations that weren't intended?

It's the last of these contexts, the cultural associations of colours with certain pre-conceived ideas, organisations or emotions, that I have been exploring mostly in this chapter, and that will remain the focus of my attention as we look to explore the question further.

Colours have a wide range of associations in culture that can vary significantly across different geographies and religions. Some colours have consistent associations, for example, when a particular culture has a colour associated with passion, it is usually red. But what about something you might consider simple, like the sun? Most Western cultures, from childhood, would draw the sun as a big yellow circle. However, in Japan, ask a child to draw the sun and you can be sure that they will draw a big red circle instead.

And what about good luck? In researching this, it didn't take me long to find that in many cultures red is the colour of good luck. With the colour revered as such in China it is a principal reason behind the choice of red for brides in that country. However, as a resident of the UK, it's something I hadn't considered – I couldn't think of a particular colour associated with good luck straight away. I'd perhaps be more likely to have similar associations to neighbouring Ireland, where the "luck of the Irish" is associated with the colour green and associated emblems such as the shamrock, the four-leafed clover.

Similarly in Islam culture green symbolises good luck through the "green man", a patron of travellers. In Thailand, there is a different lucky colour for different days – in particular, yellow is lucky because it is worn on Mondays, in honour of the King's birthday (and similarly, often throughout the first week of December regardless of weekday). And did we mention that orange, the colour of saffron, is considered lucky in India? Finally, I can guarantee from personal experience that opinion is very much divided in the UK as to whether a black cat crossing your path is lucky. Britons are agreed on the colour of the cat (black) but not the resulting fortune. Some think it is lucky, but some think it is unlucky!

It's hard for me to back up the above findings with sources – many of these colour associations come from colormatters.com and their global survey of over 130,000 respondents. Others are less difficult to pin down, and whereas we might consider them "known" facts, the example of the black cat I mention above shows that it's quite possible that cultural association with colours is not always accepted, or not consistent, in the same culture.

The key is to be aware – there's probably no coincidence in the fact that the majority of COVID-19 related visualisations associate disease, or deaths, or higher prevalence of the virus, with colours you would naturally associate with "bad" things, such as red. I mention COVID-19 since at the time of writing, there is no bigger global issue, and certainly as a result there is no issue that has been consistently visualised with such a high profile.

If we simplify some of our colour and culture associations, most of us will be familiar with a few examples such as these:

Red/orange=hot, blue=cold (from our associations with weather maps)
Red=stop, Yellow=slow down, Green=go (from our associations with traffic signals)
Green="good", Red="bad" (by extension from the above – it's better to be moving!)
Pink=female, Blue=male
Green=growth, Brown=decay (from our associations with plant life)

Here I need to add yet another caveat – I probably should have said "Most of us in the Western world …" or something similar. Remember how I said that red was a lucky colour in China? As a result, when red and green are used in Chinese stock markets, red is used to denote prices going up, and green is used when prices go down, against the convention of every other major economy! This is a telling example (demonstrated at https://www.bbc.co.uk/news/av/ business-33464903) which shows that almost no colour systems are conventional right across the globe.

Interpreting colours without legends

Recently, data visualisation expert and author Jorge Camoes posted the following visual on Twitter, with the caption: "Which munici- palities are losing population, the red ones or the blue ones? Try to guess based on your personal colour preferences" (Figure 1.2.3).

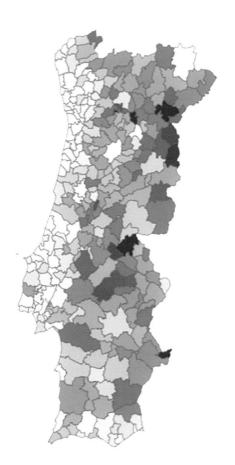

FIGURE 1.2.3   *Change in population – Jorge Camoes.*

With little context, it's genuinely difficult to know. The small amount of context I had was that I know Jorge is from Portugal, hence that helped me recognise this country as a map of Portugal. I know nothing about the individual municipalities, and probably only just about enough to know that the red areas correspond approximately to Portugal's major cities and metropolitan areas. But already by this point I was wondering if this was prior knowledge, or was it being logically suggested by the red/blue patterns I could see?

If I think of red as hot, blue as cold, does this mean by extrapolation that red might be associated with things (humans) being packed closer together/gaining population? Perhaps I should think of blue as healthy and red as unhealthy, and therefore associate blue with rising population? Or if I think of red as "bad", that the red areas are showing the category that's least favourable? And, if so, what is considered less favourable? Gaining or losing population? You could certainly argue a political case for either – is gaining population representative of stimulating economy, or of overpopulation in areas that cannot cope?

As it happens, there was a variety of answers and certainly no consensus, but the graphic was designed so that red represented population gain and blue represented population loss. It was produced by the Portuguese Statistical agency with preliminary 2021 census data, where it did have the explanatory colour legend. Most would argue that a diverging palette, which is a colour palette based on different intensities of two contrasting colours, is a correct choice but it's very difficult to pick a palette that doesn't associate at least partly with preconceptions around the relevant colour.

Let's say that we decided to choose a green colour for increase in population, and a brown colour for decrease. We might understandably associate green with growth. But when looking at brown areas of a map, we might also be thinking of urban and rural areas, respectively? Or green field and brown field areas from a planning perspective?

As it happens, the correlation between urban areas and population growth is pretty strong – would that then mean that we are implying causality? Or potentially confusing the reader by using labels associated with a similar measure to the one we are displaying (urban/rural) rather than the actual measure (population increase/decrease?).

This example goes to show that once you are aware of the cultural or pre-conceived associations, it doesn't make it easier to choose a palette. We mentioned above that another important colour consideration is accessibility. The first thing that many of us learn (myself included, very early on) is the importance of not using red and green, because of the prevalence of red/green colour blindness.

With so many pre-existing KPI dashboards and Excel spreadsheets having used red and green for many years, many visualisers will rightly push for a different colour scheme. A common alternative colour scheme is orange and blue. Orange and blue are a good pair of visually complementary colours which work well in a diverging palette – they are the default colour pairing that have replaced red/green in Tableau's default colour associations.

But what about the associations of orange and blue? It works well for associations with hot and cold, but does it have the same "good"/"bad" association as red and green? Let's say we're looking to replace a red/green scale with orange and blue – what would be associated with performing well? Orange, with its "hot" association? Others feel that orange's closeness to red makes it the more obvious candidate for poor performance, or "bad". Which colour is profit, and which is loss?

If associations are not as strong, or more tangential, then the most important thing is to include obvious clear labelling and/or a colour legend. A good practice and necessary addition but potentially something that is making your reader do more work.

Male and female

A final thing to review is the use of colours for male and female within visualisations. I should add that I'm talking about examples where your data is considering binary data, looking at male/female or men/women. In colour terms, that allows us to consider the pros and cons of colour pairs below.

Of course, it might be more appropriate to consider your gender data in less binary terms, and this is a highly important consideration regarding inclusivity at the data collection stage of your projects. That's outside the scope of this chapter, except to remind you, if the book doesn't remind you enough, that there are always additional questions you must consider at every stage of the project.

I've mentioned the obvious cultural association of blue with male and pink with female. But if, like me, you cringe at the very obvious and unimaginative stereotypes of these particular colours, you might wonder what better alternatives there are in data visualisation? The obvious first thing to mention would be to stay away from other associated pairs. You don't want red/green or orange/blue with the obvious implication, intended or otherwise, that one gender is more "good" than the other, or that one gender is more "hot". But how do established data journalism establishments deal with the issue?

Lisa Charlotte Muth, known as Lisa Charlotte Rost when she posted the below piece, an industry-leading data visualisation blogger with Datawrapper, wrote about this in 2018 at https://blog.datawrapper.de/gendercolor/. Perhaps the most surprising thing is not that there are a lot of news outlets that tend to use alternative colours, but that there were still a lot of news outlets that do not.

And those that use alternative colours are far from consistent in the colours they use, even within their own newsrooms. The examples below show the examples Lisa collected in her research, and my own strong recommendation would be to consider a colour pair similar to those from the second group of colours (Figures 1.2.4 and 1.2.5).

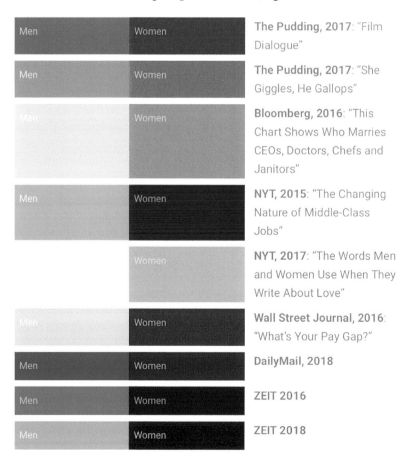

FIGURE 1.2.4   *Use of colour for gender – Lisa Charlotte Muth.*

FIGURE 1.2.5 *Use of colour for gender – Lisa Charlotte Muth.*

I'd identify two examples from the article worthy of further attention. First, the Quartz newsroom which often uses pink for male and blue for female. I admire the challenge to the accepted norm, but suspect that would normally confuse readers, especially since it's not a consistent choice – it appears they are just as likely to use blue for male as they are to use blue for female.

Lisa goes so far to describe it, correctly, as dangerous – after all, the likelihood is that if you see a chart using blue and pink for sex or gender, the preconceived colour associations are so strong, that you're not likely to consult the colour legend.

The second example is that of the Telegraph, which uses green and purple. I love this pairing – it has no cultural association with genders, no obvious connections with well-known diverging attributes such as good/bad, but better still, it has a nod to the colours of the Suffragette movement in the UK, the women who successfully fought for the rights of women to vote in the early 20th Century.

Conclusion

There are no easy answers to questions around colour other than to make sure you are considering obvious cultural associations with colours, and not misleading your readers as a result. Perhaps a peer review from someone not associated with the project to get their first impressions is the ideal solution.

But if you're not making an obvious colour blunder or introducing doubt, then perhaps the best advice is to acknowledge that there are many considerations to make about the correct use of colour, and sometimes it's OK if you don't make them all, given that you need to consider cultural associations alongside the other important colour considerations of accessibility, aesthetics and readability.

That said, I still wouldn't recommend giving anything red to a grumpy Everton fan!

First

Challenging

Idea

1.3

What does data visualisation have in common with psychology?

In reading we do not read letters but words, words as a whole, as a "word picture." This was discovered in Gestalt psychology.

Josef Albers

Design choices

Early in my data visualisation career, I was preparing some simple bar charts for a presentation. I was presenting demographic results for three separate cities, so I'd decided to give each city its own colour. So far, so good, but for my "combined" chart looking at data from all three cities on one page, I was seeking clarification on the best way to group the data. What I initially decided to do was something I still feel I should do a lot more often, which was to sketch out the possibilities (Figure 1.3.1).

So, I came up with two ideas. I can't remember what the length of each line signified but each line represented a bar in a bar chart for the metric we were interested in. Let's assume it was something like "Number enrolled in programme." I do know that each colour represents a city, and each of the three lines (bars) represents one of three points in time. Do I show the age groups within each city

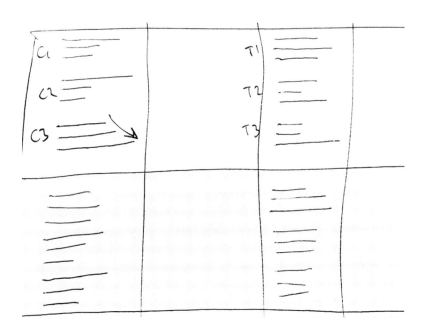

FIGURE 1.3.1   *Preliminary sketch of two alternative layouts.*

(colour), as has been shown in C1/C2/C3? Or do I split up the colours and show the cities at each time point, as shown in T1/T2/T3?

I thought about the data visualisation theory I'd learned up to that point, and it didn't take me much thought to come up with the conclusion that the former option would be best. I was pretty clear about that, without having to reason any further with myself. I knew that it felt like the bars in the first example would be easier to compare, but although it made instinctive sense, I didn't really know why.

So, I sought confirmation from my colleague next to me on his opinion – he agreed that the first option of keeping the age bands within each city was best and would allow easier distinction of age profiles, hence drawing the arrow. And then, as I turned away to fire up Tableau, he said something along the lines of – "Yes, that's consistent with Gestalt theory".

Gestalt theory

I'd churned out a few visualisations and had read a couple of books, but I had never heard of Gestalt theory. A quick google confirmed Gestalt theory as a school of psychology emanating from a number of German psychologists in the 1920s. Immediately this interested me – the multidisciplinary nature of data visualisation is one of the things that fascinates me.

When I had given a short presentation at Sheffield University earlier the same year, this was the first realisation I had that few of my audience, who were all involved in some way with data visualisation, had traditional data science or analysis routes into the field. Many came into the field from traditional or digital art backgrounds, some were statisticians, some were students/theoreticians, and some came from altogether different backgrounds. So, is there a link to psychology, in the form of Gestalt theory?

Gestalt, in German, refers to the principle of perceiving something (or, in our case, visualising something), by considering its individual parts as having different characteristics to the whole.

The word itself most closely means "organised whole". You might describe a tree by describing its trunk, its branches, its leaves, its blossom, its roots, its inhabitants, not to mention many other components of a tree we haven't considered here. But if you were to step back and look at a tree, you would do just that and consider the tree as a whole entity, and not necessarily all of the different parts we just mentioned.

Kurt Kofta, who, along with Max Wertheimer and Wolfgang Köhler, was considered one of the founding fathers of Gestalt psychology in the 1920s, summarised the theory of Gestalt with the assertion that "The whole is other than the sum of its parts" – in other words, the whole takes on its own form that only exists because of its parts. It's this way of thinking that underpins Gestalt theory, though that this is quite different to the often-used phrase "the whole is greater than the sum of its parts" – a phrase often used when considering team performance, but which is a different mantra altogether.

Principles of gestalt theory

I want to explain gestalt theory just a little bit here since it's an important principle that underpins data visualisation. And whereas this book is deliberately only discussing a few such hand-picked principles, from my own perspective it's important to include Gestalt theory because it's quite possible to overlook it as you start your data visualisation journey, as indeed was the case in my own experience. Since it's not possible to go into any great detail here, I would certainly encourage you to read, explore or study further if anything whets your appetite following the introduction in this chapter.

Having learned that Gestalt refers to visual perception, it seemed obvious that it must therefore have parallels in data visualisation. And, it seems, it does, although there doesn't seem to be a hard and fast agreed list or number of principles especially when it comes to data visualisation. I've found nine commonly stated principles which are listed below (it's not a ranked list, so the numbers and order of each principle are not important).

1. **Proximity:** we generally perceive objects that are close together as being grouped together.

2. **Similarity:** we tend to perceive objects with the same characteristics as being grouped together. In data visualisation terms, colour is a good example of this.

3. **Continuity:** we tend to consider shapes as continuous if we can, so the human eye will usually look for pathways in lines, curves or sequences of shapes.

4. **Closure:** we perceive closed shapes as a grouping, or near-closed shapes which we perceive in a group shaped as the whole shape.

5. **Enclosure:** we think of objects as belonging to a group when they are enclosed in a way that creates a border or boundary around them.

6. **Figure and Ground:** we will usually differentiate between foreground (the object in the focus of our vision) and background.

7. **Connectedness:** we will tend to consider connected objects as being in the same group, and objects that aren't connected (or which are connected in a different way) as a different group.

8. **Simplicity:** we tend to look for simplicity in otherwise complex shapes, in order to reduce our information load.

9. **Common Fate:** things that move together are seen as being grouped together. The most common example of this seems

to be a flock of birds: from a data visualisation perspective, this could refer to animations but also elements which seem to be tending in a similar direction.

Example of gestalt principles

When I learned and subsequently blogged about Gestalt in the first instance, it felt important to look at a visual example to understand the principles a bit further. I was able to create a quick visualisation (a work in progress) on a dataset I was working on at the time, to see if I could see or recognise any of the principles above.

Below is a map of police killings in the US from 2013 to 2015. Each circle represents where the killing took place, and each colour represents the victim's ethnicity. Not that the ethnicity legend is not shown, since although it will be hugely important in the analytical findings of any finalised visualisation, it is not important in the context of our discussion (Figure 1.3.2).

FIGURE 1.3.2   *US police killings 2013–2015 (preliminary work in progress).*

I haven't designed this to be a perfect example of every Gestalt principle in action, rather I began work on what might be considered a "typical" visualisation, if there is such a thing. Straight away, I think I can see many of these principles in action.

In describing what we see and explaining Gestalt, I want to take time to explain that in describing the piece we are going to be looking at the distribution, colours and proximities of circles on a map.

However, these marks are not just "dots on a map" but real people who were killed by police officers. It's very easy for us as data visualisers to overlook sensitive subjects when focusing purely on technical issues and any finalised and completed visualisation should be very aware of this. This acknowledgement is very important in the idea of Data Humanism, which we will discuss later in the book.

First of all, a map visualisation, especially when the map is shown just for background context, is a perfect example of 6 *(Figure and Ground)*. When we look at just the marks on the visualisation themselves, we don't want or expect people to look at this and think of it as a map of the USA. Instead, we see individual states with coloured circle marks (our collection which, along with the background map image, forms the Gestalt whole).

We see areas where recorded incidences are closely packed together, and we see areas where the circles are much more sparsely distributed. Gestalt doesn't tell us whether we are looking at areas of high population or high crime (or both), so we need additional context to draw further conclusions from any such clusters.

We see clusters of red and orange packed together in a Florida-shaped wedge, and a light blue mass around about the Carolinas. We see the proximity of circles forming the shape of California but with less consistency of coloured circles. We see a couple of orange clusters on the border with Mexico.

Where we see areas of dots packed together – we are using principle 1 *(proximity)*. The colour distribution encourages us to see connections between marks of the same colour, whether close together or otherwise – this is 2 *(similarity)*. Perhaps the mass of red along the east coast of Florida is an example of 3 *(continuity)* – a proliferation of red dots, which we can see despite interspersal of orange and light blue dots.

We can certainly see that the states of California and Florida are pretty recognisable from their dot patterns, even though there are small gaps between the circles – this is a good example of 4 *(Closure)*. And if we step back and look at the state boundaries themselves, then 5 *(Enclosure)* comes into play as we consider groupings of marks within states.

It's a little harder to make a case for principles 7 and 8 but again where colours are grouped together in such a way as to actually overlap, we might consider them as the group of crimes *en masse* in that particular area (such as Florida). Considering overlapping marks as one larger mass is an example of *7 (Connectedness)* and could be thought of as *8 (Simplicity)* as well. Principle *9 (Common Fate)* is most likely to be seen where there is movement or animation, so would not apply here.

The key thing is that in recognising Gestalt principles at work, it enables us as designers to notice and work on stories in the data. So, let's return to the example at the start of this chapter.

Practical example

If you've been paying attention so far, you'll notice that this is exactly the same example I mentioned last chapter in my dilemma about colours, although I must emphasise that whereas the cities, colours and groupings into 3 years are true, the values and description of the number we are comparing are entirely fictional. But it's key to notice that one of the simplest and most basic visualisations I ever had to create, which was also one of the first I had to present in public, has already led to the discussion in not one, but two principles and two chapters in the book. Everything is an opportunity to think, to question and to learn! (Figure 1.3.3).

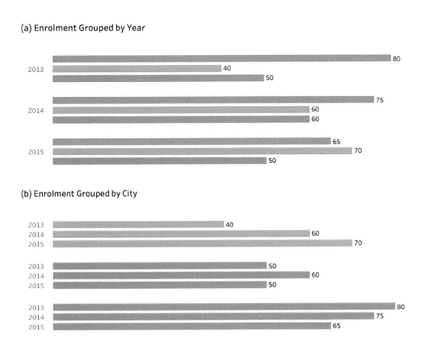

FIGURE 1.3.3   *Enrolment by year (a) vs by city (b).*

The chart above shows the electronic version of my two sketch options from the start of the chapter, and I chose the second of the two options for my combined chart. The Gestalt principle *1. Proximity* (as well as that of *5. Enclosure* from the light grey lines added by my charting software) means we are naturally tending to group the bars into objects of threes.

But, for example (a) we can't really see anything meaningful by looking at each city's figures for each year. However, example (b) accentuates these groupings. Using *2. Similarity*, we can much more easily see each city's trends. Liverpool (green) is increasing, Blackpool (orange) is decreasing, Manchester (purple) has increased and then returned to 2013 levels.

Finally, there is nothing wrong with example (a) per se, and if we were less interested in trends within each individual city and we wanted to get an idea of overall trends year on year, it would in fact be the better of the two options. Perhaps we'd rethink in this case whether using a colour option for each city was really necessary, but the point remains it is an equally valid representation of our data.

Conclusion

Our reaction in accordance with Gestalt principles as consumers of data visualisation is not a considered choice, but an instinctive response formed by the desires of our brain to consider shapes, objects, and distributions in certain ways. For that reason, we should consider embracing Gestalt principles rather than fighting against them.

Considering Gestalt principles, even if, at the time, I didn't realise I was doing so, is recommended, not just to adhere to data visualisation best practices, but also to give the best chance to find insight into your data.

Do data visualisations have to tell a story?

For sale. Baby shoes. Never worn.*

Ernest Hemingway

Defining storytelling

The topic of data storytelling is one that can't really be escaped and thus definitely feels worthy not just of inclusion but of a place in the first section of this book. But unlike some of the other chapter-leading questions, this one is not so clear-cut. After all, what does "telling a story" mean, particularly in the context of data visualisation?

In my professional role, I'm often called on as someone who can tell a story with data – in fact there have been times I've been asked to be involved in a project or included in a team for that reason. In such cases, it can be seen as the difference between a competent data analyst and an analyst who might be thought of as "next level". Clients might be looking for someone who can "tell a story" with the data rather than just perform standard analysis. Often the perceived skill might go hand in hand with an assumption that the visualisation's designer or developer has more than just basic skills when it comes to design or analysis.

DOI: 10.1201/9781003240211-5

Now it's important to say at this point that this chapter's lead quote came with an asterisk attached. How did the quote come about, and how was it attributed to Hemingway? Probably the real answer depends on whichever website your chain of Googling ends at. What seems to be clear is that the idea of a hard-hitting and pithy story described in just six words is such a noteworthy concept that it was attempted and achieved, with tweaks and refinements, before Hemingway's time. It seemed believable that it would come from Hemingway, being renowned as he was for the simplicity of his writing style, and Hemingway was in no hurry to deny it. The skill of storytelling is in demand.

Impact of vaccines

My own absolute favourite example of what might be considered storytelling in data visualisation comes from the *Wall Street Journal* (Figure 1.4.1).

The visual impact of the chosen graph is striking, and the graph tells an obvious story. Prior to the introduction of a measles vaccine, cases were prevalent in all 50 US states. After the vaccine was introduced in 1963, cases decreased to almost zero across the board within just a couple of years. The story has a "before" state, leading to a plot twist – the vaccine introduction – and an "after" state. It's a narrative arc, it even has an ending where everyone lived happily ever after!

The authors didn't have to do too much work to eke out the story, it was right there in the data. When we are considering the concept of storytelling, we are not referring to the words themselves within the visualisation, although they are vitally important, but how the presentation of the data itself tells a story.

In fact, there are even what might be considered several poor data visualisation practices in the chart, but it gets away with it. The colour scheme is not sequential, and the "rainbow" colours chosen show almost no variation between 2 k and 4 k, yet travel from white through blue, green, yellow and orange in less than 1 k. Perhaps it's not just the powerful story in the data that distracts our attention from these choices, but the overall metaphor – the colours chosen have given the overall look of a Petri dish which we might associate with culturing of bacteria in a laboratory.

Battling Infectious Diseases in the 20th Century: The Impact of Vaccines

By Tynan DeBold and Dov Friedman
Published Feb. 11, 2015 at 3:45 p.m. ET

The number of infected people, measured over 70-some years and across all 50 states and the District of Columbia, generally declined after vaccines were introduced.

The heat maps below show number of cases per 100,000 people.

Measles

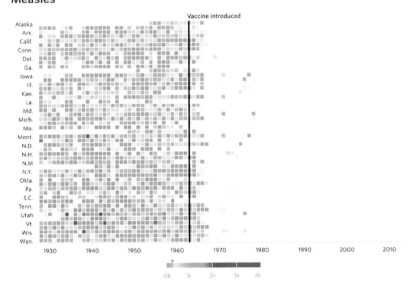

FIGURE 1.4.1   *Impact of vaccines – Wall Street Journal.*

But, if ever a book was going to encourage you to think twice about good practice in order to experiment, be creative, add impact or contribute to a metaphor, it's this book!

Before we answer our chapter's question, let's consider some more ideas as to what storytelling is when it comes to data visualisation.

Tableau Iron Viz

Every year, Tableau Software runs a flagship visualisation contest known as *Iron Viz*, which takes the part of a feeder competition, open to all, using a dataset of choice, on a topic determined by Tableau, followed by the final on-stage competition, where the three feeder competition winners compete to create the best viz on stage in 20 minutes in the presence of thousands of energised Tableau

Conference attendees in the audience. For both the feeder and final competitions, the entries are judged on three categories: design, analysis and storytelling. The first two categories should be obvious in their meaning, but how is storytelling judged?

We might not know exactly, but a result of this has been a proliferation of so-called "long-form" visualisations. Visualisations that are big on content, big on beauty, big on design skill, and because most of the content is on show, usually have little or no interactivity. Those that rise to the top of the judges' scores are seriously impressive, beautiful looking and packed with information.

The storytelling element is easy to interpret at its most basic – a visualisation packed with several individual charts all imparting information which can be read in sequence, as a story. Of course, our eyes are drawn from top to bottom, so we read each individual chart in sequence.

The example below by Joshua Smith won an Iron Viz feeder competition in 2019. Deservedly so, it's a combination of amazing design and great analysis, taking on the long-form storytelling style that does so well in these competitions, and deserved all the plaudits it received. But it's a very specific style of visualisation, is there more to storytelling than this? (Figure 1.4.2).

One person with a strong opinion of this is Joshua himself. In a post for Nightingale, the journal of the Data Visualization Society, he was satisfied that he had done very well in the design and analysis elements of the required judging elements but modestly stated that he would have given himself a score of 1 (the lowest possible) for storytelling.

> I met the judges' expectations for storytelling. I worked on presenting the information with coherence and continuity, with clear organization and a concise "so what" message. I believe I put together a really good expositional piece. But I didn't really tell a story, at least not a good one. There aren't any well-defined characters. There isn't a plot with impactful events.
>
> Pasture and Crop [...] is one of many examples of us labelling something a "story" that doesn't resemble a story at all. Storytelling is often used as a blanket statement to describe how well the information is presented in an interpretable presentation with a logical flow.

First

Challenging

Idea

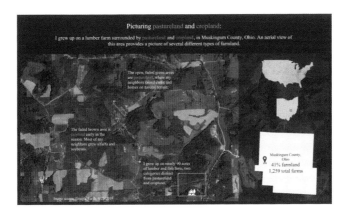

FIGURE 1.4.2   *Pasture and Crop – Joshua Smith.*

(Continued)

FIGURE 1.4.2 (CONTNIUED) *Pasture and Crop – Joshua Smith.*

(Continued)

Categorizing counties allows for a deeper dive into how we're using the land, and the distribution of the crops grown. But where should the lines be drawn to decide which counties are mostly pastureland, mostly cropland, or a blend of the two?

Tableau's cluster analysis can help us algorithmically determine some boundaries. In this use case, a bivariate cluster analysis isn't providing us with much new information, but it does help categorize farms with a bit more mathematical rigor.

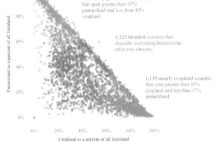

Mapping these categories shows the blended counties are often acting as boundaries between counties that are mostly pastureland and counties that are mostly cropland.

So, what crops are we growing?

These clusters make it easier to explore the differences in distributions of crops between the 3 categories, providing a more nuanced view of how we're using the land.

Counties of mostly pastureland devote more acreage to wheat and alfalfa. The distribution of crops in blended counties looks very similar to counties of mostly pastureland, but with more corn and soybean. Counties of mostly cropland devote most acreage to corn and soybean.

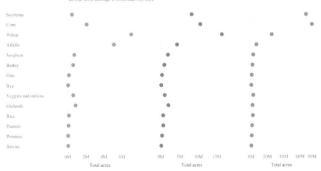

FIGURE 1.4.2 (CONTNIUED)   ***Pasture and Crop – Joshua Smith.***

(Continued)

This breakdown provides a more detailed understanding of how we're using the land and sheds some light on the relationship between pastureland and cropland.

Most cattle and sheep farmers will supplement their feed with the high-protein alfalfa (or hay). In addition, many farmers will grow their own corn for feed. Cattle and sheep farmers often grow wheat as straw bedding, and they can sell off the seed portion (or grain) for food production.

The patterns in cropland utilization seen in blended counties and counties of mostly pastureland illustrate livestock farmers growing the crops their livestock need for feed or bedding, or neighboring crop farmers acting as local suppliers to livestock needs.

The distribution of crops grown between the clusters explains some of the land treatment patterns we observed above.

Patterns of weed control in blended counties and counties of mostly pastureland are very similar.

This is more evidence that the differences in chemical use is largely due to the differences in crops grown.

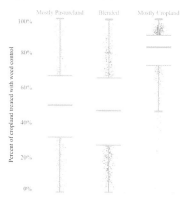

Patterns of insect control in blended counties and counties of mostly pastureland are very similar.

The distribution difference in counties of mostly cropland isn't nearly as strong for insect control, suggesting other variables (such as a wet climate for larvae growth) might be at play.

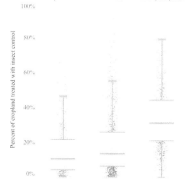

We see a steadier increase in soil conditioning from counties of mostly pastureland to blended counties to counties of mostly cropland.

The different distributions of corn may explain this, as corn is often considered a "needier" crop by farmers.

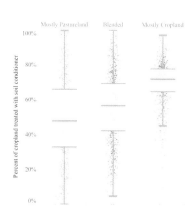

Only one county of mostly cropland reported using more animal manure than chemical fertilizer, whereas animal manure use is more common in blended counties and counties of mostly pastureland.

This is likely due to the local availability of manure, as stale ..

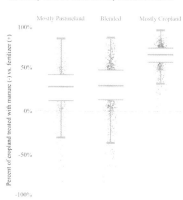

FIGURE 1.4.2 (CONTNIUED) **Pasture and Crop – Joshua Smith.**

(Continued)

There's *one more* nuance to pastureland vs. cropland:

farmland that was used for both in 2012.

There's a number of counties where the percent of farmland devoted to pastureland and the percent devoted to cropland add up to greater than 100%, meaning that the same acreage is used for both.

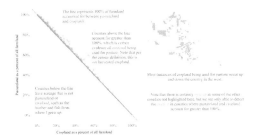

There are a number of reasons why farmers would choose to

pasture their cropland.

While we can't quantify the true prevalence of crop rotation on farms when all seasons and all farms are rolled into one year of county level census data, the cases where more than 100% of farm land is accounted for suggest a few of the places where it is certainly happening. In particular, the overlap of cropland and pastureland suggest a practice known as cover cropping.

Cover crop is grown during the winter to prevent soil erosion and replenish nutrients. Farmers will often allow their livestock to graze cover crop, and the animals naturally fertilize the soil with fresh manure for the next season.

Pasturing wheat is also a common practice if, for some reason, a poorer quality of the wheat won't bring a sufficient price for harvesting.

In line with these practices, counties with more overlap show higher proportions of wheat relative to other crops, and wheat is one of the more common winter cover crops.

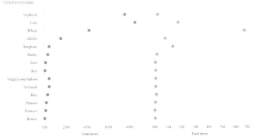

Counties with certain overlap exhibit lower patterns of soil conditioning.

Because other counties certainly have overlap that we can't detect, these patterns aren't too dramatic. However, this still suggests that the practice of pasturing of unharvested cropland

Counties with certain overlap actually show *more* reliance on chemical fertilizers.

This may be because farmers may need a boost of more targeted macronutrients to cover some gaps in what the cover crops and animal manure didn't replenish.

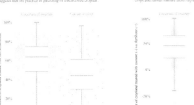

This agricultural census data illustrate complex geographic, economic, ecological, and biological relationships between pastureland and cropland. Our sustainability efforts should be designed to work through these relationships for real impact.

New policies that target livestock will also impact crops, and vice versa.

Our discussions of sustainable food farming **must** come from a deeper understanding of the ways we farm our land.

As is usually the case, the truth isn't as black and white
— or pasture and crop — as we make it out to be.

Love y'all.

JOSHUA DEAN SMITH
@data_jackalope

TABLEAU #IRONVIZ 2019

FIGURE 1.4.2 (CONTNIUED) *Pasture and Crop – Joshua Smith.*

It would be nice to think that every Tableau qualifying competition could be won with just one simple chart such as the *Wall Street Journal's* vaccinations visualisation above without resorting to several charts in long-form sequence. But, in fairness, the Iron Viz competition is looking to recognise design and analytics talent too.

If we consider the long-form style and, though I don't mention it here, the more interactive but otherwise similar in many ways "scrollytelling" style, as just one interpretation – a subset of storytelling style dashboards, it's worth considering what we consider to be the definition of storytelling more generally.

The narrative arc

Consider the narrative arc, which we've already mentioned in passing in this chapter, often considered as the mantra both for fiction and non-fiction storytelling. There are many similar versions – the version below is from Cole Nussbaumer Knaflic, who is the author of *Storytelling with Data* (Knaflic, 2015). By identifying the story you want to tell with the data, the onus is on the chart creator to skilfully present the data in such a way as the takeaway message from the data is left in no doubt to the readers (Figure 1.4.3).

FIGURE 1.4.3   *The narrative arc – storytellingwithdata.com.*

It's this underlying definition that encourages chart designers and visualisation practitioners to deliver outputs focusing on *Story* (with an upper-case S). Among Cole's principles to help designers adhere to this are: not to over complicate; getting rid of non-essential elements; making it clear where to look; increasing accessibility with words; creating an "aha" moment; and most importantly remembering that everything we are doing when we communicate with data is for our audience.

I would argue that each of these principles can be seen in the vaccination example above – the "aha" moment ("Look at that! – as soon as the vaccination was introduced, the measles cases tailed off in all states!"), the lack of unnecessary detail, the annotation and the simplicity are clear for all to see. There is a clear beginning, middle and end, and as a reader of the chart you take part in the narrative arc of the story too, being involved in the plot (setting the scene of the USA with high levels of measles), the rising action (its continuation from the 1930s through to the early 1960s, the climax (measles vaccine introduction) and the resolution.

Other leading thoughts on storytelling

The difficulty comes in other ways we might consider framing a data visualisation, if not as telling a story in the true sense of a fiction story with a narrative arc, then how? The following thoughts are just some of many, which share some similarities but differ in the extent to which they might consider the importance of storytelling as crucial to good data visualisation.

Moritz Stefaner is a renowned independent data visualisation specialist from Germany, host of the Data Stories podcast. On well-formed-data.net, he says that data visualisations can be considered as tools, and some as portraits. Tools can reveal stories and help us tell them, but they are not the story (or the storyteller). Alternatively, he considers that visualisations can be considered as portraits. We capture many facets of a bigger whole, rather than telling a single story. Expressed alternatively, good data visualisation "tells 1000 stories, but not all at once".

Chad Skelton is a prominent data journalist from Canada, who says that we should not consider data storytelling in the same way as a fictional story, but rather as a news story. The priority of a visualisation is to inform rather than to entertain, and this fits the metaphor of a journalistic news story, whose author must, by definition, inform their audience by use of facts, much more than a fiction story, whose author has the luxury of making things up to ensure their story is as entertaining as possible. The facts of a journalistic story may not stir emotions or fit into a satisfying story.

Bridget Cogley is a five-time Tableau Zen Master/Visionary, who uses her sign language and interpretation background to consider the act of data visualisation as communicating pieces of information, and the means of communication as grammar. To that effect, we then think of data visualisation as language – in any given situation there are many ways we can use different language to describe the same object, action or situation. And yes, this communication can be used to entertain, inform, transmit culture, teach or achieve the role of communication in any of its more conventional form. She also asserts that perhaps the nearest equivalent to data storytelling may be reciting an anecdote.

Jonathan Schwabish of PolicyViz, a leading data visualisation author and speaker, would agree that we can tell stories with data, but we are usually just using our own interpretation and findings from within data to make a point or elucidate an argument. So, you might usually only use the "storytelling" term when people are asked to feel deeply.

Alberto Cairo has gone so far as to suggest the term storytelling should be banned! Preferring to use terms around "narrative" he argues that the term is less loaded and ambiguous, and that storytelling can too often lead people astray by the desire to tell a story rather than arguing facts (Figure 1.4.4).

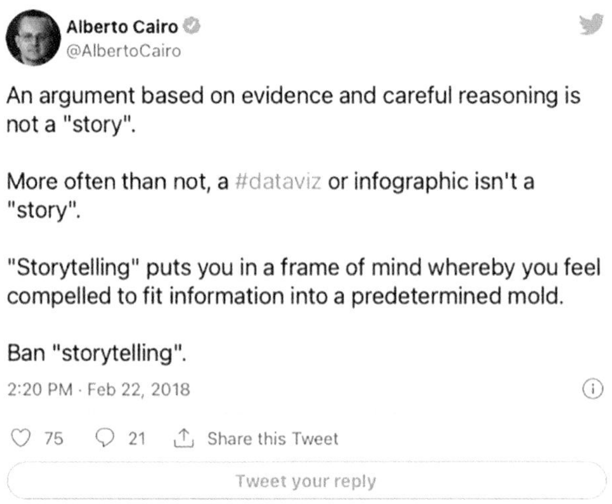

FIGURE 1.4.4   *Tweet from Alberto Cairo.*

I present the majority of these without counter-argument – my own opinion is a composite in agreement with the majority of those above, namely that "storytelling" when considered purely to data visualisation can be considered in many more nuanced ways, all of which are good considerations that help us understand the process of communicating our insights more.

Getting your story across

More important is to understand that the more seriously, or literally, you consider storytelling then the more emotive the subject becomes and the livelier the debate becomes! It's probably best summed up by saying that data storytelling is about getting your point across in a clear and engaging way to your audience – this might sometimes be done by use of a good narrative.

And the key thing is that a visualisation should aim to convey the message that it's intended to convey. Cole's blog then makes a distinction between a "Story" (with upper case S) and a story (sic), with the latter lower-case definition covering the use case of the intended message of your visualisation. Perhaps the conclusion is that every visualisation should tell a "story" (lower case s)?

If I had to zone in on one of the opinions above, I would link the metaphor of data storytelling with recounting an anecdote, and perhaps then we get close to what those advocating storytelling are describing. Meet me and I tell you some stats/numbers, and you forget the numbers. Chances are you forget me too. Meet me and I tell you a great anecdote, you're far more likely to remember both me and what I told you. That's surely a key aim of good data visualisation.

There's an additional principle that Cole mentions which I didn't include earlier: be clear on your intent. This brings me on to the concept of exploratory and explanatory visualisation. Regardless of what data you are using, what stories you might find and think are there in the data for you to visualise, or what chart types you use, you have two contrasting options as a designer.

Your first option (*explanatory visualisation*) is to lead your reader to the conclusion you have found, to present the data and explain these findings clearly. This doesn't mean you have necessarily come up with some ground-breaking analysis or assembled some data that is unique, but that you have chosen the message you want to convey with your data visualisation. Logically, most visualisations considering storytelling will fall into this category, since the storytelling skill is in getting a message across in such a way that our audience will understand and engage with.

Your second option (*exploratory visualisation*) is to present your data in a neutral manner without a "headline" or takeaway message and allow your readers to draw their own conclusions, or perhaps interact in their own way with selections, filters and different journeys through your visualisation.

The story of Leicester City in 2015–2016

Here's an example, again from early in my career, of a visualisation which I look back on now as somewhat rough around the edges, but at the time launched me into a love of non-standard creative data visualisations. In the spring of 2016 Leicester City, an unfashionable football team in England who had been given odds to win the Premier League of 5000-1 at the start of the season the year before, had just done exactly that. They'd won the Premier League.

As a football fan I wanted to create a visualisation. I had three main thoughts in mind:

- Tell the amazing story of how Leicester City won the Premier League against all expectations.

- Do something fun, challenging, creative and eye-catching.

- Use a full, detailed dataset so that my visualisation would be able to include all teams, matches, goals and key events, not just Leicester City.

The resulting visualisation is shown below. There's no major significance in the fact that I've included the phrase "story of the season" in the title, other than it just seems to make sense in normal conversational usage. For that reason alone, would it perhaps be a good example of data storytelling? It also included interactivity so that readers could see all individual results and positions on hover, highlight teams or filter the graphic on the number of game weeks through the season (Figure 1.4.5).

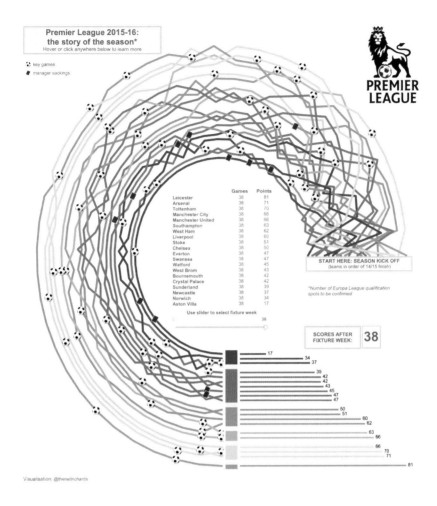

FIGURE 1.4.5   Premier League 2015–2016 – the story of the season.

While I was designing the visualisation, I soon reasoned that I couldn't make this all about Leicester City while including so much other information. I wanted to show the story of all 20 clubs. Now most readers would have known that Leicester City was the real "story" of the season. They were not just the story in the data, but the story in all newspaper and online reporting. But there was so much more to be seen in my data.

Where Leicester succeeded, much bigger clubs such as (at the time) Arsenal, Tottenham, Liverpool and the Manchester clubs failed. Leicester didn't reach the top of the league for the first few months as Manchester City dominated the initial part of the season. Managers were sacked, surprise results happened every week, and Aston Villa finished a long way off the bottom of the league. And any reader coming across the visualisation who was interested in any of the other 19 teams apart from Leicester would want to be able to find their own story.

Essentially, in the storytelling analogy, there were too many sub-plots for me to ignore. To tell one story was to condense the narrative. In a business situation, when presenting charts to your executives, or when summarising key findings from a customer survey, that's exactly what you do want to do. But in a personal, creative and non-standard visualisation about football? Quite the opposite.

If I only cared about one story, for example, Leicester's success, then with Cole's guiding principles I could have created a much simpler and entirely different visualisation that told that story. It could still include some, or all, of the other data, but we would "grey them out" literally and/or metaphorically to guide our reader through the narrative arc of our sole story to reach the conclusion we wanted to share.

You could consider that an exploratory data visualisation which might be heavy on data, interaction and granularity is similar to a "choose your own adventure" type story, the kind of which was popular when I was growing up. I have used one story, that of Leicester City's success, to prompt me into investigating, visualising and presenting data for the reader to delve further by themselves. We are asking the consumer to discover and enjoy their own story. Or perhaps endure, rather than enjoy, in the case of Aston Villa fans!

Storytelling caveats

Another thing to be clear about is that often the story is that "there is no story". Our data might be the equivalent of a fiction story where our main character goes to the shop to buy a loaf of bread, nothing extraordinary happens and she goes back home again. Or, in more scientific terms, we might have data on something where we'd desperately hoped to see results to get excited about, but our data suggests there is not a significant enough change – cases where our p-value > 0.05, for those who will be familiar with statistics and research.

Maybe we want to visualise a drop in opinion poll ratings or a definite swing from one candidate to another, but the reality is that our findings are inconclusive or meaningless. In these cases, it's so much better to present them without a clear story or to make clear that we are not trying to lead our readers into a conclusion they can't legitimately make.

Another reason to be cautious around telling a story is that as a visualiser, we don't always have the scientific background or access to the original resource/journalism which has generated our data, so we need to be careful not to overstate our conclusion. For example, as mentioned earlier, at time of writing, there is no bigger global issue than the global pandemic COVID-19 which has generated many data visualisations all around the globe. But subjects like this will always be a difficult issue, and we should only tell a story if we're absolutely confident of the underlying facts.

In my case, as an analyst with a mathematical background I can design charts which are accurate, and I would consider myself qualified to make observations on how the data is changing. But without being a scientist (and certainly not an epidemiologist) I can't draw conclusions from the data. I can't explain the stories, which means I can't really tell them with any authority.

In such cases, it's better just to design your charts accurately and well enough that your reader can read and infer their own conclusions if they have greater subject knowledge than you do. As a data storyteller, we can perhaps state the basics (the plot points – in the case of COVID visualisations, the obvious rises and falls of cases, for example) but it's important not just to say no more that the data is actually telling you, but also to say no more than you can actually tell with authority or certainty.

We all need to examine the stories we tell with a critical eye. Are there biases or assumptions we are introducing into the narrative? Does the data itself warrant the claims we are making? Are they statistically valid statements? Or, better still, stay well away from subjects and stories we cannot confidently tell.

Conclusion

In conclusion, not all of these chapters will be neatly summarised with an answer to the question, and this one is no exception. But I do think it warrants a summary of some of the thought processes.

When considering storytelling:

- Think what we mean by storytelling in the context of data visualisation – there are many interpretations on the theme: which, if any, interpretation do we want to follow?

- Think whether the data has one obvious story you want to emphasise – are the "sub-plots" best left un-highlighted, or do you want your readers to be able to find them just as easily?

- Connected to the above, think whether you want your audience to explore the data you are visualising to find their own insight, or to focus on the story you want to tell them.

- Think if there really is a story – is your well-intended desire to create and tell a story with your data telling (or at least exaggerating) a story that isn't fully formed? Perhaps a story that is not statistically proven or factual?

- Decide if it's really necessary to focus on storytelling – perhaps your pleasure is going to be from creating an exploratory (or data art style) visualisation and allowing your audience to consume, explore and enjoy at their leisure.

I'll conclude by saying that "storytelling" is enough of a buzzword to evoke a wide range of often diametrically opposed opinions. If you explore and understand your data and can present it truthfully in a way that engages and intrigues your intended audience, then the argument as to whether you are telling a story is a moot one. And whatever your definition, sometimes the mantra of "Show, don't tell" comes into play – you don't always have to feel obliged to tell a story with every visualisation.

Chapter 1.5

Is it OK to steal?

Write the book you want to read.

Austin Kleon – Steal Like an Artist

Is it OK to heavily base your output on another person's work?

Is it OK to steal? Of course not. In the data visualisation context, that would be passing someone else's work off as your own. Anyone would agree that would be the wrong thing to do. The issue of plagiarism is also a serious one within data visualisation – this chapter doesn't go into detail on this, but it does discuss situations where you are very obviously influenced by someone else's work. It could be phrased: "is it OK to base your visualisation heavily on someone else's work, to the point where it's quite obvious that's what you've done?".

Here's a case in point – first up is a visualisation by Sonja Kuijpers, a freelance data visualisation artist working as Studio TERP in the Netherlands, which visualises the FIFA (Men's) World Cup history of all 80 nations who had taken part up to and including 2018. It's no coincidence that I came across this visualisation as I'm a huge fan of

DOI: 10.1201/9781003240211-6

Sonja's work. Sonja uses Adobe Illustrator to visualise each country at a granular level, with geometric shapes and coloured marks to give a unique representation for each nation (Figure 1.5.1).

FIGURE 1.5.1   History of the FIFA (Men's) World Cup – Sonja Kuijpers.

So, when I wanted to visualise the historic Women's World Cup data, my first thought was to use Sonja's visualisation as an influence. What if I openly did it exactly the same way? The fun challenge for me would be to recreate Sonja's Illustrator work in my own tool of choice (Tableau), and of course, it would look significantly different, with 36 nations instead of 80.

Because it felt so similar, I contacted Sonja before I created the visualisation (or before I published it, at least), to ask if she minded if I recreated a version of exactly the same visualisation using Tableau, using data for women instead of men. Sonja's reply was clear – yes it was absolutely fine, so long as I used an alternative colour scheme using orange as the dominant colour! Fortunately, I knew Sonja well enough to know that she was teasing slightly – the choice of orange was in honour of the Dutch team who play in orange. But that was one particular stipulation I didn't mind at all! Having taken this only stipulation into account, my own version is below (Figure 1.5.2).

The data is different, the layout is different, and it's unmistakeably orange, not pink. But the idea and chart design are identical, and I'd be first to admit it's pretty much the same visualisation. I've been

FIGURE 1.5.2 *History of the FIFA Women's World Cup.*

clear to cite Sonja as inspiration (see the note in the bottom-right part of the visualisation) while linking to the original, because to produce this without acknowledging the original would have just been plain wrong.

It has the same pros and cons as the original. If you want easily readable, accessible, and comparable stats, you can just go to Wikipedia or any good football website, indeed the figures were sourced from Wikipedia in the first place. But I chose a visualisation to emulate that had many features I liked – an exploratory poster-style viz which builds intrigue through showing each nation's history in a colourful and geometric way. I could see no better way to improve on it than to replicate those elements I liked so much using a different dataset.

Using existing work as a template

Another example from my own back catalogue is derived from the initial inspiration of the following work, which shows the character appearances, and deaths, of Game of Thrones characters over time. The visualisation was initially published by Adam McCann on his duelingdata.com website (Figure 1.5.3).

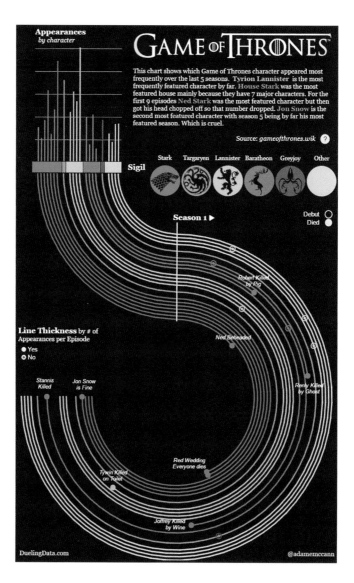

FIGURE 1.5.3 *Game of Thrones appearances by character – Adam McCann.*

If it looks familiar, it's because it was the template I used for my Premier League visualisation featured in the previous chapter. The subject may have been very different, and therefore the underlying data; the design elements may have been different in terms of colour choices, additional design element and curve shape, but some crucial parts were so similar.

In particular, the three-quarter circle with separated grouped lines, merging into one final chart depicting appearances by character, where the continuation of the lines is in fact a simple bar chart designed to look like a line continuation, that much of the visualisation was derived not just from Adam's idea, but from Adam's code.

Fortunately for me, Adam blogged about his process – the clarity with which he moved from sketch to visualisation and the techniques he used proved to be a lightbulb moment for me in my early career. I was able to first understand, and then use his techniques to create what was, for me, a breakthrough visualisation in terms of the creative and non-conventional visualisation style I wanted to emulate.

When I released my Premier League visualisation, I was quick to attribute inspiration to Adam's visualisation. In fact, I still now cite it as one of my favourite and most inspirational visualisations of all time, despite having never watched Game of Thrones, nor having any interest in doing so! And perhaps most importantly as a result, because both Adam and Sonja were appreciative that I'd taken the time to cite them as attribution and inspiration, both were happy to promote and publicly appreciate my own creations as next-level incarnations of their own work among their networks, which were both much larger than mine at the time.

Done properly, using inspiration from earlier data visualisations is a "win-win" process. If you are inspired by someone else's idea and if you then use it with little (but enough) change, and you acknowledge and interact with the original creator, then there's plenty of room in the huge community of data visualisation for both versions and more.

Steal like an artist

One phrase that sums up the philosophy of data visualisations influencing future visualisations is the phrase "Steal like an artist". As I began to visualise data and share my work online, it was a term I was hearing more and more from data visualisation practitioners in the community, by which I mean in the online community where I was learning, interacting and sharing my visualisations. It was a phrase to encourage data visualisers to look for great examples that matched their style and ambition, and to find influences and influencers in the field. This was certainly what I was doing in emulating Sonja and Adam.

What does this mean? Essentially, the main thing is that everyone should almost be encouraged to "steal". If there's someone whose work you admire, copy it! Copy it well, understand it, learn from it, acknowledge it, and in due course adapt it, so that you find your own style.

In the artistic world, some people think Dali influenced Picasso, others think the reverse, but it seems there was a certain amount of "stealing like artists" going on, helping both become arguably the two biggest names in early 20th-century art. A non-expert like myself can certainly see similarities in the work of both artists and has capacity to admire them both in equal measure.

Going back further in time, most of the true master artists did this. The greatest artists of all eras will have eventually found their own style and therefore their own place in history, to the extent that an art expert can usually recognise and categorically define a work as having been done, or not done, by a specific famous artist, even if it is one of the finest imitations or most accurate fakes.

But there's an irony about "Steal like an artist" which has become almost "meta". The truth is that when I first mentioned and enthused about the phrase, I quoted it in my blog, aware at the time that it was from a book, but without due attribution. I knew only that it was a favourite principle of some of the visualisation designers I admired early in my career. My use of the phrase and adherence to the concept was second or even third hand. Below you'll see that I was quite rightly called out by the author, Austin Kleon (Figure 1.5.4).

I was happy to correct my oversight in the best way I knew how – not only by backtracking and editing to make it clear, but also by buying the book. This wasn't exactly a guilty decision – it was very obvious that in citing the philosophy as an inspiration to the way I work, then the book should be a perfect read for me. Perhaps it's karma that I gave my copy away to someone I wanted to inspire to take their first steps in creative data visualisation, so I have since replaced it – I have now bought two copies!

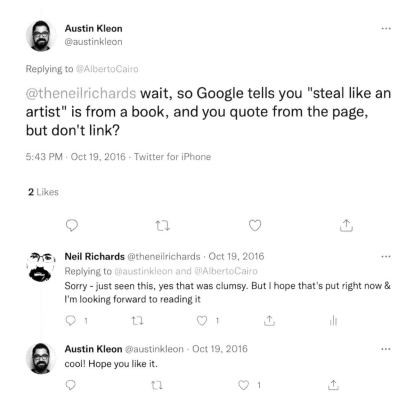

FIGURE 1.5.4   *Tweet by Austin Kleon.*

Nothing is original

The book was, as I expected, a delightful and inspirational read, and this was my key takeaway:

> *Nothing is original, so embrace influence, collect ideas, and remix and re-imagine to discover your own path.*

The concept has helped me hugely in two ways. First, to understand that, as Kleon mentions, to embrace influence and understand that it's very unlikely you will think of something entirely 100% original. As I encouraged myself to be inspired by other practitioners, by designs from other fields, by nature or by metaphors found all around us, and as, through this book, I encourage you to do the same, it reinforced the idea that most, if not all projects, will come from an adaption of a visualisation, a concept or an inspiration that already exists.

Second, it has encouraged me to think of myself as an artist. I get a huge amount of impostor syndrome just writing that sentence because I am not an artist in any other sense of the word. But as I have mentioned before, the field of data visualisation is a unique field which allows us to be creative to the point of being artistic, using data as our medium. If it allows me to extend the metaphor to being an artist, with data as my medium and my visualisation tool of choice as my palette, then to me that's a feeling I would never replicate in any other artistic field. I would genuinely be not even close!

Kleon makes the distinction between "Good Theft" and "Bad Theft". In summary, *Good Theft* consists of the concepts Credit/Transform/Remix. *Bad Theft* consists of Plagiarize/Imitate/Rip Off. Consequently, if I were to give a definitive answer to the chapter's title question "Is it OK to steal?" I would answer in the affirmative. Yes, so long as it is Good Theft.

Bad theft

Before signing off on this chapter, I want to provide an example of where it's **not** OK to steal – an example of where stealing has gone on, but very much not like an artist. In other words, an example of *Bad Theft* is briefly described above. I should add, that when using Tableau Public, where the vast majority of my own work is hosted, I have made the decision to always allow my work to be downloadable. This helps others to see my methods, to learn how I created a particular piece of work and to use or adapt any of these visualisation methods how they seem fit.

It's not a particularly altruistic decision, it just feels like the right thing to do, not least because it helped in my own learning journey immensely. Being able to download Adam McCann's Game of Thrones visualisation, for example, was key to being able to understand some of Adam's techniques and apply them to the Premier League visualisation.

The visualisation in question visualised access to sanitation in a number of nations across the globe. Consisting of a stylised map, with all countries displayed as coloured circles of different sizes, the countries are not in their exact geographical locations but do make a recognisable outline of the continents in most places. Crucially though, this is a bespoke design that I created myself.

Note, the visual itself is shown as Figure 3.7.4 in Chapter 3.7. *Is it possible to tile the world?* where we discuss the design ideas in the context of unconventional map design. But for now, the issue is one of ownership rather than design. So imagine my surprise when I was alerted to an almost identical visualisation a few days later. This visualisation had the same data, the same map, the same black background and Viridis colour scheme, and only very minor text changes.

The person who had downloaded and attempted to republish my visualisation as their own had made just one key mistake. The world map was upside-down! It was only their lack of geographical knowledge that gave them away. Perhaps, the landmasses created by my unconventional mapping weren't familiar enough, but either way, the mistake was made.

I don't want to call out the person who did this, nor display their chart here, since that won't achieve anything. From what I can see, after it was pointed out to them, the chart and user promptly disappeared, and I'm willing to accept, perhaps naively, that it was at least in part an innocent mistake. To give them a modicum of credit, they had downloaded my version and opened it up to take a look, rather than republishing it unseen and unchanged – in doing so, they had obviously inadvertently flipped the vertical axis!

It's not cool to publish other's work as your own or to not make enough effort to attribute your influences and make it look like your own. Chances are, if you can get hold of the original creator, they will be happy to share advice, offer assistance or even spread the reach of your new creation, so long as you haven't just blatantly stolen.

Conclusion

In the interests of balance, it's worth considering when you might not need to cite or attribute a visualisation. I'm not sure I have a clear answer to that. After all, you wouldn't cite William Playfair each time you use a bar chart. I'm hoping that there doesn't need to be a hard and fast set of rules that stipulates which criteria you need to have met in order to create a visualisation without needing to share attribution.

I would hope that in most situations the correct course of action is pretty obvious. If you know you are using something that's commonly used, and your own idea doesn't borrow heavily from an obvious chart, feature or bespoke design of another designer, then you're probably OK. It doesn't hurt to be on the safe side though, and you alone will know whether you significantly borrowed or stole the idea in the first place.

In other words, it's OK to steal if you *Steal like an artist.* And to quote from Austin Kleon's book one more time:

Be nice. (The world is a small town).

1.6

Is white space always your friend?

I don't think there is anything wrong with white space. I don't think it's a problem to have a blank wall.

Annie Leibovitz

Creating an annotated line graph

This chapter centres around a visualisation I created in response to a community challenge set by data visualisation expert Cole Nussbaumer Knaflic through her *Storytelling with Data* website. The challenge was simple: *Using any data you care to source, create (and share) an annotated line graph.*

The obvious choice for a line chart was to look at change of a particular number over time, and before long I settled on a chart about baby names – baby names are always a fun, uncontroversial and freely available source of data. And, as is my wont, if my visualisation is going to be conventional, at least I'll try and make the particular angle of the visualisation relevant to me and unlikely to be chosen by many others.

I decided to focus on the name Neil (my spelling only!). My visualisation is shown below (Figure 1.6.1).

DOI: 10.1201/9781003240211-7

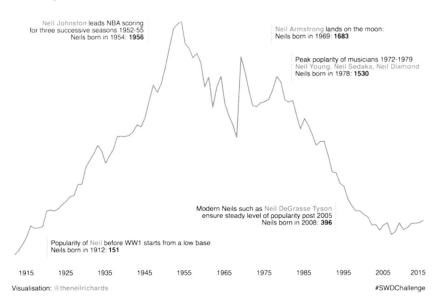

Rise and Fall of the name Neil in the USA
Births 1912–2015

Source: data.gov

Neil Johnston leads NBA scoring
for three successive seasons 1952-55
Neils born in 1954: **1956**

Neil Armstrong lands on the moon:
Neils born in 1969: **1683**

Peak poplarity of musicians 1972-1979
Neil Young, Neil Sedaka, Neil Diamond
Neils born in 1978: **1530**

Modern Neils such as Neil DeGrasse Tyson
ensure steady level of popularity post 2005
Neils born in 2008: **396**

Popularity of Neil before WW1 starts from a low base
Neils born in 1912: **151**

| 1915 | 1925 | 1935 | 1945 | 1955 | 1965 | 1975 | 1985 | 1995 | 2005 | 2015 |

Visualisation: @theneilrichards   #SWDChallenge

FIGURE 1.6.1   *Rise and fall of the name Neil in USA.*

Data-ink ratio

Crucial to the principles used in attempting to create a clean, uncluttered visualisation which highlights the important data elements is the data-ink ratio, introduced by visualisation expert Edward Tufte in his seminal publication *The Visual Display of Quantitative Information* in 1983.

Data-ink is defined as the "ink" necessary to show the data in a given chart (which cannot be removed without altering the integrity of the chart). All other (non-blank) elements of a data visualisation are referred to as "non-data-ink"; in other words, the "ink" used in creating any elements of the chart deemed not absolutely necessary to show the data. Tufte considers this unnecessary and distracting. The data-ink ratio is therefore the ratio of *data-ink/non-data-ink*.

Given the importance placed on showing the data and nothing else, we can conclude from this that a high data-ink ratio is good – the higher the better. As a result, we are encouraged to remove all clutter from charts. Anything considered "non-data-ink" is effectively thought of as clutter.

Chartjunk

In discussing the issue, Tufte introduces the principle of "chartjunk", a phrase he is considered to have coined himself. Chartjunk is described, perhaps loosely, as those visual elements of charts and graphs that are not necessary to comprehend the information represented on the graph, or that distract the viewer from this information.

I'm not particularly enamoured with the phrase because it's not exactly neutral. Nobody wants to be thought of as producing or displaying "junk" so the term comes with a negative preconception. Nevertheless, it's repeatedly used by Tufte and thus well understood, so we'll continue to use it here.

And I'm also not 100% sure what constitutes chartjunk by this definition – I would see this definition as being very similar, if not the same, as the definition of "non-data-ink", but I do know that one of the classic images often used to illustrate chartjunk is the chart below from Nigel Holmes (incidentally, he is described by Tableau Research Scientist and industry expert Robert Kosara as the "anti-Tufte").

Nigel Holmes was graphic director for Time magazine at the time of the publication of *The Visual Display of Quantitative Information* in 1983. There's no doubt that, from a purely analytical viewpoint, there are non-necessary and potentially distracting visual elements here, and it's this chart that Tufte launches into in his follow-up book *Envisioning Information* with the following diatribe (Figure 1.6.2):

> *Consider this unsavory exhibit – chockablock with cliché and stereotype, coarse humour, and a content-empty third dimension. [...] Everything counts, but nothing matters. The data-thin chart mixes up changes in the value of money with changes in diamond prices, a crucial confusion because the graph chronicles a time of high inflation.*
>
> *Lurking behind chartjunk is a contempt both for information and for the audience. Chartjunk promoters imagine that numbers and details are boring, dull and tedious, requiring ornament to enliven. [...] Credibility vanishes in clouds of chartjunk; who would trust a chart that looks like a video game?*

FIGURE 1.6.2 Diamonds were a girl's best friend – Nigel Holmes.

At this point, I present Holmes' chart without comment, simply as context and explanation for Tufte's definitions and subsequent comments above. But it's hard not to form your own opinion on this! I'll discuss this in a postscript towards the end of this chapter.

Back to the annotated line chart

For now, it's back to my own chart – I used as many good data visualisation practices as I could think of to come up with a clear, concise example of an annotated line chart to hone my chart presentation skills and create something fit for the challenge.

I chose to use a single highlight colour. Orange had no particular significance, but once chosen it was important to remain consistent and not introduce other spurious colours into the chart. I ensured that the chart had no borders, no grid lines, and just the very faintest of grey for its vertical axis.

The horizontal axis was removed entirely as I added direct labelling, focusing only on peaks and troughs of interest. I made sure that I added no icons or extraneous graphics, certainly nothing that might be considered as "chartjunk".

By now, my chart looks like this – before deciding where to add value labels, and before adding the additional annotation labels (Figure 1.6.3).

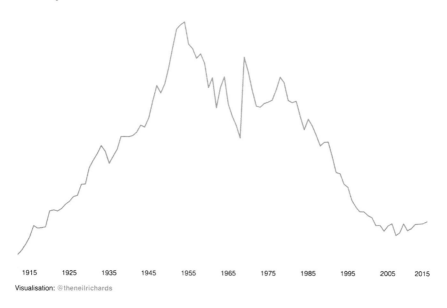

Rise and Fall of the name Neil in the USA
Births 1912–2015

Source: data.gov

| 1915 | 1925 | 1935 | 1945 | 1955 | 1965 | 1975 | 1985 | 1995 | 2005 | 2015 |

Visualisation: @theneilrichards

FIGURE 1.6.3 *Rise and fall of the name Neil in USA – earlier version.*

By this point, I have probably ensured that the data/ink ratio is as high as possible, or, at least, pretty high. In using very little non-data-ink, I have a data-ink ratio that Tufte would be proud of. But the chart isn't finished at this point. We already know that from this most minimal point I have then added more content. In particular, in line with the original challenge requirement, I've added text annotations throughout to give context to numbers and highlight interesting and important areas of the chart.

In using these annotations, I would even assert that I am bringing the chart to life to the point where it is then telling a story. In highlighting the interesting and important areas of the chart, I'm setting the scene, I'm accentuating the rise and fall, I'm facilitating the narrative arc, I'm leading the reader to the climax. In short, I'm bringing in all the elements of storytelling that would not be possible without annotation.

The addition of annotations is probably the main design complication here. How many annotations do we add? Where do we put them and how do we format them? How much space do we take up with them? After all – the addition of every non-data element is lowering the data-ink ratio of the chart. In this case, I've tried to be succinct and leave the graph clear enough to speak for itself but have used the annotations to offer up some analytical insight.

White space

I entitled this chapter "Is white space always your friend?" However, though it's an integral element of chart design, I haven't mentioned the concept of white space yet, only data-ink and non-data-ink. Crucially, the data-ink ratio only considers the latter two elements and holds firm (however much you choose to adhere to the principle of whether or not to keep it as high as possible) regardless of whether your charts are surrounded by a lot, or a little white space.

So, what is "white space"? Put simply, any area with no "ink" would be considered white space. This would really consist of your plain chart background, so although it is often white (as in my example), your chart's white space can technically be any colour, even black. And the reason that white space is crucial to this chapter, and the principles of designing in a minimalist way that highlights the data elements, is that every time you make the decision to remove non-data-ink (or chartjunk) you increase the amount of white space in your chart.

Why else did I entitle the chapter: "Is white space always your friend?" Generally, if you google anything to do with "white space" in the context of design and data visualisation, in particular, you'll come back to two phrases, in particular.

"White space is your friend", or

"White space is not your enemy"

Probably the most famous iteration of the phrase is from the book of the same name by Rebecca Hagen and Kim Golombinsky – a book aimed at graphic, web and multimedia designers aimed at helping its readers to produce effective visual communication.

Many other publications have thoughts on the concept of white space. Cole Nussbaumer Knaflic's *Storytelling with Data* book says "We need to get more comfortable with white space" and mentions the "powerful effect that white space used strategically can have on our visual communications". The *Big Book of Dashboards* authors (Messrs Cotgreave, Shaffer and Wexler) state that "white space used subtly creates distinct zones on your dashboards" and highlights use in a dashboard where "adequate white space allows the data to stand out and not be overwhelmed by complexity". Alberto Cairo's Functional Art website reiterates that "White space is your friend. Empty space is needlessly unused space, white space has meaning".

Empty space

Each of these assertions leads to one important distinction, between that of white space and empty space. White space is a choice. The exact placement and amount of white space is a strategic design choice that allows data or annotation elements to be more readable or allows for aesthetic design and placement of data and annotation elements. It reduces our cognitive load as we focus on the crucial elements of the visualisation.

That leaves "empty space". Have we left areas of the chart that would be better used by adding more data-ink or non-data-ink? Perhaps our chart is not well-enough explained, and there are non-useful blank areas that would be better served with an explanation, a title, a legend or a logo? Empty space might be considered any non-used space that isn't there by design. In other words, non-used space that isn't doing any of the great things white space can do in the paragraph above.

Back to my un-annotated chart, it's undoubtedly clean and uncluttered, but there's no context, no story, and the reader would be hard pressed to find insight from it. I'd be certain here that not all of the white space (in the literal sense) is my friend. The chart is sparser than it needs to be, and some of the non-used space is definitely what we have defined above as empty space.

For example, I made the choice to remove the vertical axis in the original submission, because I include the values in my annotations. But without these annotations, we have no idea of scale, and no explanation of peaks and troughs, so the empty space is crying out for the inclusion of an axis, or some contextual explanations.

Once those decisions have been made and annotations added, I hope then I've left the right amount of white space to keep the graph readable and not overwhelming, to allow it to breathe and to give it a clean, minimalist look. I've determined a small number of interesting areas of the chart to highlight and annotate. Since the nature of the ups and downs of the name's popularity is that these areas will occur at the start, middle and end of the timelines, this then breaks up and reduces the empty/blank space nicely.

Finalised chart

Now let's review my finalised chart. Are my annotations going too far? Am I more Holmes than Tufte? Might my annotations be considered chartjunk? It seems to me that the key is to think about usage of space in two ways. If we're reviewing any given chart, we can categorise any area as "filled" or "unfilled".

Consider *filled space*: Does this space really need to be filled, completely or at all? If not, then using less space, or white space here will lead to a clearer and less cluttered visual.

Consider *unfilled space*: Is this empty space better served by adding in something else, such as annotation, a legend or additional information? If so, then we're talking about *empty space*. If not, and it helps with the clarity of the pure visual element, then leave it alone (this is your friendly *white space*. Unfilled space is an opportunity (it is your friend, perhaps?) to shape your design, to add context or story.

So, to me anyway, the key element to this challenge was in balancing the three elements of empty space, white space and annotation. To answer the chapter's question – most people would agree that *white space* is your friend, but *empty space* is not.

Story behind a line

Just in case you thought this was starting to make sense and you had an idea of what the perfect example of a good data-ink ratio or ideal opportunity to take advantage of unfilled space might be, below is a section of the visualisation "Story behind a line" by Federica Fragapane, found at https://www.storiesbehindaline.com (Figure 1.6.4).

S.S., 20 years old
Gao, Mali

1394 days
7771 kilometers

He lost his parents.

Vercelli
Italy

Gao
Mali

Paths
Map
Date

Distances

Home Legend
About

FIGURE *1.6.4   The story behind a line – Federica Fragapane.*

This is one of a collection of pages that visualises long journeys taken by individual asylum seekers from their home towns and villages to the end of their journeys in Italy. Beautifully minimalist in terms of the data-ink ratio (the data-ink is made almost entirely of each individual's route, with annotations and explanations only where necessary), it is also very high in unfilled space.

In many circumstances, this may leave the visualisation looking bleak and empty, crying out for more data or information. However, in this case the designer has chosen to leave large amounts of white space, much more than you would expect to see on most visualisations. In doing this, she's choosing to emphasise how each journey is long, crossing huge continents – the unfilled space accentuates this space beautifully.

And it's the only element of the story she wants to tell, there is no additional context other than the very simple story at the top left for each individual – anything more (whether data-ink or non-data-ink) would be not only unnecessary but also detracts from the metaphor. In this case, the unfilled space remains unfilled.

Whether you would consider it white or empty in the context of our definitions here is a moot point, but the ability to use it within this powerful design means that in this case, the presence of large amounts of it is our friend.

Postscript

As a postscript, I want to add a potentially interesting additional question to this chapter at this point. What was your favourite chart in this chapter, or to put it another way, which chart do you most remember? Of course, in putting the question in different terms, I acknowledge that the answers to each phrase could be very different!

There's obviously not a correct answer to the above, but I can say with certainty that if a collection of people read this chapter up to now and answered the above question, then at least some of them will give the Nigel Holmes diamond price visualisation as an answer to one or both versions of the question. If I were to give my own opinion, it would be full of praise for Holmes' diamond visualisation, if only because in the unlikely event that someone were to ask me what the trend was for diamond prices in the early 1980s, I would remember the image with a smile and quite easily remember the general shape of the timeline.

You might consider the image itself to be somewhat "over the top" but the impact, the visceral reaction and even the discussion points within the design choice, all lead to increase the memorability of the chart itself and the data contained within it, even if, aesthetically, you find it pleasing or displeasing. And perhaps for all the reasons mentioned above, I love it!

I asked earlier in the chapter, when discussing adding non-chart elements, "Am I more Holmes than Tufte?" But I intentionally didn't imply whether that was a good or bad thing – I leave you to infer one or the other. It may well depend whether you are part of the intended audience for one or other of the charts – is it important that you have analytical information at your fingertips? If that's not the case, your answer probably comes from the context of the visualisation, or your own personal preferences. Or both!

Impact leads to intrigue, and intrigue leads to insight. The skill of a designer, if indeed it is their intent, is to bring out the insights from the data, albeit how they choose to do that is a whole different discussion! But there is a better chance of those insights being found if your reader's attention is first attracted and then held. Similarly, others will choose the powerful visualisation from Federica Fragapane as their favourite chart image of this chapter, with its deliberate, stark, empty space.

Conclusion

I'm pleased with the outcome of my own chart, not least because it was featured in Jon Schwabish's book "Better Data Visualisation" as an instructive example of an annotated line chart, even if my pride at being included was dampened slightly when I found that I had equal billing in the book's index with Neil Armstrong, Neil Sedaka, Neil Diamond and Neil deGrasse Tyson. And perhaps surprisingly, as someone who loves to experiment, create impactful and unorthodox visualisations and look for unique and creative ways to express himself with data, when I'm asked which of my visualisations I'm most proud of, I often refer to this simple annotated line chart.

It might also surprise many who know me that I do own two of Tufte's seminal data visualisation books and that I re-read them in order to prepare a good grounding for this chapter. Indeed, Tufte's books and principles are not necessarily the first (or even the tenth) that I turn to when looking for creative data visualisation inspiration.

But it's important to acknowledge that 90% of charts and visualisations I might produce in my "day job" in business intelligence will adhere to Tufte's principles, including minimising data-ink ratios where possible, even if 90% of the charts and visualisations I create in my personal portfolio and demonstrate in this book do not!

End of Section I

We come to the end of the first section of this book which has covered only a selection of guiding principles that everyone would be advised to be aware of and to learn. As you progress through the next two sections, you will encounter more and more examples where I encourage you to question what you have learned, and more principles you might have come across, to help you come up with more inspiration or ideas for creative data visualisations.

There's an important adage that states that you need to understand the rules to know when to break them. A cliché it may be, but it's certainly true – I try and assert that there may be well-established guidelines but there are very few hard and fast rules in data visualisation, and it's with this mindset that you can grow your skills, increase your creativity and widen your repertoire.

I'm not saying the remainder of the book will lead you fully down the lines of "chartjunk" visualisations, nor should it! However, if, like me, you rather like the idea of becoming an anti-Tufte, you can't do so without learning, understanding, appreciating and applying Tufte's principles in the right situations.

The rest is then up to you!

First

Challenging — Idea

—

CHALLENGING QUESTIONS

Why do we visualise data?

Let the dataset change your mindset.

Hans Rosling

Definitions of data visualisation

Many people have tried to define data visualisation. It wouldn't be right of me to come up with a definition that was much, or even at all, different from the definition as given by Andy Kirk in his book *Data Visualisation: A Handbook for Data-Driven Design*, given the absolute underlying importance of the concept. Andy defines data visualisation as "The visual representation and presentation of data to facilitate understanding".

And although, in defining the concept of data visualisation, we might think that this answers the question of "what" but it doesn't answer the question of "why" per se, in actual fact the second half of the definition does give us a good "why". The reason we visualise data is *in order to facilitate understanding*.

Another way of putting this would be to look at the mission statement of data visualisation software suppliers Tableau, whose

DOI: 10.1201/9781003240211-9

73

mission is "to help customers see and understand data". If you take the customer/client relationship out of this, then you can certainly reword this to substitute in our chart readers instead of our clients. And because I'm not trying to be too exact or tool-specific about this, and I want to generalise this instead for most applications of data visualisation, I can happily say that "we visualise data to help people see and understand data".

This is definitely a definition that works for me in the conventional sense. There's an element of tautology there, since the word "see" is used in conversational English not just in the visual sense, but in the sense of understanding. Think how often you have used, or heard, the phrase "I see ..." when referring to understanding or acknowledging an explanation.

But I want to answer the question a lot more specifically. Why do *I*, the author of this book, visualise data? If I haven't made it clear already in the introduction to this book, I love visualising data. That's why I regularly visualise data as a hobby, or for fun. It's why I attend and speak at user groups, why I look forward to conferences as the highlights of my year and why I spend much of my non-work spare time on my own creative data visualisation projects. And, of course, it's why I chose to start a blog and ultimately write this book on data visualisation.

If I'm going to lay myself bare by offering thoughts, opinions, advice and visualisation examples that represent my very personal data visualisation ethos and journey, then to understand why I personally visualise data will be to help understand the mindset behind this book.

I'll attempt to answer that with two separate examples, both of which occurred during personal data visualisation projects, and both of which illustrate the fulfilment I've been able to get from data visualisation.

The President of Nauru

The first instance was from a local Tableau User Group, in Birmingham (UK, not Alabama!) which took place in early 2018. Perhaps there's already a clue to my enjoyment found in visualising data and being part of visualisation communities, in the fact that it's not actually the user group most local to me. But in any case, the group was a chance to hold a gathering of users from the Birmingham area to meet, network and listen to data visualisation related presentations.

On this particular day, we had an informal "hackathon" which was a chance to get together in small groups to get to know each other, and then visualise the data based on a common dataset supplied to all the attendees. What visualisation could we create and present back to the group in the course of about an hour?

The group had been pre-supplied with data on medallists from the Commonwealth Games, to celebrate Birmingham's awarding of the tournament for 2022. For those not familiar with the Commonwealth Games, the Games are a four-yearly multi-sport tournament that are, in British terms, second only in size and stature to the Olympic Games, featuring nations from the Commonwealth of Nations, a group of nations which are almost, but not quite, equivalent to the list of nations formerly part of the British Empire, including Australia, India, Canada and many Caribbean and African nations.

We'd had the opportunity to look through the data and prepare something in advance, but my case, I only allowed myself half an hour or so on the train journey up to Birmingham to try something. I was quite pleased to have got to a good starting point by producing this bump chart.

A bump chart is a type of line chart usually looking at rankings over time, with circles on each node to encode or display further information, such as the rank or dimension, in this case the country, being tracked. It was far from finished, but I had attempted to do some analysis, looking at the following questions: who have been the top ten nations over the years, how have they changed from competition to competition and how did being host nation affect them? The host nations in my chart below are shown with double-sized circles (Figure 2.1.1).

OK, so I've got some analytics here. It's not earth-shattering though. I haven't added a colour legend yet, but my version of the visualisation had the countries identifiable on hovering, and the main countries generally use the national colour associated with their national sports teams. Australia (in a gold colour) usually ranks top, with England (white) and Canada (red) doing well. Host nations usually get a spike in medals – this just about holds true

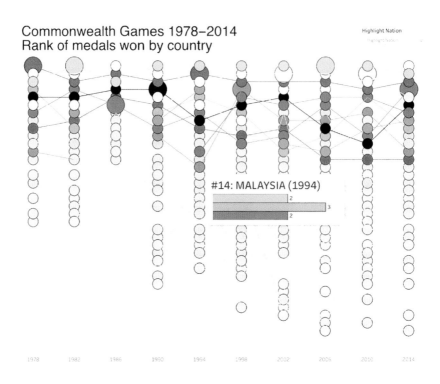

Commonwealth Games 1978–2014
Rank of medals won by country

Highlight Nation

#14: MALAYSIA (1994)

1978   1982   1986   1990   1994   1998   2002   2006   2010   2014

FIGURE 2.1.1   Commonwealth Games medallists by country (draft).

but it's quite a well-known fact, and the host nations are generally always from the top few performing countries anyway, so it's hard to make much of that.

It's a quick analysis, and it looks OK. But one thing stands out to me that I wasn't looking for at first. What's going on in 1986? Why such a short column, with far fewer countries obtaining a medal of any kind? Maybe that's where the story is?

At the hackathon element of the evening, we paired together with users we hadn't met or worked with before. My partner for the evening, Andrew, hadn't started on any visualising of this dataset, but he had sourced a dataset including national population data for all countries and was keen to look at correlation with population. With the population data included we decided to look at first medals, then country rankings, considering number of medals pro rata. As Andrew was less experienced than me, I was more than happy to put my visualisation to one side and work on something with this additional data source (Figure 2.1.2).

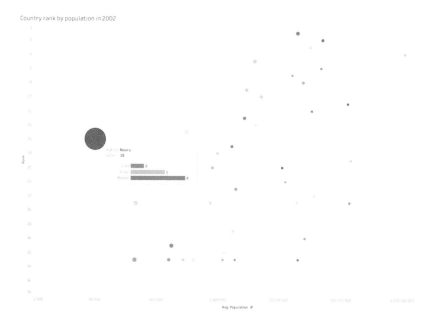

Country rank by population in 2002

FIGURE 2.1.2 Commonwealth Games medal table rank by population (draft).

We devised a rough and ready Hans Rosling-style scatterplot of country population on the x-axis versus medal table ranking on the y-axis, with each circle sized by number of medals per million of population. Note that a log axis was needed just to get India in on the same scale – this is not potentially a final design decision we were likely to make, but an intermediary decision while we were exploring the data.

Hans Rosling

It's worth deviating at this point to explain who Hans Rosling was. Rosling, who died in 2017, was a Swedish physicist who co-founded and chaired Gapminder Foundation. He gave a number of instrumental TED talks containing data visualisation, themed around his optimistic view on international development. In each of these talks, he would usually stand in front of a huge screen explaining the movement of animated data points in scatterplots behind him, where each coloured circle represented one country.

Usually with a trademark long pointer to reach particular areas on the screen that he wanted to talk about, his energy, positive attitude and charisma were utterly captivating. Many, myself very much included, would cite him as a key influence in introducing them to the field of data visualisation, as he demonstrated the power that data has in communicating globally important issues, when in the hands of an expert data storyteller.

Chapter 1.4: "Do data visualisations have to tell a story?" highlighted the debate around storytelling in data, but regardless of opinions on the definitions and importance of the storytelling concept, most in our field are unanimous that when it came to telling stories with data and mastering the act of communicating with data, in particular, Hans Rosling was peerless. In terms of career influencers, then for me, Hans Rosling is a big part, probably the biggest, in the

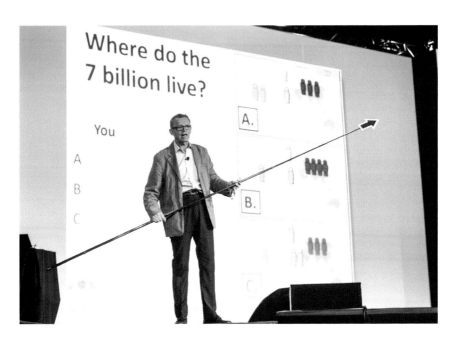

FIGURE 2.1.3   Hans Rosling (2014) – photo Red Mar Photography via eagereyes. com.

answer to this chapter's question of why I visualise data (Figure 2.1.3).

Back to our Commonwealth Games chart, and any charts we made which were looking at medals per person, here represented by the size of each bubble, kept showing up two outliers that skewed the graph and hid any correlations. First instinct had been to ignore India on the right (huge population) and Nauru on the left (tiny population) but on reflection, it became pretty obvious that Nauru was the story.

We cycled through the scatterplot for each competition year, and here we just show the picture in 2002, when the red Nauru circle was at its largest. The process of exploratory data visualisation had moved us away from one potential story to a totally different one.

But I wasn't done yet – the last several minutes of the session were spent away from Tableau, scrolling through Wikipedia. I was still intrigued about the countries taking part in 1986, or more to the point the countries not taking part. Why so few? There were well-known boycotts in the 1980 and 1984 Olympic games which I remember well, but the 1986 Commonwealth games? Look at the countries whose line graphs have a gap there: Nigeria, Kenya, India, Jamaica, …

Visualising this data led me to discover there was a widespread boycott of the Commonwealth games in protest over South African sporting links. It was very obviously an overwhelmingly "White" games as the predominantly non-White countries stayed away. This just wouldn't have been obvious had the data been shown in a less visual way, and that's why I love visualising data, for those times when we look for a story to tell and find another one we weren't expecting.

I then still found time to learn about Nauru's proud weightlifting tradition and their resultant regular success at the Commonwealth games. Furthermore, a total of seven gold medals were won by just one athlete over the course of four tournaments: Marcus Stephen. Given the tiny population of Nauru, this one highly successful athlete had a huge effect on his country's medals per population ratio, far more than any other athlete.

And whatever happened to Marcus Stephen? Undoubtedly helped in part by his national hero status for bringing sporting success to his small nation, he went on to become President of Nauru from 2007 to 2011, that's what!

Again, this is something I would never have known about and found very hard to find without the exploration that visualising the data allowed me. With more time we could have really focussed on this aspect or completely redesigned the visualisation to tell the story of Nauru. I had arrived in Birmingham that evening with one unfinished visualisation, and I left not with a polished final version, but with two unfinished visualisations. But I had acquired several snippets of extra knowledge that genuinely fascinated me, as well as making a contact who I would eventually stay in touch with and work together with further down the line. That's the opportunity that data visualisation offers.

Decimal fractions

Another reason I visualise data is to create something I enjoy. One of the most important considerations in creating any data visualisation is to consider your audience. In particular, when you have a client brief, or if you work for a specific team or department, this consideration is of paramount importance, and it is crucial to have a clear understanding of exactly who that audience is.

But for some personal projects, your audience might be less clear. Essentially, your audience might be people who share the same interests as you, people who have similar design tastes to you, in data visualisation terms or otherwise. Either way, if it's not a commissioned piece, then your audience will be a relatively small subset of people who spontaneously come across your creation. In my case, they most likely will have found it posted on my blog or on Twitter.

Therefore, for personal creative projects, you might accept that your audience is "niche". The enjoyment from the project will come from your own creation, your own involvement in the process or your own satisfaction with the project.

With that in mind, I often design with *myself* as the audience. And specifically, a significant number of my visualisations are designed with the idea that I think they might look great poster-sized and displayed on the wall. My wall. They may never see the light of day as posters, or be displayed on anything other than a phone, tablet or computer screen, but that is often my incentive.

My intended audience can often, therefore, be summed up as the imaginary Venn diagram intersects between "People who find the same things interesting as I do" and "People with similar design tastes who think this might look quite good on a wall".

One such example was a recent visualisation I created when looking at numbers; specifically, the fractions of the numbers 1–100 in decimal form. I'll talk about this later in the book, where this was one of a number of visualisations I created looking at mathematical patterns. But as I was creating this and forming ideas of how I might want to design it, my mind went back (a long way) to my youth. Wouldn't posters, which were fun, colourful and impactful ways of looking at numbers make great adornments for walls in classrooms?

My own mathematics classes were often spent gazing at multiplication tables when younger, or M.C. Escher tessellations in posters on the classroom wall when a little bit older. These posters formed part of my lessons in formative years which led all the way to a Mathematics degree when I was older. Now that my focus is on designing with data, wouldn't it be cool to come up with something that would look good on mathematics classroom walls of the present or future?

My visualisation looked at the patterns in recurring decimals. Using bright and bold colours for every digit, I imagined these hypothetical classrooms and created something I was really pleased with. I knew that wasn't going to set the world alight or gain widespread recognition.

But, going back to "consider your audience" – I was basically just aiming at those who find number sequences and bold geometric colour blocks fun, and maybe, just maybe, hypothetical classrooms full of young children studying mathematics who were as keen and number-obsessed as I was when I was younger.

I published the visualisation, first on my public profile and social media, and second on my *Questions in Dataviz* blog as part of a larger discussion around visualisation of numbers and decimals. You can see the full-size visualisation and the discussion around it in *3.8 Can you create visualisations using only numbers?* However, several months later I received the following message via e-mail to my website:

> Hi! *I'm a middle school math teacher, and I'd love to print the visualization of the repeating decimals as a large(ish) poster for my classroom. It would be an awesome way to show repeating vs. terminating decimals!*

Now **that** is why we visualise data!

It's certainly why I personally visualise data creatively and in unorthodox fashion sometimes, to get creative pleasure in the process, to have fun and to hope that the end users will enjoy it in exactly the same way I hoped they might, even if that potential group of end users is both very small and very specific.

There are just two posters of "Decimal Fractions" in existence. One is now in my office in the UK, and one is now on the wall of a classroom in Oregon in the United States. That, to me at least, is better than a million upvotes on Reddit! What's more, the poster is below a series of images featuring figures of a cartoon man making a series of different curves with his arms – every shape is approximating the figure of the graph equation underneath. Forgive my mathematical excitement – I love these posters, they are such fun visualisations and I would have spent ages in the classroom poring over these, enjoying their wit and appreciating how they were a great way of remembering the shapes of curves (Figure 2.1.4).

FIGURE 2.1.4   *Decimal fractions – photo Martha Sherman.*

First

Challenging

Idea

Now before I lose you as I go hazy-eyed over mathematical formulas, my point is not just that I am happy to see my visualisation on the wall as a poster, but better still that I am delighted in the fun mathematical poster company it keeps. I might not have known it at the time, but I designed a visualisation that found its spiritual home almost 5000 miles away.

Conclusion

The two examples in this chapter are just that really, two anecdotes. There were many other moments that might not have "make the cut" for this chapter that also had those unexpected moments that made the process worthwhile. Both demonstrate visualisations I created for pleasure, subjects where I continued learning during the process, with unexpected twists in the outcome, leading to encounters with new people being invested in the visualisations.

Sure, we visualise data to help our end users and clients see and understand their data. But we do it for pleasure knowing that every visualisation might lead to something unexpected such as the examples in this chapter. And that, to me, is a good enough reason to keep visualising data.

Why do we visualise using triangles?

The laws of Nature are written in the language of mathematics […] the symbols are triangles, circles and other geometrical figures, without whose help it is impossible to comprehend a single word.

Galileo Galilei

Length versus area

Despite the question – the triangle is not an especially common shape, or theme, in data visualisations. In zero-dimensional form, data is represented simply by dots, usually encoded by position in space on the page or screen. If "zero-dimensional" doesn't make sense to you, don't worry, I just mean that it has no dimensions that can be counted or quantified – in data visualisation terms that means there is no additional encoding possible from the shape itself. In one-dimensional form, our dots become lines, so we now have the length of a line allowing us to encode further information.

If we want to consider two dimensions, we need elements of length and width. That might be extending our data mark in perpendicular

DOI: 10.1201/9781003240211-10

direction, such as a square or rectangle, in all directions equally (a circle) or any number of directions, which then leads to any polygon you care to imagine, such as a triangle. But the introduction of a second dimension can introduce uncertainty.

Are we trying to encode quantity using the shape's area? Or using just one of the shape's dimensions? And if the latter, are we using its height, or its width? Its radius? A line from one corner to the middle of an opposite side? The point is, that once we have a shape of three or more sides (thinking here of a circle as a shape with an infinite number of sides), we already have myriad ways of measuring it. All of which may lead to different results or interpretations of our data.

Some of you might be nervous at this point – is he going to carry on the sequence and advocate three dimensions? Aren't 3D pie charts bad, especially "exploding" ones? There's no need to worry, I won't be discussing three-dimensional visualisations anywhere in the book. If you haven't realised already, I always encourage you to think about the advantages of the unusual or unconventional visualisation style, so perhaps it won't surprise you that I don't necessarily think all 3D visualisation is bad *per se*, in fact far from it! But that's as far as I'll go in this publication.

In fact, if we're considering the length of a triangle, are we measuring the length of its base? One of its sides? Its height above the base? All of these measures can be quite different in any given triangle (Figure 2.2.1).

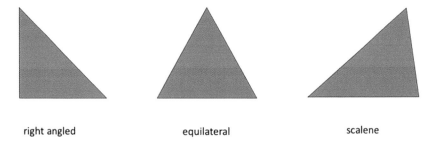

right angled   equilateral   scalene

FIGURE 2.2.1   *Types of triangles.*

The irregular nature of triangles means that our ability to compare areas of triangles against each other is affected – it's harder to do so with triangles than with squares. And that's already hard. Consider the below figure which represents questions and results from a survey designed by Steve Wexler, co-author of the book *The Big Picture* (Cotgreave, Shaeffer, Wexler, 2021), in order to make this point.

The two left-hand charts represent the two questions: first "if circle F=100, what is circle G?", and second "if bar A=100, what is bar C?" (Figure 2.2.2).

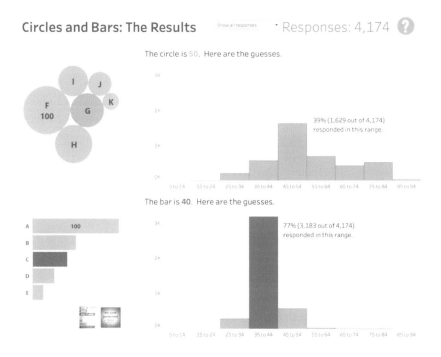

FIGURE 2.2.2   *Circles and bars: results of survey estimating values from a circle and a bar – Steve Wexler.*

These results can be seen in print in the book, but I include them here with more up-to-date results. That's because I had to take the survey myself to get to this page. I, despite knowing the pitfalls of the questions and the points that they were trying to make, and, despite the fact I'm pretty sure I already took the survey a few months ago, got the bar question exactly right, but the circle question wrong. My guess of 45 for the latter question got me *just* into the teal bar but was an underestimation of 10%. The inference is clear – estimating and comparing areas are much harder than estimating and comparing lengths.

These are all principles around cognition that may be dissuading you from using triangles. If accurate interpretation is needed, especially where areas are concerned, then why indeed are we using triangles?

Why visualise using triangles?

So, let's go back to why we visualise using triangles. My blog post of the same title was a deliberate nod to a previous post asking why we visualise using circles, and the previous post in question was very much an homage to *The Book of Circles* (Manuel Lima, 2017). In this book, Manuel Lima was able to use images throughout history from art, astronomy, biology, cartography as well as data visualisation. To distil his observations down to just two points, the use of circles comes down to two major advantages:

> *Firstly, the metaphor of a circle represents a number of things: infinity (through eternity, immensity, etc.); movement (with the concept of continual force, rotation, cyclicality, periodicity, etc.); unity (representing wholeness, completion, containment, etc.) and perfection (simplicity, balance, harmony, symmetry).*
>
> *And secondly, there's no doubting the aesthetics of a circle, they just plain look good. Whether a circle is the overall shape of the visualisation or graphic (encapsulating its contents in a pleasing circular form), or circles represent constituent elements of a larger visualisation, there is always a choice to be made in just how good, or appropriate, the circle might be.*

So how do these ideas apply to triangles?

I briefly started down the line of googling "symbolism of triangle" here, but really there are as many interpretations as there are articles, and I'm not particularly interested in spiritual connotations, since it's unlikely that visualisations I might create or enjoy consuming are on a spiritual theme. But one recurring theme is the theme of strength. The triangle is a sturdy shape – of all the regular polygons it has the smallest internal angle, and as a result, it's the hardest polygon to "squash".

First

Challenging

Idea

And we know that six equilateral triangles combine to make a regular hexagon, and hexagons can tessellate to form honeycomb structures, one of the most solid, regular structures known in nature (Figure 2.2.3).

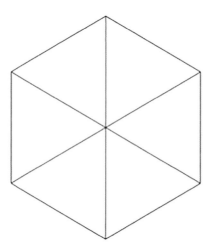

FIGURE 2.2.3   *Hexagon consisting of six triangles.*

Where metaphors for the triangle are concerned, we can imagine triangles to represent things that are roughly triangular in shape. The strength metaphor is also considered when we might think of triangles to represent trees, valleys or mountain peaks, all natural features of great stature and endurance.

The final relevance of the triangle is perhaps the most obvious. Whereas a circle might be thought of to represent infinity, with its infinite number of sides, similarly a triangle represents the number three. Maybe the three side lengths could represent three metrics or measurement you're trying to count. Or the distance from the centre to the three outer points could also be counting three quantities. After all, isn't a triangle just a radar chart with three measurements?!

Triangles encoding area values

Yet still they remain relatively uncommon in the field of data visualisation. In July 2021, Jonathan Schwabish posted the following observation on Twitter:

I found two triangle data visualizations in the last few days... now I need a third.

Seriously, is the triangle an underutilized shape in #dataviz?

He then showcased the two visualisations in question, which are excellent examples of very different visualisation types featuring triangles. The first comes from the *Washington Post*, and it highlights how reservoirs in and around California were running dry due to the extreme droughts in 2021 (Figure 2.2.4).

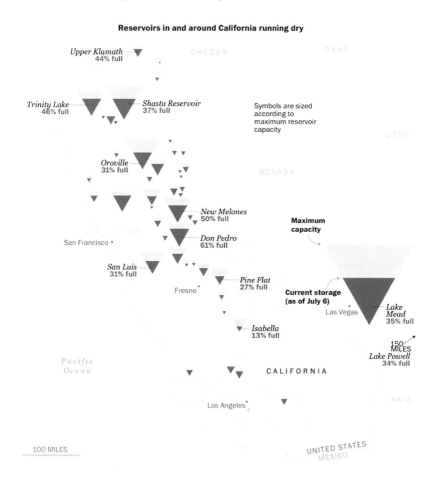

FIGURE 2.2.4   *Reservoirs in and around California running dry* – Washington Post.

Starting with the downsides – a detractor of the visualisation, and of the choice of triangles, in particular, might say that it's very difficult to interpret the ratio of volumes. Look at the largest triangle on the map, that of Lake Mead, also the rightmost example on the map above. The dark blue triangle, representing how full the reservoir is, looks to be a little more than half the height of the light blue triangle, from the bottom point to the horizontal surface. Would you estimate that as 35% full, without the prompt? I'm not sure I would. It looks about half full – maybe the triangles are really confusing here?

But I think the triangles work really well here. It wouldn't make sense in a form without water at the bottom and emptiness at the top. And in terms of the shape, we know that a reservoir is likely to be narrower at the bottom than at the top. Of course, they are unlikely to be completely triangular in cross-section, but it's not too much of a stretch to think that this is what the cross-section of a reservoir might look like in simple two-dimensional form.

And, crucially, for every major reservoir on the chart, we are told the percentage full amount. The image draws us in – maybe the triangular nature even adds to the impact of the image, the difference in triangle sizes tells the story – we are instantly shown in a visual manner how much lower levels are than their maxima, and then the annotation gives us the numerical detail if that's important to us.

Imagine if, instead, this was a map of California and surrounding areas with a couple of dozen pie charts. We might be able to visually judge the percentages of water in each reservoir, but we wouldn't get nearly such a clear representation of what each shape was representing.

Triangles for visual appeal

The second highlighted chart is from Budapest-based visualisation designer Krisztina Szücs – each graphic representing the goals scored in one of the knockout games from the UEFA 2020 finals (in 2021!) (Figure 2.2.5).

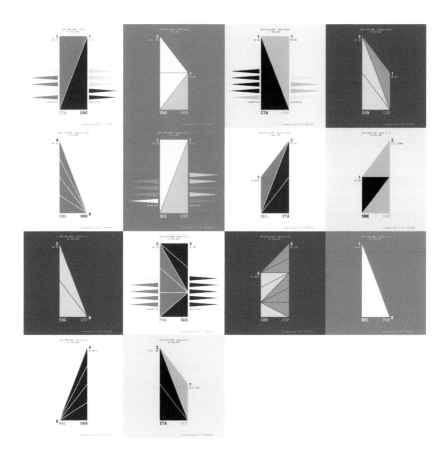

FIGURE 2.2.5   UEFA 2020 Finals – Krisztina Szücs.

Whereas the first *Washington Post* example can be critiqued along the lines of storytelling, analytics, effectiveness or whatever criteria we might be interested in, the above chart bypasses criticism. Clearly, it's not just supposed to show the results, goals and timings of each match. If we just wanted that, we'd read them in a list or see them in a table. Although in terms of encoding, the only thing we need to do is judge the lengths of lines on the two vertical axes.

The triangles themselves are just drawn almost as a by-product of the points on the horizontal lines, representing goals. And the long pointy separate triangles on the sides? They are simply shapes counting successful and unsuccessful penalty kicks. So, no encoding is required there other than being able to count. Moving away from the analytical work this chart is doing though, there is a clear reason this chart got noticed and has been included in both the initial discussion and this book right now, and that's because it is an eye-catching and very pleasing chart that just looks great!

Now, beauty is in the eye of the beholder – a "very pleasing chart that just looks great" is my own choice of words, as someone who appreciates a small multiple, geometric-looking visualisation about sport, to say that the above chart looks beautiful. As you'll find out during the course of this book, if you didn't already know, the above categories pretty much tick all of my boxes.

To me, this is entirely about a visualisation that chooses to show the patterns of goals scored as triangles resulting in what might be considered a piece of data art, and which is, to many, aesthetically pleasing. My instant visceral reaction is to love the chart, and once I'm hooked in, the visualisation itself does the rest.

Triangle areas encoding non-area values

My delight at the relatively new discussion around triangles was because I had used triangles in my visualisations several times before. I had pre-dated the *Washington Post* in visualising percentage of a whole using smaller triangles as fractions of larger triangles (the only difference being mine were inverted in relation to the *Washington Post*'s orientation).

There's no obvious choice here for choosing right-angled triangles to show the percentage of women in each country who do not want to avoid pregnancy – no metaphors or shape approximations fit the choice of a triangular motif. In this case, I'm just experimenting and choosing to express the data geometrically without further justification, other than, not for the first time, to emulate and take influence from the work of Sonja Kuijpers at Studio TERP (Figure 2.2.6).

FIGURE 2.2.6   *Contraception choices for women.*

Triangle grids

Other uses of the triangle motif had more relevance to the themes alluded to in this chapter. Often, a visualisation, or an element of a visualisation, will take the form of a triangle, because a full square visualisation would leave half of the square unused. This is particularly the case when your visualisation is in the form of a grid. If the same dimension is shown on both the x and y axes, you can get redundancy.

Here there is no need to show the top right-hand corner of what would otherwise be a square because the data would be exactly the same. It's the same distance from, say, Edinburgh to Leeds, as it would be from Leeds to Edinburgh. As a result, a triangular graph results, in order to frame just the necessary data (Figure 2.2.7).

Similarly, the data may only make sense in one half of the grid. For my next example, I was inspired by a similar chart I had seen in the *Financial Times* where the chart had the year of purchasing a house on the x-axis with, perhaps unusually, most recent year at the top, and year of the same house's sale in the y-axis left to right.

EDINBURGH									
290	BIRMINGHAM								
373	102	CARDIFF							
496	185	228	DOVER						
193	110	208	257	LEEDS					
214	90	165	270	73	LIVERPOOL				
412	118	150	81	191	198	LONDON			
222	86	173	285	41	34	201	MANCHESTER		
112	207	301	360	94	155	288	141	NEWCASTLE	
186	129	231	264	25	97	194	66	82	YORK

FIGURE 2.2.7   *Driving distances between major UK cities – Open University.*

Since the *x* value is never greater than the *y* value, that results in almost half of the square grid never being used (specifically, everything above and to the right of the top-left to bottom-right diagonal which divides the chart where $x=y$).

In other words, in the same way we ignored the top right section in our mileage chart above because the data is unnecessary/identical; here we ignore it because there is no data in that area, or the data is "null". And once again, this results in a triangular chart.

Note that here, we just arrange each individual data element into one large triangular array on our screen or page. So this itself is not affected by the issues of cognitive perception discussed at the start of this chapter, this is purely a case of intuitive arrangement of our data points.

In this version, I made the decision for each position in my triangular array to be a full map showing how geographical patterns differed across England and Wales. But the overall result was still a triangular shaped visualisation.

Of course, one disadvantage of a triangular shape overall is that you are still going to print it on a rectuangular piece of paper or, more likely, display it on a rectangular screen. But on the plus side, this leaves plenty of room for legends, explanation and however much white space feels appropriate in the otherwise unused area of the page.

The result was a visualisation that pops out from the screen in an interesting and unconventional way, while still, I hope, telling the story of house price rises and falls in England and Wales in a way that can be easily understood. A choropleth matrix! (Figure 2.2.8).

First

Challenging

Idea

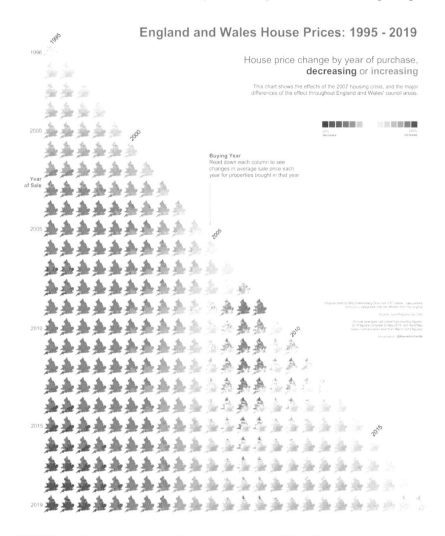

FIGURE 2.2.8   England and Wales house prices 1995–2019.

Ternary charts

A mention for ternary charts – these charts in the form of equilateral triangles are often the best way, inasmuch as I would ever describe any chart choice as "best", to look how three different quantities vary in relation to each other.

I was alerted to these examples by data visualisation designer Zan Armstrong, who explained that a ternary chart was an example of an unusual chart type, generally thought to be "unintuitive" in data visualisation circles, but which is almost ubiquitous in certain domains. The below examples come from the field of materials science, where ternary charts are used, and loved, as a great way of visualising a metric associated with three quantities that add up to 100% (Figure 2.2.9).

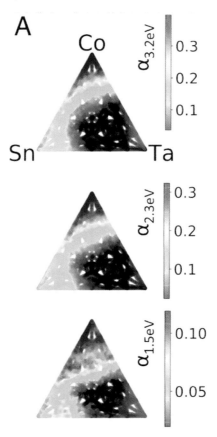

First

Challenging

Idea

FIGURE 2.2.9 *Optical phase analysis of Sn-Co-Ta oxides: composition plots of the optical absorption signal at 3.2, 2.3, and 1.5 eV. Zan Armstrong/Lusann Yang.*

The ternary chart allows for compositions of 0%–100% of each of three metallic constituents of metal oxides to be examined (in this case tin, cobalt and tantalum) with the chosen measure (optical absorption signal) to be encoded. The ternary charts above are actually built from 49 line charts, where the designers were interested in how slope was changing across a number of cuts through the triangle, with the resulting triangular lattice effect shown above.

It's certainly unconventional to visualise data in this manner. As we consider our audiences, of course many readers might not take the time to understand or explore the fact that we have a third axis denoting a third measure, which is not immediately simple for the layperson to easily interpret. This factor, that of ease of comprehension, should always be an important consideration, though I would counter it in this case by adding that materials scientists, the intended audience for these particular triangles, will be much more familiar with triangular ternary charts than most. We can expect these charts to be much less daunting or unfamiliar with their intended audience than they would be to most people not in the field of materials science.

Triangles for three-sided radar charts

A final example of my own goes back to the core of what Jon Schwabish was talking about in his tweet at the start of this chapter, a visualisation consisting of triangular marks. Below was a fun visualisation in response to a challenge from the then fledgeling Data Visualization Society to visualise their first 3500 members. What better way to do this than 3500 triangles? As with most of the questions in this book, you don't have to answer that! Or, if you do, you are welcome to disagree.

In this case, as alluded to earlier in the chapter, I have essentially taken the three self-scored ratings from each of the members, which were, incidentally, ratings for Data, Visualisation and Society, respectively, and created a radar chart for each member. As a result, our individual polygons have as many vertices as there are metrics to visualise (three) – hence the use of triangles (Figure 2.2.10).

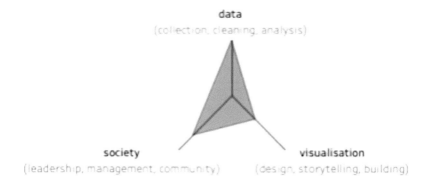

FIGURE 2.2.10   *Individual DVS member represented using triangles.*

Admittedly, it wasn't the first thing I tried, but when I stumbled across this idea, I loved it. My arrangement and colour scheme gave the additional impression of trees in a forest at different phases of their life cycle. Unlike other triangular examples in this chapter, these triangles have a property that circles and squares do not – they are all different shapes as well as being different sizes.

All size lengths and, as a result, angles, are different, resulting in many more individual forms and a more amorphous overall feel. This felt like a great representation of individuality within a community – a "strong" community too as we remember the "strong" analogy of a triangle mentioned at the start of this chapter, so once I had created this multi-triangular visualisation, I settled on it.

I'll discuss this visualisation further in the next chapter, which looks at multiple overlapping marks, and there you will be able to see the final visualisation, incorporating 3500 separate triangles!

Conclusion

In each of the examples discussed in this chapter, I believe that the shape of the triangle, whether at the "micro" level or the overall level, stands out because we're expecting something round or something rectangular – something that fills our screen or page in a conventional manner. Perhaps we undergo the same visceral reaction as seeing a triangular flag or a triangular postage stamp? Both are examples where a triangular shape is very rare, but once we get past the anomaly of the triangular shape, we don't have any problem understanding the object's purpose, nor do we think they are any less fit for the aforementioned purpose (Figure 2.2.11).

FIGURE 2.2.11 *Triangular stamps issued 2021 – Isle of Man.*

There are many reasons why we might want to visualise with triangles. Of course, usually if triangle marks or triangle-shaped marks are an option, then there are other equally valid options too, which might well be better when considering pure analytical best principles. But there are plenty of positive reasons to consider triangles or triangular layouts. It might be the perfect option for your layout, it might best fit the values in your data, or it might be a reasonable choice that fits with a metaphor related to your data.

Or the shorter answer might just be "Why not?". Perhaps, if we are looking to provoke intrigue, impact or an aesthetic appreciation, we might just like the way it looks?

Does it matter if shapes overlap?

In all chaos there is a cosmos, in all disorder a secret order.

Carl Jung

Visualising the Data Visualization Society's membership

Data visualisation is all about presenting data in a visual manner for your readers to be able to understand and interpret the values you present. We already have a definition of data visualisation, from Andy Kirk in Chapter 2.1: "The visual representation and presentation of data to facilitate understanding". This chapter essentially poses the question as to whether, if shapes, or other elements of our visualisation were to overlap on the page or screen, it would take away some of our understanding and counter the very definition of data visualisation.

DOI: 10.1201/9781003240211-11

We choose to encode our data in a precise way – perhaps each dimension on a shape is representing a particular measure. Maybe the colour is relevant, or its position on the screen. If a line starts and finishes in a particular spot, then every twist and turn it takes is representing a particular data point. If we choose to cover up any element in part or in full, are we not obscuring vital information?

At the end of the last chapter, I introduced a visualisation where I chose to visualise every member of the Data Visualization Society individually, using a triangle to encode the three measures of self-reported skills and experience. Small multiple visualisations, also known as a trellis, or tiled visualisation, are a particular favourite of mine, and as a way of showing disaggregated data, a small multiple visualisation can be a great way to compare and contrast every individual element in the dataset, whether that represents a country, state, person, year's data or anything else. To do this, you will need to clearly depict each element with enough white space to set each element apart so you can read, compare and interpret what you need.

For example, this small multiple visualisation below, in typical trellis formation, looks at female representation over time across a number of world nations. Every country has its own non-overlapping grid square, so you can see the superior female political representation in Rwanda, Cuba or Bolivia, compared to the likes of Papua New Guinea or Vanuatu (Figure 2.3.1).

Back to the triangle visualisation for the Data Visualization Society. Similar to the trellis-style small multiple grid above, my first draft looked like this (Figure 2.3.2).

It was fun and colourful, and it matched my self-imposed brief of a poster-style visualisation, but I wondered if I could do better. If I created the visualisation in a different way, I could take attention away from the "grid" style of the visualisation.

Female Representation in political power 1997–2019

Overall, there is an upward trend in female representation in parliament from 1997-2019 However there have been very few occasions of 50% or higher female representation.

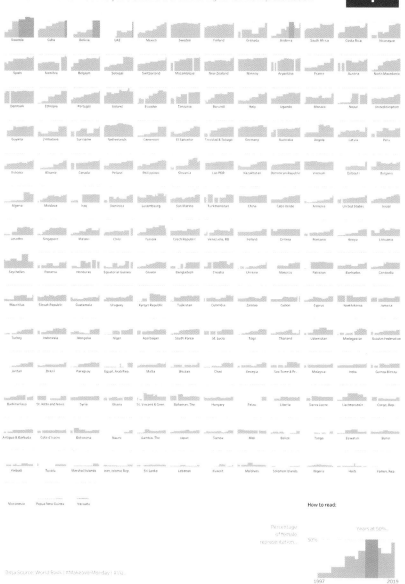

FIGURE 2.3.1 *Female representation in political power.*

FIGURE 2.3.2 *Data Visualization Society membership – draft.*

First

Challenging

Idea

Introducing overlapping marks

You could determine that the grid nature might have been essential in the first grid, for Female representation in Power, to highlight inequality in female representation and make it as clear as possible which country refers to which chart by separating them clearly and uniformly. However, I didn't think that grid lines, or a grid-like overall presentation, were so essential here. Incidentally, it's not the lines themselves that determine the grid, but the regular placement of each chart – you could remove the grey grid lines, but even if made entirely invisible, I would still consider them "present" because of the job they are doing!

If you consider, in general, terms that introducing any constraint is potentially restricting creativity, then you can always consider its corollary. What if we could remove a restraint, might that allow for more creativity? A restraint such as the need to keep all of the elements apart from each other, in a grid formation?

Allowing my triangles to be longer and wider led to the final figure (Figure 2.3.3). I've already mentioned in the previous chapter how this really helped the metaphor of trees/forests and strong community. But you might think there's an obvious downside to this. So many of the triangles now overlap – it's hard to tell which is which. There's no analytical value in this, only confusion and lack of clarity, might you not think?

Consider the first, non-overlapping version. The triangles may be less haphazard, not overlapping and easy to distinguish. But the data is still anonymised so each individual triangle can't be traced back to an individual member. So, does it matter? Each shape still shows analytical data as hard-to-read triangle dimensions.

The aim is to show the variety of self-reported skills, the geographic locations and the overall fact that everyone is different. In that sense, nothing has changed. We're not obscuring anything **vital** – generally speaking, overlapping areas suggests a cluster of larger values, nothing more.

The overlap itself didn't matter, and it served only to emphasise the design choice, accidental or otherwise. And it's important to emphasise the element of design choice. It didn't matter **to me**, and I also considered that it wouldn't matter **to my readers** in the context in which it would be displayed.

First

Challenging

Idea

FIGURE 2.3.3 *Data Visualization Society membership – final.*

Unknown Pleasures

Where overlaps in visualisations are concerned, arguably the most famous (or infamous) examples are derived from an unlikely source, an iconic album cover from the 1979 album *Unknown Pleasures* by English band Joy Division (Figure 2.3.4).

FIGURE 2.3.4 Unknown Pleasures – *Joy Division/Peter Saville.*

The album cover image itself is of course, a data visualisation. It turns out that the original artwork was based on radio/magnetic waves from a pulsar star, which was published in the *Cambridge Encyclopaedia of Astronomy* in the late 1960s. The original image consisted of a series of pulse waves, stacked and centred.

Peter Saville, who was responsible for the artwork in question, recommended the image to one of the band members (which member is unclear) and subsequently recreated it as the album artwork. The only difference Saville made to the original scientific diagram was to invert the colours, so that white on black gave it more of a space-like feel.

As the image regained a certain amount of popularity in popular culture, a spate of data visualisations began to appear around 2017, when the "ggjoy" package was created in R. The term "joy plot" had been coined for visualisations that emulated the look of the *Unknown Pleasures* cover, although the term, originally named after the band Joy Division has now widely been renamed the ridgeline plot, with the R package renamed to "ggridges".

I was one of the many who used the former term back in 2017, including in my blog that these chapters are derived from, but the consensus for the change in name is due to the unsavoury connections of the term "Joy Division" – suffice it to say the term is not as joyful and innocent as it might seem. The term "ridgeline plot" is a more visual explanation, and I will continue to use that from here on.

The ridgeline plot looks great, and was a very popular, albeit experimental recent chart type, but it's difficult to come up with an accurate, exact definition given that its prevalence is still particularly new, and it is not widely approved by data visualisation purists. So instead,

I'll give a vague definition here:

- A succession of horizontally close-packed area charts over time, usually showing defined peaks

- The lines are sufficiently close together that the peaks overlap/obscure the lines behind (giving a sort of 3D effect)

- Looks a bit like the cover of "Unknown Pleasures".

Creating a ridgeline plot

It won't surprise you to know, given that I have argued that a visualisation featuring overlapping elements may have advantages that counter the disadvantages of having elements partially hidden, that I was keen to try a ridgeline plot. The "spate of data visualisations" I mentioned above included a couple of my own creations. For my very first attempt, I wanted to emulate not just a ridgeline plot, but the specific overall look of the album cover itself. I didn't want to just create a meaningless image though, I wanted my visualisation to be derived from real data, albeit not frequencies emitted by pulsars. Here is my first Joy Division inspired ridgeline plot (Figure 2.3.5).

I've made the decision to include 40 lines of data. At the time, I had a great set of data of Men's singles tennis results at Wimbledon for another project, and so it seemed the perfect dataset for my needs, given that my needs, in this example, were purely creative

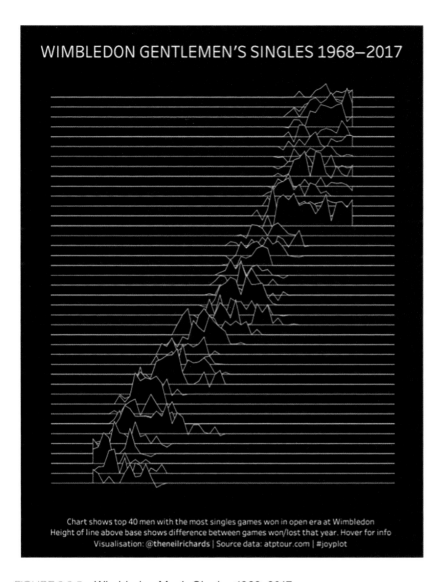

FIGURE 2.3.5   Wimbledon Men's Singles 1968–2017.

and experimental. Each row is not labelled, nor is the timeline on the y-axis, but the interactive version published on Tableau Public allowed the user to hover and explore to interpret the values behind every point on the line – well, admittedly, every point on the line that was visible.

Reaction to overlapping data elements

The difference in career start and finish of each of the players has led to a gradual left to right drift reading upwards, unlike the original. This is because I've ranked the players in order of debut – the most prominent, nine from the top, is Roger Federer. But that wasn't important to me and didn't detract from its overall look and feel as a ridgeline plot paying homage to the original album cover. However, there was an understandably mixed reaction to this at the time (Figures 2.3.6 and 2.3.7).

FIGURE 2.3.6   *Tweet from Matt Francis.*

FIGURE 2.3.7   *Tweet from Andy Kriebel.*

Both Matt and Andy were, and still are, prominent voices in the visualisation community, the Tableau community, in particular, whose opinions I value enormously. And you can't deny that they are both absolutely fair, polite and correct in their comments!

The important thing is to acknowledge the limitations and determine whether they are enough to detract from your choice. Had I wanted to avoid overlap, and visualise the same information in the same size of image, with other minimalist design considerations remaining the same, my visualisation would have looked like this (Figure 2.3.8).

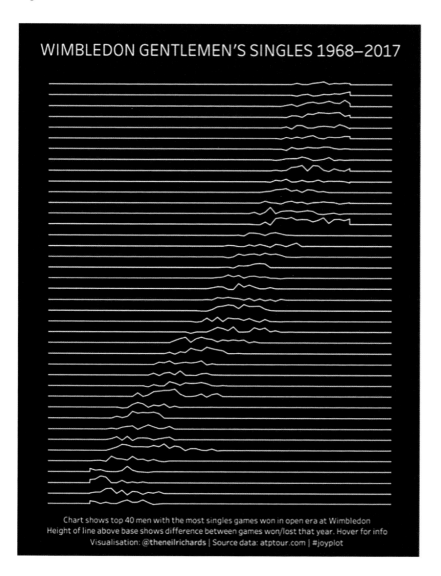

FIGURE 2.3.8   Alternative: Wimbledon Men's Singles 1968–2017.

This version looks far less dramatic and far less aesthetically pleasing. It's also harder to see the magnitude of peaks, and it's not a ridgeline plot. The first two of these points are just my opinions, but the second two are factual. If I wanted to really make the data clearer, I could have created this chart within seconds and easily pinpointed the dominance and longevity of Federer, Connors and Becker (Figure 2.3.9).

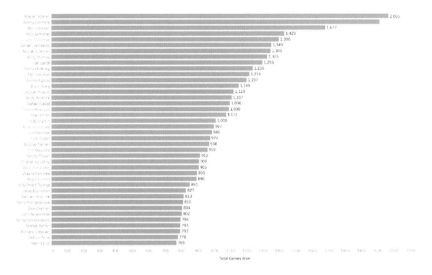

FIGURE 2.3.9   *Wimbledon Men's Singles 1968–2017 – bar chart alternative.*

But where is the joy in that? (no pun intended – OK, pun definitely intended). This wouldn't be remembered, discussed or explored. Investing time in exploring and understanding a visualisation can lead to a greater understanding and recollection of key information. That's not an asserted fact, it's just my own hypothesis, based on how I interact with my favourite visualisation types. Being eye-catching, unusual and fun can be plus points to any visualisation, if used in appropriate situations.

Considering your audience

I didn't create this for analytical accuracy or even for anyone to be able to look at this chart and confidently identify the most successful men's singles tennis player at Wimbledon. But, although it's a cliché, by thinking "outside the box", I learned great design skills and

First

Challenging

Idea

technical skills that I would otherwise not have learned just by plotting a series of bar charts or line charts. And I had fun in the process, the challenge and in the resultant output and surrounding discussion.

It's worth noting that, as mentioned at the top of the post, this is absolutely not to everyone's taste. There's a strong argument to describe similar visualisations as "data art" or "dataviz art", and I'm certainly OK with that. It's precisely because you are unlikely to find examples such as those above in any data visualisation textbooks that I'm keen to include them here. Non-standard and unconventional visualisations will usually only occur as a result of questioning the norms and taking the decision to move away from them.

The key advice that will always be offered when considering a data visualisation is "consider your audience". Therein lies the answer. If my audience were the general public; if I'd been commissioned to write an article for tennis fans or newspaper readers; if I were writing a report showing findings of my research of 40 years of results, there's no way I'd create a ridgeline plot, and certainly not a minimalist, stylised ridgeline plot on a dark background. I'd probably spend time making the above bar chart look slightly prettier, include that, and move on.

But my audience isn't the general non-visualisation consuming public. My audience consists mostly of the following:

- Data visualisation enthusiasts, whether sticklers for analytical best practices or fans of artistic less functional projects

- Blog followers, many of whom enjoy a debate on the pros and cons of various methods, and now book readers

- People professionally interested in a variety of visualisation techniques and chart types

- People who know what I'm like, and who enjoy my questioning approach and unconventional foray into data visualisation

Ridgeline advantages

My second example highlights an alternative styling and two other plus points of ridgeline plots. Below is a visualisation depicting medals won by the most successful Winter Olympics nations in history (from 1928 to 2014) (Figure 2.3.10).

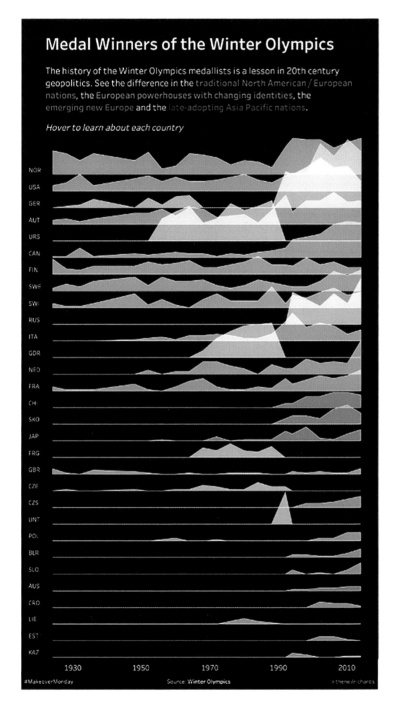

FIGURE 2.3.10   *Medal winners at the Winter Olympics.*

Like the above Wimbledon example, showing every nation's timeline to the same scale without overlap just wouldn't make sense, it would take up far too much vertical space. But here we can make the choice to show transparency in each layer. That way, we are not hiding information. Look at East Germany, for example (GDR in the chart) with its huge peak from approximately 1970–1990. Using transparent peaks means that we can still see the record of Italy (ITA) behind it, so no information is lost.

This particular design choice gives two advantages. First of all, the lines are only overlapped from below if a nation has won over 12 medals in a given year. This means that there aren't many overlaps, but when there are, this adds to the effect. Any year where a nation overlaps the line above is a successful year, for example, Finland, though consistent throughout, only exceed this once, in 1984.

The second advantage is a metaphorical advantage. Remember how I decided my overlapping triangles visualisation had the look of trees in a forest? The cold light blues of jagged, overlapping, translucent irregular shapes from foreground to background have a look of icebergs, adding to the cold, wintry feel. It was an effect I was particularly pleased with in what was otherwise a very simple design.

Sometimes your colours, shapes and positioning can give you a pleasing design element through luck. But you can sometimes make your own luck by experimenting, iterating and trying different shapes, sizes, colours and chart types, before the final look presents itself.

Conclusion

Returning now to the original chapter question – does it matter if shapes overlap? To some readers and designers of charts, it will always matter if the shapes overlap. And that's OK. The use of overlapping chart elements will always be a creative decision rather than an analytic decision. Be aware that it's a question in your data visualisation armoury that it's OK to ask, consider the response and choose your design accordingly. By allowing the concept of overlapping elements, you can increase the number of design styles and chart types in your repertoire. Then it's up to you when, or whether, to use them.

Chapter 2.4

What is data humanism?

Every individual matters. Every individual has a role to play. Every individual makes a difference.

Jane Goodall

Peak infographics

In a TED talk and several talks and articles from 2016 onwards, Giorgia Lupi, who founded and ran data visualisation design company Accurat, and is now a partner at the design studio Pentagram, argued that we had reached "peak infographics".

The concept of big data, a term that was becoming impossible to avoid, had been leading to more and more vast amounts of information being collected. However, this didn't necessarily translate to data visualisation, where the emphasis still remained on drawing conclusions that were easy to digest. Charts and visualisations were used to convert vast, impersonal aggregated amounts of data into a simple visual output for audiences to understand quickly.

DOI: 10.1201/9781003240211-12

Lupi introduced her vision for how data visualisation could, or perhaps should, change, after the "big data" and "peak infographics" era, by introducing the concept of *Data Humanism.*

Data humanism

Now I'd never heard of the term humanism in any context – it turns out that humanism was a Renaissance term when scholars and artists began to consider that humans, not God, were at the centre of the world. This new way of thinking led to them including considerations such as empathy, imperfection and human qualities in their cultural output of the time.

It would be unfair of me to include or give commentary on the talks and articles in full detail here, since to appreciate and understand the idea in full there's no better way than to listen or read as Giorgia intended. However, it's true that many of the points raised have particularly resonated with me and influenced both my way of thinking and my personal preferences within data visualisation.

These are my takeaways of how the way we think of data visualisation would change in a "post-peak infographics wave" centred around data humanism in my own perspective.

Data visualisation must be more meaningful

Instead of simplifying and heading towards a crowd-pleasing infographic, thinking in a way that involves data humanism leads to visualisations being more thoughtful where both the data and the output are concerned. It's up to us to question what the data means more. And I'm all for asking questions!

Data visualisation will be more about personalisation

This reminds us that data is almost always connected to humans. To that extent, very often a particular record of data that we are visualising is related to a particular human. We might not have personal details of that individual person, and in the age of data protection, privacy and GDPR, this is almost certainly for good reason, but remembering that we are looking at data on a human level is likely to influence how we think about the story we want to tell, in turn making it more meaningful.

Embrace complexity

One of the key concepts might be counter-intuitive at first, but as data has expanded and become larger in quantity, to reach any analytical conclusion, the result has usually been an increase in simplicity. Giorgia quotes the example of the US election predictions in 2016 where huge amounts of data were condensed into just one or two numbers. My UK compatriots will also undoubtedly be able to come up with some very high profile and similar recent election predictions!

For example, FiveThirtyEight, a prominent American website whose name derives from the number of seats in the US electoral college and focuses on political opinion poll analysis, condensed its pre-2016 US Election results into one forecast giving Trump a 3% chance of winning.

Of course, that didn't mean Trump couldn't win, but the simplified (arguably over-simplified) nature of the headline prediction, however correct, confused the public, including experts, into believing there was only one possible election result. Or at the very least, it surprised many of the public when results were called. This was a great example of this effect.

We can learn so much more by introducing, visualising and explaining more levels of complexity, to elaborate the context, margin of error and any other extenuating circumstances that an over-simplified projection hides.

Data capture process is becoming more personal

The data capture process is becoming more personal, and as a result, this process brings in **empathy** with it. In the so-called peak big data era, it was difficult to find empathy within data visualisations, but the humanisation ethos is changing this. The personal process of data collection also allows us to acknowledge the imperfection of data, and we can demonstrate this imperfection within the visualisation of the data.

It's also important to acknowledge that this is also the case even when data appears to come from a non-human source. What if the data comes from a sensor, or a survey, or a systems database? All of these systems, or any data collection or storage system, are designed by humans. Humans who decide which data to collect, and which not to collect. Data collection and representation are never fully objective, but a filtered representation of the overall situation, with the filter applied in some way by a human designer, programmer or protagonist.

Disaggregate data

Bringing in humanism and personalisation very often leads to disaggregation of data. If big data is aggregating huge quantities of personal information, then in order to think in a more human-centric way, we need to do the opposite. A first example of this that I became aware of was from Rob Radburn, an expert Tableau analyst participating in the Makeover Monday initiative, who created this very simple but powerful visualisation looking at deaths in police custody in 2015. With 1200 rows of data to represent 1200 police killings in 2015, Rob chose to visualise each of them individually, highlighting the human nature of every case. Further information adding to the human context of every killing is shown in the tooltip for every shape (Figure 2.4.1).

In some ways, there's a dichotomy here since my previous takeout was to embrace complexity, yet this visualisation is very simple. But

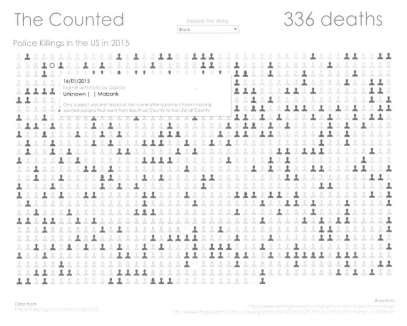

FIGURE 2.4.1   *The Counted – Rob Radburn.*

here the complexity is in the necessarily large amount of information on display. We are encouraged to explore and learn about 1200 humans, rather than see, for example, aggregated bar charts which could be consumed more quickly and simply. And it enables us to see the imperfect detail of the human-collected data.

It's telling that my first thought was how complex the visualisation was, because in my novice stages of learning my software tool, I had no idea how to create the above. The default behaviour is to aggregate or to summarise. If there are 1200 data points with a numerical metric attached to each, your software tool is most likely going to want to show one number that summarises, whether that's a sum, an average or something else.

This simple observation about the default behaviour of Tableau and other visualisation tools is a telling indication that disaggregating data is a new, non-first-wave behaviour that needs re-learning.

Promote slowness

There's an often-cited quote from Seth Godin, a highly influential US marketing author and blogger, that states:

> I don't think that is what graphs are for. I think you are trying to make a point in two seconds for people who are too lazy to read the forty words underneath.

I'll be honest that while I can appreciate the context of the quote, it will never be a philosophy that aligns with the way I like to visualise data. I could certainly have posed a question and chapter challenging this concept that wouldn't have been out of place here. My takeaway, in the context of post-peak infographics data visualisation, and of data humanism, in particular, is that a natural result of data humanism is the need to encourage engagement with our visualisations. We actively want our readers to slow down, to explore, engage and appreciate the detail, the direct antithesis of Godin's quote.

Remember, as is the case throughout this book, that my frame of reference is for the non-business chart, the creative data visualisation, usually the personal project. Godin's quote might perfectly encapsulate the busy business exec for whom you are including a chart in a presentation at work, but these are not the circumstances we are considering here. Personally, and perhaps selfishly, if I am taking time to curate something creative, I want my audience to spend time appreciating it!

Move beyond standards

This observation feels worth emphasising and is again probably essential to the philosophy of data humanism. I interpret this as looking past the standard chart types, or not being restricted to depict data visually in the most conventionally accepted ways. In circumstances where data is becoming less perfect, and more disaggregated and personal, we have opportunities to be more creative and less conventional in how we show the data. After all, if we accept that we want our audience to spend more time with the data, then perhaps that gives us the green light to move away from bar charts?

I don't intentionally malign bar charts here, by the way, I simply use them as an example of the simplest, most conventional and easiest to understand charts – I wouldn't disagree that they are often the clearest and best choice. But, in a quote from Amanda Cox, now editor of the *New York Times* data journalism section The Upshot, that it would be criminal of me not to include it in this book somewhere given my approach to data visualisation:

> *There's a strand of the data viz world that argues that everything could be a bar chart. That's possibly true but also possibly a world without joy.*

Sketch with data

This could be interpreted in different ways – in the most literal sense, moving to humanism-based data visualisation allows us to consider non-digital output, why not?! The human-centred, imperfect, individual nature of data is a perfect candidate for using pen, pencil and paper for your output; sketching data in its traditional sense. And we'll see some inspirational examples of this later in the chapter.

Data sketches

However, I don't think this has to necessarily mean that the process of data visualisation should start, or even finish, with a traditional sketch, though there are many times where this is great advice to gain an early understanding of your data and intended process. Generally, it's more a concept I would tie in with the message above, about moving away from standards. The concept of data sketches could not be better summed up than by the Data Sketches project from leading data designers Nadieh Bremer and Shirley Wu.

In proposing a collaboration of personal creative projects, they decided to embark on 12 themed visualisations each where they would gather their own data, create their own designs, code their visualisations from scratch and document the whole process, all the while trying new creative approaches and exploring new tools, and having lots of fun along the way.

The result was an award-winning online project which has now become a book in the very same series as this one, and a series full of personalised, unconventional, creative data visualisations where the reader has the opportunity not just to enjoy the final process (slowly!) but also to appreciate the nuances of the full journey and the underlying data included in the final products.

Operation Fistula

With all these concepts in mind, the visualisation below is a good example of one of my own creations encapsulating as many of the data humanism elements discussed above. It definitely involved a preliminary sketch or two, and it shows disaggregated records of individual patients assisted by Operation Fistula in five countries across Africa. It certainly moves away from standard visualisation conventions, and it requires a slowness to interpret, understand and appreciate the content.

The data has understandable imperfections given the nature of individually collected data on each patient, and every flower has its meaning – the potential extension of quality and quantity of life of an individual woman (Figure 2.4.2).

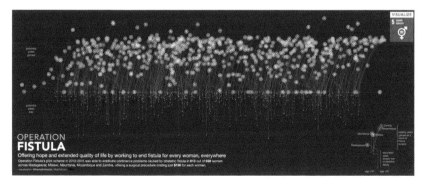

FIGURE 2.4.2 *Operation Fistula.*

Dear Data

But having concentrated almost entirely on the ethos of Giorgia Lupi's data humanism to explain the ideas behind data visualisation's new wave, it seems only right to represent this further with two examples of Giorgia's work which are both very representative of data humanism but also very influential to my own design ideas and data visualisation principles, along with those of many others.

First off is Dear Data – a year-long collaboration in 2016 between Giorgia and Stefanie Posavec, a fellow information designer based in London (Figure 2.4.3).

FIGURE 2.4.3   *Dear Data – Giorgia Lupi and Stefanie Posavec.*

Each week, over the whole year, they collected and measured a particular type of data about their lives, used this data to make a drawing on a postcard and then posted it to their co-collaborator. Eventually, the postcard would arrive at the other person's address in a process they described as a type of "slow data" transmission.

Fast forward to 2021 and the postcards are now exhibited in MoMA in New York, as well as being featured in a book of the same title, a permanent exhibition as a reminder of Giorgia and Stefanie's journey of discovery. By collecting and reporting data in a slow, personalised, unique and hand-drawn way, the process made them learn about themselves and each other in a way they would never have anticipated. As stated on their website:

> *Instead of using data just to become more efficient, we argue we can use data to become more humane and to connect with ourselves and others at a deeper level.*

And of course, thankfully for those of us who appreciated their unique and imaginative way of presenting personal data, it resulted in 104 truly unique and creative hand-drawn data visualisations.

But putting data humanism to one side, this project was a "light bulb" project for me as it instilled a more basic realisation in me, namely the realisation that you can visualise data in any way you like. The only thing you need to be able to do is to sketch and draw your output. In fact, you don't even need to be able to do that – your software tool or coding language of choice can do that for you.

In my case, the satisfaction comes from being able to do so in a way that's more skilful and accurate than my own hand – I just need to be able to come up with a drawable idea, whether I can draw it or not, and then, with the appropriate amount of skill, precision and patience, I can create the visualisation I had in mind.

The data we don't see

The second of Lupi's projects to include was a collaboration with musician Kaki King. Entitled "Bruises – the data we don't see", it tells the highly personal story of a child's bruising, as a result of a rare medical condition, and a mother's emotions. Because of the musical contribution of Kaki King, this means that the final project has a musical soundtrack to it, and the visualisation builds over time as the music plays. Obviously in a book it's only possible to show the final figure (Figure 2.4.4), but this represents only part of the final project.

FIGURE 2.4.4 *Bruises – the data we don't see – Giorgia Lupi/Kaki King.*

To quote from some of the accompanying text:

The song has 120 measures in 3/4 time, covering the 120 days that I collected data. There are elements that you will hear that reference the amount of petechiae on her skin, my changing mood... And the main guitar part is a musical map of the bruises on her skin, changing, bleeding into each other.

Kaki King

As you probably can see, this isn't by any means a scientific representation of data. Still, we believe it paints an accurate sensorial picture of this personal journey.

Giorgia Lupi

The important thing is that the whole experience involves the story, the visual and audio elements of the performance, and the annotations and explanations not shown here. All in all, an inspirational example of data humanism that requires the reader to really spend time immersing themselves in understanding the output to appreciate the highly personal nature of the data being shown.

Conclusion

To sum up, the concepts of data humanism can be shown in this slide below (Figure 2.4.5).

FIGURE 2.4.5 **Data humanism.**

And as I embraced the concept of data humanism, or "post peak infographics" thinking, this is probably the point that I realised the one overriding principle of all. Every point made in the chart above involves questioning established "first wave" principles and challenging them or flipping them round. The act of questioning and challenging existing principles and established ways of doing things will always open up a whole new way of thinking and allow you to think of creative and alternative ways of visualising data.

What is design-driven data?

Being creative is not so much the desire to do something as the listening to that which wants to be done: the dictation of the materials.

Anni Albers

A bet at breakfast time

This chapter features what was, at the time when I produced it, probably my most unorthodox visualisation to date. One morning, during a business trip, while having breakfast in a hotel bar in Manchester, I saw the following unremarkable, uncredited artwork on the wall (Figure 2.5.1).

At this stage in my data visualisation journey, I was frequently tempted to create visualisations based on design inspiration from other sources, with such sources of inspiration taken from almost anywhere. I joked with my breakfast companions that morning that

First

Challenging

Idea

FIGURE 2.5.1   *Artwork unknown – photo Neil Richards.*

you could bet I would end up creating a visualisation based on that poster. I took the photo above on my phone, and sure enough, a couple of days later, true to my word, I released the following visualisation, where I visualised Irish whiskey sales (Figure 2.5.2).

Irish Whiskey Sales 2002–2016

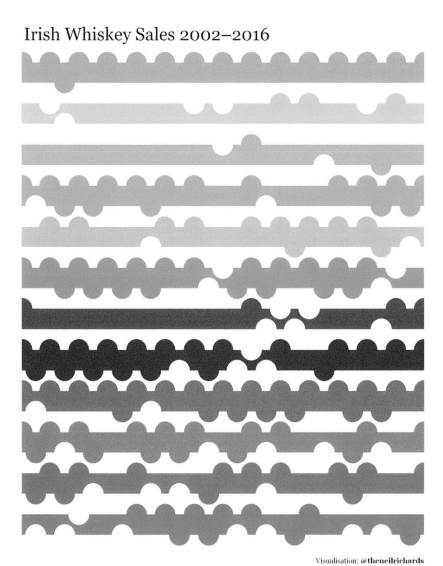

Visualisation: @theneilrichards

FIGURE 2.5.2   *Irish Whiskey Sales 2002–2016.*

For me, this represented design-driven data in its purest form. First, I chose a specific design for my visualisation. Second, I found data that generated a visualisation that approximated, but didn't exactly replicate, that design. And from that point, the process took its traditional linear form – using the data to generate an accurate, albeit artistic and abstract, data visualisation.

Design-driven data

Before I explain the visualisation above, my inspiration for the concept of "design-driven data" came from the data humanism slide introduced at the end of the previous chapter. I knew that in starting to experiment with different design ideas, such as recreating ridgeline plots to emulate the Joy Division album cover, for example, I was finding designs to inspire me to create interesting and unorthodox data visualisations, and then finding data that enabled me to complete the output. The Data Humanism slide was validation for me – because "design-driven data" was a new concept that had recently been coined there, I had my green light to go ahead with more such designs!

It's important to note that by introducing the concept of design-driven data, I directly challenged my thoughts in the earlier chapter. In Chapter 1.1, we asked our very first question: Should the data drive the visualisation? I'm always happy to consider both sides of a visualisation-related argument and change my viewpoint as my experiences change. It's often said that you need to know and understand the rules in order to know when to break them. This could certainly be said to apply to data visualisation, particularly if you replace "rules" with "best practices".

And indeed, some of the visualisations you have seen up until now, and many that you will see in subsequent chapters, would also be classified as design-driven data. If you want to undertake projects that you would consider design-driven data, you need an appreciation of the fact that it's the counter-intuitive way to design a visualisation.

Is this what Giorgia had in mind when she introduced design-driven data in her data humanism talk? Not exactly – in subsequent and later discussions on the topic, she confirmed to me that she had different thoughts on its meaning and considered the term as the opposite of data-driven design because she was envisioning a renaissance where we would design the ways we collect, analyse, interpret and present data.

First

Challenging

Idea

In other words, not so much having the design in mind first before even considering the data, but more like baking design into the data process from the beginning. But we both celebrate the fact that the phrase, concept and philosophy behind it has inspired my alternative interpretation and resultant way of working.

Explaining the visualisation

Let's return to the whiskey visualisation. The visualisation is actually in two parts – a second page which is less prominent but equally important (Figure 2.5.3).

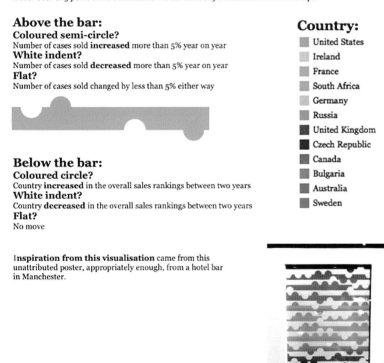

How to read this visualisation

Along the top edge of each coloured bar, each shape or flat area represents sales for each year 2002-2016. Along the bottom of each bar, each shape or flat area sit in between each yearly slot above the bar, and represents change in overall sales ranking between the two years.

Hover over any point in the visualisation to see details of the data behind each shape.

Above the bar:
Coloured semi-circle?
Number of cases sold **increased** more than 5% year on year
White indent?
Number of cases sold **decreased** more than 5% year on year
Flat?
Number of cases sold changed by less than 5% either way

Below the bar:
Coloured circle?
Country **increased** in the overall sales rankings between two years
White indent?
Country **decreased** in the overall sales rankings between two years
Flat?
No move

Inspiration from this visualisation came from this unattributed poster, appropriately enough, from a hotel bar in Manchester.

Country:
United States
Ireland
France
South Africa
Germany
Russia
United Kingdom
Czech Republic
Canada
Bulgaria
Australia
Sweden

Visualisation: **@theneilrichards**

Data: Board BIA via the IWSR

FIGURE 2.5.3   *Irish Whiskey Sales 2002–2016 – how to read.*

As a reader, you'll need to appreciate how to read, interpret and understand a visualisation such as this. After all, we may all know how to read bar charts these days, but an unmarked and irregular visualisation is a tough data literacy challenge for most people and will need explanation for anyone but the author.

A design-driven data piece, in order to most closely resemble the original influence which, if it is a design rather than a data visualisa, is unlikely to contain text or annotation in the same way. In such cases, it's therefore important that explanations can be found, usually either on an accompanying page or behind the tooltip on the hover of a mouse.

Reaction to design-driven data pieces

I feel like I need to make one last caveat here – this visualisation and other design-driven data examples like it are entirely for fun, and personal benefit. Its aim is to look nice, interesting, impactful, creative, artistic, or any similar adjective you might think. The intended audience may be a niche group of those who agree that the visualisation will be fun to explore at their leisure and/or enjoy its overall look. And this is a very subjective opinion.

It's true that for everyone who applauds or appreciates it there may be many more who roll their eyes or ignore it. And there will be more who decry it for lack of easy to interpret analytical takeaway. It's a choice I've made, and the thought processes behind that choice have evolved from many of the questions we've raised and principles we've challenged up until now.

This probably raises a lot of questions – principally, why doesn't it look the same as the original design? After all, if I've chosen the design for my visualisation, why stop at an approximation, why not make it look exactly the same?

The answer is that the original design is the inspiration – it drives first the data and then the final output, but the data stage can't be omitted. And after all, data is real. Chances are, having decided the way I want to encode every data point in the same manner as my design inspiration, it couldn't possibly look identical. The key point in the process is to identify what I want to visualise and how I want to encode it. How close it gets to the actual original is a matter of luck and circumstance, but that's not a priority of mine at all.

Process of design-driven data

So, the process is as follows. Let's say I have the design I want to emulate (the Manchester picture). What data can I potentially encode that could potentially look like this?

First of all, there are 12 horizontal elements to the picture, all with up and down semi-circle elements, and all with their own colours. This could quite easily be tracking something over time left to right for 12 different categories/regions/countries/whatever – 12 different dimensions. Each of these dimensions could then have its own colour, using the same palette, or an approximation thereof, as the original.

So far, so good. Our other main shape is the semi-circle, which is used in one of two places – the top or bottom of each horizontal strip, and in one of two ways – either "sticking out" or "cutting in". There's no magnitude to these circles, and they are always the same size, so that rules out coding the magnitude of anything, such as sales over time, medals won per Olympics, etc., but it does mean I can code something that exists in three states, namely for each circle "in", "out" or neither.

At this point it's sensible to consider that the process is iterative. What I needed was a promising dataset with measures over time and split into different dimensions such as countries, with potential to encode my data in the way shown above. At the time of creating this visualisation, I was partaking regularly in a community data project called Makeover Monday. Every week there was an existing visualisation, with its dataset made freely available online. Participants would then have the opportunity to explore the data, and create a visualisation. The initial thought behind the initiative was to use your data visualisation skills to improve on the original image, but it was also always a great practice opportunity to explore the creative possibilities with a different dataset every week and take a more creative or unorthodox approach than the original visualisation. You can probably imagine which of the two aforementioned directions I would usually take! The current dataset at the time when I was formulating this idea was looking at sales of whiskey over a number of years for a dozen or so countries.

This was perfect for me. As you'll see from the "how to read" panel, I could encode my circular tabs and indents with whether a country's sales increased or decreased year on year (above the bar) and whether its rank increased or decreased year on year (below the bar). With a little fine-tuning and iteration: for example, which gives me about the right number of tabs and indents above the bar, a 5% or 10% change in sales? – I had my final visualisation.

And, once again, it is just that, a data visualisation that looks like a pre-conceived design. As a piece of analytics, it's tricky, at best, to understand, although all the tools are provided to enjoy this at your own pace. But as an output, some will enjoy it, some will appreciate the wit and skill behind it, and, what's more, if you're anything like me, you'll very much enjoy creating it and getting better with your technical skills as a result.

But is it data art?

This, or the related question "What is data art?" would have been, you might think, a perfect chapter question for this book. But the simple answer is that this is a very objective opinion. After all, the cliché statement from those of us who are not experts in art usually goes something like "I don't know what's art, but I know what I like". And that's probably true of creative data visualisation. Many will like a given visualisation, often many more will not. Is the original piece on the wall in Manchester a piece of art? That's open to opinion. Is it good? Ditto.

But I do maintain that the most important word in "what is data art?" is the word "data". There's a huge trend at the moment for generative art. Because I don't consider myself an expert, or even a beginner, in generative art, I'm going to take the lazy definition here from Wikipedia:

> *Generative art refers to art that in whole or in part has been created with the use of an autonomous system. An autonomous system in this context is generally one that is non-human and can independently determine features of an artwork that would otherwise require decisions made directly by the artist.*

For me, the key difference between generative art and data art is that generative art is not necessarily generated by real data. My own creations, and any creations that fall under the description of design-driven data, are underpinned by data and are data visualisations first and foremost. Data curated and chosen by humans, with encoding and design decisions also taken by a human (me). I don't consider myself an artist, but I do make design decisions based around the encoding of data. Data humanism, you might say.

However, one thing you may encounter if creating design-driven data visualisations is the comment that it is "artistic", or "creative".

Of course, that's every bit as subjective as the data art question. But that's a nice compliment to receive, in my opinion. After all, it's creative display of data that drives me to improve, to create visualisations for fun and to inspire you to do the same with this book!

Sesame Street sponsors

I want to show you another example of mine of a design-driven data piece. The inspiration for this, to many people, will need very little introduction (Figure 2.5.4).

FIGURE 2.5.4   *Sesame Street sponsors.*

When I heard that the puppeteer of Big Bird and Oscar had died in 2019, in the 50th year of Sesame Street, I decided that I wanted to do a design-driven data tribute in some way. You'll see, obviously, that my design inspiration was the character Big Bird, from Sesame Street. But this shows that inspiration can come from anywhere. It doesn't have to come from an art piece, or a kind of diagram with two-dimensional shapes that lends itself to data visualisation. The inspiration can be absolutely anything two or three-dimensional.

Some ideas that represent just a fraction of the possible range of design-driven data ideas: artwork, music scores, existing visualisations, wallpaper or carpet patterns, flowers/trees/plants, embroidery, flags or emblems, costumes, animals, … as you can see, the list goes on.

There was a time, as I introduced the concept and presented it to conferences and user groups, that people began to send me photos of their wallpapers and carpets, patterns on their clothes and other such things, accompanied by messages such as "Hey, this looks like it could be one of your visualisations!"

And sometimes design-driven data requires a bit of luck. Sesame Street themed data was hard to come by and my potential design idea was obviously quite restrictive. But a round, feathered, face lends itself to a radial visualisation. The perfect quantitative measure to visualise seemed to be the "sponsor" letters and numbers mentioned at the end of every show. Differences in measures would lead to different feather lengths, but that's OK. The organic nature of a creature's feathers means that different lengths will make the face less smooth and circular. But how could I deal with the extra vertical tufts around the top of his face, and the additional lower white feathers underneath?

You can see from the final visualisation that's where I was lucky. There were enough additional options with larger numbers to encode than the rest (numbers 2–12 come up a lot more often than letters A-Z), and enough with much smaller numbers to encode than the rest (numbers 0, 1 and 13–20 are featured a lot less regularly).

This led to a much simpler design in terms of the data it shows, but it is a design-driven data example, nonetheless. And it's true, this really could have been a bar chart. In fact, I got around this by showing a simple bar chart under the tooltip for every feather, since again, it's important that the analytical information is there for those that want it. Call it frivolous, call the unnecessary touches "chartjunk" but in creating something more memorable it feels more of a tribute to Carol Spinney than any bar chart would have been.

Conclusion

Design-driven data is a fascinating data visualisation design concept which unleashes creativity and imagination, allowing the designer to learn new skills. Without this approach, we may miss the opportunity to try a particular variation on a chart type that works for your data but hasn't been tried yet. It flies against the principle we have already discussed, which is that the data should always come first before the design.

In that sense it might be unusual and unconventional, but it's been essential to my own development, both technically and creatively, and resulted in most of my favourite personal data visualisation projects. What have you got to lose?

Do we take data visualisation too seriously?

Only those who attempt the absurd… will achieve the impossible. I think it's in my basement… Let me go upstairs and check.

M.C. Escher

When is a map not a map?

There's a danger that your first thoughts on this question might be influenced somewhat by the fact that I, as a fully grown man, have just illustrated my last chapter with a visualisation in the form of Big Bird from Sesame Street. But nevertheless, this question then leads us, once again, to challenge some of the principles we may have held until now, or have discussed in previous chapters.

Prompting this discussion was a visualisation I created a few years ago that depicted the number of pets of different types owned in the United Kingdom. An important consideration is that the information held in a very simple dataset consisted only of two fields: pet type and total number owned in the UK, so opportunities to be creative were somewhat limited.

Perhaps it's also pertinent that this project was also a project for Makeover Monday, as mentioned in the previous chapter, which

DOI: 10.1201/9781003240211-14

143

means that a number of often early-career data visualisation enthusiasts in the online community were tackling the same dataset at the same time and sharing their outputs.

This was my visualisation (Figure 2.6.1).

FIGURE 2.6.1   *Pet ownership in the United Kingdom.*

Now, armed with the information that there are 15–20 million fish kept in ponds in the UK, 15–20 million fish kept in tanks, 8.5 million dogs, 8 million cats, 900,000 rabbits, etc., how would you report that if you had to disseminate that information (a) to your boss and (b) to the general public in an accurate and visual way? There's never a correct answer, but I would hope that you would think or at least strongly consider the answers: (a) a bar chart and (b) a bar chart. You certainly wouldn't eliminate the option in either case.

In those circumstances, or indeed any circumstances other than the circumstances I found myself in, which was wanting to have fun with a creative alternative visual depiction of the data, I would almost certainly have produced a clean, tidy, simple bar chart in no time at all, I would have presented it to whoever my stakeholder was and moved on.

Adverse reaction to the visualisation

When I shared the above visualisation online, it agitated some readers, and here are some of the reasons I think why:

First, it's obviously not a map. It's perhaps unfair to use the word "obviously" here, because, after all, I've chosen to make it look like a map of the United Kingdom. With each area seemingly represented by just one animal, perhaps each circle represents the most common pet in each geographical area?

But do people really think that all dog and cat preferring areas are always diagonal to each other and never meet? That people who prefer to own fish as pets only live in the sea? It doesn't take much to realise that this would never be the case, but that time is longer than many people's attention span and longer than the time it can take some people to get outraged!

It's certainly not my intention to be derogatory here, because I include my own attention span in there too, specifically in the context of a visualisation published on social media. The medium of Twitter and fast-paced snippets of social media information mean that people need to understand things instantly.

Scrolling past something that is designed to look like a map will lead readers to assume it is a map, and for the majority who then don't spend time to consume and understand it, it will remain a map until the point they scroll away. Rather than make the leap, people told me they just assumed there was geographical relevance, or directly asked me if there was any geographical relevance to the placement of the animals.

Second, readers aren't able to make comparisons. Are there more cats than dogs? More hamsters than horses? Even if there are no geographic meanings to placings of coloured dots, we can at least make comparisons if we, say, group the animal types together. My first assertion, when I discussed this in my initial blog post, was to say that this example does not follow Gestalt principles. But that was incorrect.

Gestalt principles are determined by our cognition, and not the visualisation – they describe how our brains instinctively collate and process information. For example, we are fooled by the Gestalt principle of proximity into thinking that the area of checkerboarding light and dark blue colours represents one combined area, and perhaps that the remaining combined predominantly green and brown area is representing another area. So, it's more accurate to say that with knowledge of how Gestalt helps us to interpret visualisations, I've chosen to go against this in asking readers to interpret the chart. In that sense, you could use this as a very good example of anti-Gestalt!

Third, it's not a bar chart.

In defence

But here are my responses and why I think people may have taken this a bit too seriously:

All the points I mention, to me, make it obvious enough that it's not to be considered a map. I even had one response, in fairness, not from a UK reader, who didn't recognise the overall shape and had no idea it was map-shaped in the first place until they read some of the tweets debating it.

The key thing to me is that my audience in this case is not people who want to know the key take-out information quickly. It's not a key report for Pedigree Mars telling them in which areas of the UK they should focus dog food over cat food. It's not a report for Pets At Home telling senior directors where they need to think about opening a new store. It's not a journalistic piece explaining the prevalence of dogs over cats in the UK overall or determining the regions where cats outnumber dogs.

It's a visualisation with all pet types in correct proportions, to deliberately catch the eye by being arranged in the approximate form of the UK's land mass and surrounding sea (with apologies for casting the Republic of Ireland adrift).

It's a visualisation that could, though I'm over-selling it here, I'd be the first to admit, be used in poster form, with a certain amount of improvement and embellishment, to tell the story in a fun way. My audience is people who like visualisations and are interested in the wide range of visualisation skills, possibilities and chart choices in the field. People who consider themselves aficionados of data art as well as visualisation, however we might define the former term. So, by definition, my intended audience at that point consisted of people who didn't just consume visualisations but would come onto Twitter and other online spaces to enjoy, search for and discuss visualisations.

I was happy for my visualisation to be noticed and talked about, even if not all of the discussion was positive, since I really enjoyed and learned a lot from the discussion. Perhaps it doesn't help that one of my favourite popular artists, namely M.C. Escher, sets out to deceive, ironically often using land, air, and water-based animals (Figure 2.6.2).

I love to solve word puzzles or chess puzzles, but in addition to that I enjoy creating them, where my aim is to lead the brain down one direction, to make my reader think, to use his or her brain laterally, and only then find the correct path. What's more, I know some people will fail spectacularly in the puzzle whereas some will instantly recognise the solution. Perhaps, here, I'm doing this, in my data visualisations too?

FIGURE 2.6.2   Sky and Water I – *M.C. Escher.*

Accurately visualising data

One element of the visualisation that was important to me is that I wanted it to be accurate too, which is why, despite being happy to discuss its good points and bad points, I do fiercely defend it as a data visualisation and not just a pretty picture. This was an accusation levelled at my graphic in some of my feedback, even by those who defended it: "It's lovely but it's just a picture, you don't need to defend it!" to paraphrase one discussion.

OK, it's a picture, but using the medium of data, which is portrayed accurately if not intuitively. One accusation against design-centred visualisations is that they are "vizdata" and not "dataviz". Quite a clever point which I can appreciate, but I don't believe that the two terms must represent entirely separate entities. A design-driven data visualisation, as described in my earlier chapter, should, absolutely, still be a particular type of "dataviz" – a subset of data visualisation as a whole.

For these reasons, I spent a lot of time on design. The total number of pets I had in the data was 55.5 million. I could represent this with 555 separate circles, 100,000 pets for each one. Considering the prime factors of 555 led me to a rectangle of 37 by 15 giving exactly 555 squares. Could I then fashion a map of the UK so that 350 squares were filled with alternating fish and 205 with land-based pets?

It became a low-tech exercise using an outline map of the UK on half of my screen and colouring in square in Excel on the other half, counting exact numbers so that all correspond exactly with the data. A lot of painstaking tweaking was done to get the 350/205 ratio exactly right and the sea "coloured in" with the two types of fish owners before the land-based pets were included.

Yes, the placings of the land animals are completely arbitrary, with my only design constraint being that I didn't want to place two of the same colour circles next to each other. Apart from that, the visualisation includes "easter eggs" in the form of UK geography puns, known only to me since publishing the visualisation, at least until now!

Only I know that I put one of the reptile circles on Lizard Point, the UK's southernmost point in the far southwest. I chose to put a caged bird, represented by a salmon colour circle, in London to approximate where Canary Wharf can be found, though London is big enough also to include Isle of Dogs and Catford. There's a black circle representing a rabbit approximately over the Nottingham suburb of Bunny. The reader knows none of these things, but I create data visualisations for fun, so I'm going to have fun including these elements, while still adhering strictly to the correct proportions.

And knowing the reasoning above, in my original blog post on the subject I challenged my readers to tell me why I deliberately put a hamster on the East Anglian coast – I don't think I ever did get a correct answer to that one so I will leave that unanswered until someone comes back to me with the correct answer!

Form versus function

My takeout from the controversy, which is an emotive word that perhaps oversells the discussion somewhat, was that if you want to be so unconventional as to almost deliberately puzzle or deceive your readers, then perhaps it needs to be done in the right forum, or with a little more explanation or warning. I illustrated it in my original blog post with the simple Venn diagram below (Figure 2.6.3).

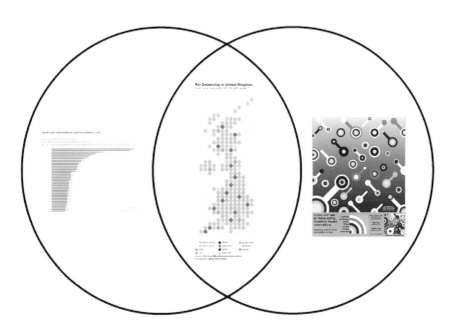

FIGURE 2.6.3 **Visualisation types.**

On the left: a visualisation that looks like a standard visualisation, and which follows standard best principles. This is illustrated here by a bar chart. We know that people like and appreciate visualisations such as this for all the right reasons.

On the right: a visualisation that looks nothing like a standard visualisation, illustrated by one of my design-driven data visualisations – this one has not yet been introduced but you'll see it in a future chapter. Perhaps you might consider it data art, and it certainly doesn't follow many of the standard analytical principles or make the best use of Gestalt theory. But although it's not everybody's cup of tea, there are many consumers who appreciate this and don't mind spending time and doing work to understand the viz. Those who don't like this respect it for what it is, they recognise it as something they can ignore.

In the centre: A visualisation that looks a fair amount like a standard visualisation, but actually it's deliberately ignoring principles for design's sake. This is what gets some people upset – they have to think contrary to first instincts. They weren't expecting to have to invest time to understand it, and the chances are they never planned to. They may feel they've been tricked. Just because you, the designer, were not taking the design seriously from a purist data visualisation perspective, that doesn't mean that your reader was expecting that or had the same mindset as you.

So, if you aren't taking a particular visualisation seriously, if you're in the middle of the Venn diagram above, focusing on design over data analysis, then be prepared for a reaction from those who interpret your design differently on first viewing. I received lots of feedback for my visualisation which has enabled me to understand, reflect and frame different visualisation projects into the categories above. I would always add though, if you get criticism which is good, bad or indifferent, you should listen.

In this case, while engaging in feedback conversations, there's a genuine case to state that it demonstrates Gestalt principles rather nicely, simply by showing how the design of the chart disrespects them as our brains try to organise and facilitate information in a way that's different to the intended outcome. Proximity, continuity, closure – in flouting all of these we are making it impossible to group together all circles representing one animal type in order to make comparisons.

Many data visualisation or data literacy classes like to demonstrate how to present a well-designed chart taking account of best visualisation principles. But there's often no better way to emphasise the importance of doing something well than by showing the consequences of it being done badly. The exploding 3D pie chart with numbers that don't add up teaches us to use only flat versions with few segments and only when demonstrating a part to whole relationship. The misleading bar charts with y-axis starting at non-zero values show us the importance of never starting a bar chart away from zero. There's no better way to emphasise the importance of a particular practice than by demonstrating the consequences of when that practice is ignored or applied in a different way.

As a final answer to the chapter's question of whether we take data visualisation too seriously, my argument is this: outside of business and professional use, when considering a personal project outside of work, every project is an amazing opportunity to interact with burgeoning data visualisation community who all have their own principles, philosophies and levels of visualisation experience. Once again, remember, your intended audience is key – if you have identified that your intended audience will consist of those who will share your curiosity for an unconventional approach, in this case a non-serious one, then you should be comfortable to explore such visualisations.

Your personal projects are a chance to practice new skills and to think of new design ideas, but only if that's where your passion and next ambitions lie. And you can't do that every week with bar charts. There's nothing wrong with taking every data visualisation project, seriously, framing every submission as something you might present to a client, but there's also nothing wrong with not doing so, if it comes with the understanding of what is the better, more conventional and professional alternative (that you have chosen to ignore!).

Postscript

From my perspective, there was a really interesting postscript to this argument, in the form of the Information is Beautiful Award's Gold-winning visualisation in 2018. The visualisation, entitled "Here's How America Uses Its Land", by Dave Merrill and Lauren Leatherby from Bloomberg, shows a map of America divided into arbitrary regions whose sizes are proportional to the area of land given over to each use type, but whose location has no relevance to land use.

First

Challenging

Idea

The visualisation, which I'm unable to show here, got a lot of traction at the time, and it's fair to assume the positive feedback sufficiently outnumbered the negative feedback given that it received a major award. Personally, I loved it, you won't be surprised to know, but that reaction wasn't universal. "It's not a proper map". "Those areas don't mean anything". "Wait a minute, does this mean that the 100 largest landowning families own all of Florida?" It's deceptive at first, but it requires you to forget geography and to spend some time understanding its unconventional nature. Once you, the reader, can do that, it comes into its own once more.

In the United Kingdom, it's often joked that when a large area needs to be described, it's always the size of a certain number of football pitches. And when a really large area needs to be described, such as global fires or deforestation, it's always "an area the size of Wales". In this case, similarly, we can visualise areas in relation to land masses we are familiar with. For example, the 100 largest landowning families own *an area roughly the size of Florida.* And every other comparison can be made in a similar way.

And UK Estate Agent Savill's did something very similar in their recent land-use survey published in January 2019, illustrated using the below visualisation in a report from Emily Norton and visualised by Joe Lloyd. To my own personal delight, it has even more similarities with my own pet ownership visualisation, inasmuch as the areas are shown as consisting of circular units. And, more obviously, it's a UK-based map!

Again, here, we might be led to thinking that, for example, the 20% of UK's current land use, shown by the dark red/orange circles, takes place exclusively in the south of England where that is the sole usage type, and nowhere else in the whole UK. But once common sense takes hold, it's clear that's not the case, neither is it the intention to contest that it is. At least Gestalt principles allow us to visualise the proportions of each particular land-use type by grouping each set of coloured circles together. And we have the additional visual cue that land used for arable cropping occupies an area roughly the size of, say, England and Wales south of Oxford (Figure 2.6.4).

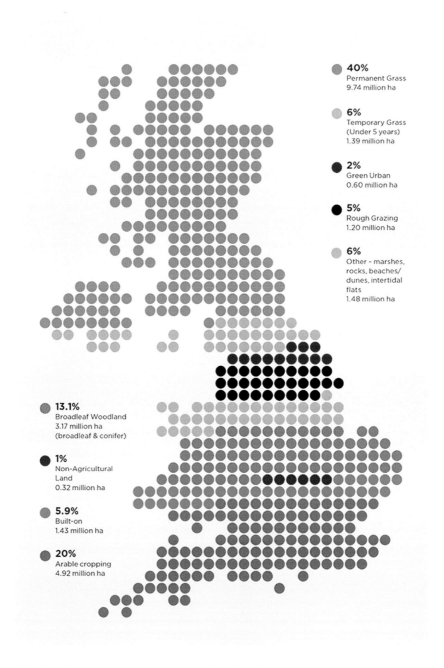

40%
Permanent Grass
9.74 million ha

6%
Temporary Grass
(Under 5 years)
1.39 million ha

2%
Green Urban
0.60 million ha

5%
Rough Grazing
1.20 million ha

6%
Other – marshes,
rocks, beaches/
dunes, intertidal
flats
1.48 million ha

13.1%
Broadleaf Woodland
3.17 million ha
(broadleaf & conifer)

1%
Non-Agricultural
Land
0.32 million ha

5.9%
Built-on
1.43 million ha

20%
Arable cropping
4.92 million ha

FIGURE 2.6.4 *UK current land use – Savill's UK (designer Joe Lloyd).*

Conclusion

I do think we occasionally take data visualisation too seriously. It's true that my first example is a low-key example of a frivolous way to show UK data that's not geographic in any way. But the examples from Bloomberg and Savill's acknowledge that arguably the industry's leading awards, as well as industry-leading estate agents, recognise that unconventional visualisation methods that actively ask the brain to look at visualisations that might seem like maps in a counter-intuitive way are an engaging, acceptable and understandable form of visual chart or report, and so there is always a place at the table for charts of that nature.

2.7

Why create unnecessary data visualisations?

I'm starting to understand that topics which make me really enthusiastic are quite niche topics. Not many other people know them.

Nadieh Bremer

Necessary data visualisation

This chapter is inspired by the publication below from Andy Kirk. Many of you will know him for running visualisingdata.com with its regular feast of industry-related resources, or will have benefitted from his book or training courses. But this was very much a personal project for Andy, and not a project for personal gain, since profits have been donated to charities, which was described on the cover as an "unnecessary data exploration". Why would anyone undertake an unnecessary exploration? After all, if we consider anything unnecessary, why would we do it? (Figure 2.7.1).

For my employer, I am involved in making *necessary* visualisations. Or, at least, visualisations that have been deemed necessary in discussion between our clients and our team. It's likely that this will

DOI: 10.1201/9781003240211-15

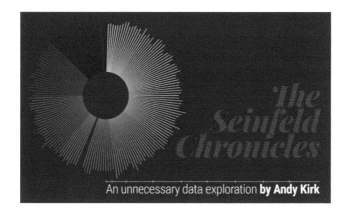

FIGURE 2.7.1 The Seinfeld Chronicles – *Andy Kirk.*

be the case for many of you reading this if you have jobs requiring you to visualise data.

We don't underestimate the importance of making sure that all elements of data visualisations are absolutely necessary – the requirements gathering phase of any business visualisation is one of the most crucial to the success and efficiency of a project. Data visualisations must help give insight, which enables our clients to make data-driven or data-informed decisions. All the things you have probably heard that data visualisations are supposed to do.

On the flipside, we're strongly encouraged to make sure anything that is unnecessary is removed – it could be detracting from the intended analysis, or it could be detrimental to the performance of the dashboard or visualisation. Professionally, these things drive me to do well, to promote best practices and to channel my time and experience into helping my clients.

Unnecessary data visualisation

But outside of the professional environment, when exploring a new project, it's easy to get bogged down in how "necessary" it is. I think for me it's obvious that I favour the unnecessary. Did we gain any new insight from visualising Irish whiskey sales to look like an art piece? Or from overlapping countries' medal-winning timelines on top of each other to achieve a ridgeline effect that looked like clouds or mountains?

Probably not, or at least not as much as would have been possible using more traditional visualisation methods. For me, these were both exercises in creativity, expression and fun, and the aim for my audience was not so much for them to glean anything useful, rather just for them to enjoy the visualisations for what they were.

At this point it's interesting to consider not so much *why*, but *how* you might define a visualisation as unnecessary in the first place. Consider a visualisation that concerns a much more serious topic. In my original blog post devoted to unnecessary visualisation, I'd included my visualisation around Contraception Choices for Women where I visualised choices available to women in a number of countries across the world.

I won't re-show the final visualisation here, since it sits, appropriately, in Chapter 2.2 where I discuss the use of triangles in data visualisation. But why did I originally frame it as "unnecessary"? My motive from a technical and personal challenge point of view was to explore a new graphical way of displaying the data. Inspired, as so often, by Sonja Kuijpers, I set about the challenge of emulating a new (to me) visual form of displaying data.

But in this case, I participated in the project as a passionate follower of the initiative to promote visualising gender inequality – indeed I have participated regularly throughout. I was happy also to negotiate the trade-off, that what a visualisation lacks in data storytelling or immediate analytical impact, it can gain in other ways through exposure via interest in its design or chart form. I was perhaps confusing unconventional design, with its slow speed of consumption and analytical takeaway, with unnecessary visualisation.

By the time I'd finished my argument in the initial blog post, I was happy that, to me, unconventional design **does not** necessarily correlate to unnecessary data exploration. I was participating in a project which gave focus to an important subject and did so in my own unique and distinctive way. So, I retract my initial categorisation!

Of course, the description I am going to give is a moot point, since it is not something everyone is going to strive to achieve on a regular basis, but I would consider an unnecessary data visualisation to be:

1. A visualisation around something trivial. Yes, it might bring joy to the creator and subsequently those consuming the visualisation who share similar interests or outlooks, but it's not a topic of importance to the majority of consumers.

2. A visualisation that doesn't feel it has to try hard to go all out for analytic results, data storytelling or best principles … so long as (1) above is already the case.

Motivation of unnecessary visualisation

Andy's book is a reminder of the importance of fun elements to visualise. As a reader, we really get the understanding that here is a well-respected professional in the field who just wanted to have fun visualising his favourite TV programme in great detail. His intended audience, I would imagine, without wishing to speak on his behalf, is niche – those who love the show, those who love data visualisation in all its forms and those who wanted to support the charity who was benefitting from the profits from the print run of this particular book. For me, there were two ticks out of three, because I don't really know the show. But I still take great pleasure from a project where the designer is really expressing his or her joy in the topic.

And it's visualisations like this, where we visualise our favourite topics, mostly for our very own benefit, that can give me the most satisfaction, can motivate me to get out of creative slumps and have fun visualising. Even if, to the wider world, it might seem unnecessary. Whether it's being the recipient of another designer's passion project, or whether you yourself are the designer of something that others would consider utterly unnecessary, the global data visualisation is much poorer without such visualisations.

As data visualisation designers, whatever your role, for example: presenting business charts, being a data journalist, creating a data art piece, you are focusing on three areas of your craft:

1. **Attention / Beauty**: you're interested in the aesthetic and impact of your visualisation and hoping that it gets attention and interest

2. **Analytics / Understanding**: you're using data and showing it visually to really explain your data and help your reader, whether that be your client, your audience, your boss, your executives, see and understand their data

3. **Take away message / Call to action**: you're proving or demonstrating a trend, summarising findings, evoking follow-up actions

The merits of all the above three sections could be debated at length and could easily fill a whole chapter or book. Very few visualisation pieces achieve all of the above three categories 100%, that's practically not possible. Our intentions for a given visualisation are

First

Challenging

Idea

more likely to prioritise one or more categories at the expense of the others.

Essentially, most books, lecturers or presenters will tell you that (2) is the most important. Most data visualisation roles would hone in on the principles, skills, tools and mindset required to maximise analytical understanding. Attention and beauty (1) are not important, in fact they detract from (2). That's why we cut the chartjunk, I hear some of you cry! Category (3) is also important – our explanation and our work done in creating our charts and visualisations need to lead to an emotional or a rational response.

All these books, lecturers, presenters and other experts are absolutely right! But they are not considering the specific situation of a visualiser or designer who just wants to throw themselves into an unnecessary project. I would argue that the key element for these projects is element (1) – create something that grabs attention and looks great, with an element of (2) – understanding is important, but not so important because of the more trivial nature of the subject.

For so-called unnecessary visualisations, it's (3) that's less crucial. In fact, there is no real follow-up, no intended call to action. We just want our readers to either enjoy or ignore what we have produced, in many ways the benefit has been to us as the producer of the visualisation.

Celebrate the unnecessary

With these thoughts in mind, I have in the past given presentations entitled "Celebrate the Unnecessary". Since much of the focus of my book is on encouraging visualisation designers to challenge the status quo, bend or break the rules, and not take visualisation too seriously for personal projects, it won't surprise you to read that all these are related to encouraging designers to have fun, to really enjoy the process of creating projects and to reap the benefits of enjoyment while learning new skills and techniques in the process. I list a number of reasons why you might want to celebrate the unnecessary in your data visualisations.

Celebrate nostalgia

Projects such as this are a perfect excuse to throw yourself into your favourite book, TV series, pastime, etc., from your childhood or from years gone by – a subject and/or place in time that's important to you, the creator.

Dive deep

You can get as detailed as you like – visualise things in ridiculous detail that nobody really needed to know. That's not to say the outputs won't be appreciated, they just won't be life-changing!

Learn new stuff

If you're diving deep and researching your subject, you'll learn so much in the process. An early visualisation of mine, not shown here, was an abstract and exploratory visualisation based on the top 75 UK singles of every week of the 1980s. I knew that data was going to take me a while to collect anyway, but it took me even longer than it should have done, as I regularly recalled, researched and played music I had either forgotten about or never knew in the first place – all of which was an unnecessary distraction but which added to the enjoyment of the experience as a whole.

Go light touch / be unconventional

By this, I mean that for an unnecessary visualisation your subject can be as trivial as you like. I refer you back to the visualisation of letters and numbers used in 50 years of Sesame Street episodes from the previous Data-Driven Design chapter. And as for being unconventional, it's a recurring theme throughout this book that I don't need to emphasise again here, except to say that if ever there was a time to be unconventional, it would be on a visualisation that might be considered unnecessary. After all, you wouldn't, for example, present COVID-19 infection rates to the nation in the form of a ridgeline plot, or an obscure artwork.

Overcome Creative Block

If you're struggling for ideas or inspiration, your best chance is to investigate a topic you love without worrying what insight you can provide. If you will enjoy it, you'll hopefully regain confidence from the process of immersing yourself into something trivial or nostalgic, and hopefully get satisfaction from the creative result.

Design influence of generative art

Here's a visualisation I completed in 2020 on *The Hitchhiker's Guide to the Galaxy*, specifically the book, from 1979 written by Douglas Adams (Figure 2.7.2).

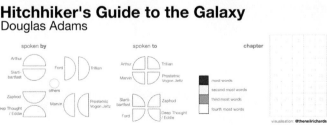

FIGURE 2.7.2 The Hitchhiker's Guide to the Galaxy.

This book, and the series that followed it, is certainly my favourite book of all time. Now there's little doubt this probably qualifies as "unnecessary" – not only is it "just" about a light-hearted science fiction book, albeit a classic, but within that, what I have chosen to visualise is which characters speak most to which other characters in a given chapter.

I had, for some time, wanted to explore geometric style–generated art as a design influence. The art I mentioned comes from Dutch coder and designer Saskia Freeke who has created a daily image every day, at time of writing, for over 5 years. And many of these images have sparked curiosity in me, wondering if the ideas could form the basis of a data visualisation.

Not surprisingly for me, it's another example of design-driven data, which is a theme I have referred to many times when citing inspiration for my work. Some of Saskia's examples are below – it's easy to see where the inspiration for my viz may have come from! I decided ultimately that I loved the shape combinations of the first piece on the left, with the colour palette from the second piece, and that formed the design inspiration for my creation (Figure 2.7.3).

FIGURE 2.7.3 *From Daily Art – Saskia Freeke.*

And as for the visualisation itself – it's one of my very favourites because it hit exactly the personal brief I was aiming for. I created a visualisation, very much of the design-driven data format, which emulated the designs I was inspired by, while "ticking many of the boxes" for unnecessary visualisation.

It helped me out of a creative block (tick), it's light touch and unconventional (tick), it's a very deep dive as it counts and looks at individual sentences (tick) and it visualised a book I'd loved for years (nostalgia – tick). And as for our (1), (2) and (3) categorisation above? Of course, attention and beauty are a subjective measurement, but I think I've concentrated on that most of all. I've made sure my data is understandable, but crucially I know that there's no real significance or takeaway from this visualisation. There's only really aesthetic appreciation of what it looks like.

"Minimalist" visualisations

A celebration of my own unnecessary visualisations wouldn't be complete without a mention of my "minimalist" series. The *Mr. Men* books, by Roger Hargreaves, were a popular series of books in the 1970s when I grew up, and the *Little Miss* books were added later when I was a little older. Why they were front of mind while I was considering a project, I honestly don't know, but I do know that I was inspired, indirectly, by the idea of data humanism – creating a small multiple visualisation showing the imperfect attributes of every individual character.

Once I realised there were exactly 49 of the *Mr. Men* characters, a perfect square number, I knew there would be a visually pleasing square grid way to visualise them, even if what I chose to analyse and display was completely (you guessed it) unnecessary (Figure 2.7.4).

Unnecessary, nostalgic and fun, it genuinely enhanced my interest in small multiple designs and disaggregated visualisation. And better still, I happen to know that this adorns at least a couple of my friends' walls in poster form. Friends of a similar age to me who had the same nostalgia towards the subject that I do, and who appreciated that their young children might appreciate the overall look of the poster in their nurseries.

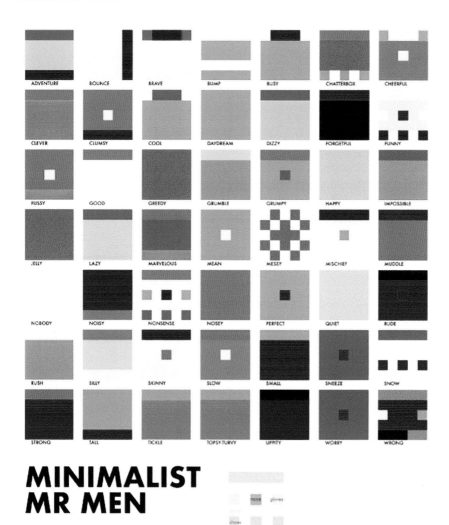

FIGURE 2.7.4   *Minimalist Mr. Men.*

Conclusion

I'd summarise by asserting that there's a difference between "meaningless" and "unnecessary". We've spoken about telling stories with data, and we are starting to see many examples of where the designer – often myself – is not really trying to tell a story with data, rather just to use data as a creative medium for output. But even in the latter case, the data is always on display, and so I would never categorise a data visualisation as meaningless. Not totally meaningless, anyway!

Of course, some might be considered unimportant. I'd agree with that – it's less important for you to know which characters spoke in Chapter 9 of my favourite book from 1979 as it is for you to know recent COVID-19 infection rates in your region. But the field of data visualisation will always encompass all, from the sublime to the ridiculous, the important to the unnecessary.

After all, I know a little bit more about Seinfeld now than I did before *The Seinfeld Chronicles* landed on my doorstep. And any of you who chose to spend a little bit of time exploring my own unnecessary work will have a slightly better subconscious knowledge of the colours of Mr. Men noses. Surely a ringing endorsement for unnecessary visualisations!

2.8

When are several visualisations better than one?

Isn't life a series of images that change as they repeat themselves?

Andy Warhol

This chapter looks at two questions, both of which are important considerations. But although the questions are very similar, the thinking behind the discussion and the answers is different.

When does adding an extra copy improve the original?

At face value, this would appear to make not much sense. If we're trying to consider the cognitive load of our readers, or if we're trying to create an impactful design, then why would we want an extra visualisation in addition to the one we've already got? And what about if we are trying to use our white space wisely, or arrive at the right data-ink ratio? Why then would we have two visualisations when one would do?

One situation where this could potentially come in useful is when you want to display the same data in two ways – you might have two variations on the same data visualisation when one is less familiar.

DOI: 10.1201/9781003240211-16

169

That's all very well, and it does represent a situation I've chosen to replicate a couple of times, although a better solution may be to hide the second visualisation type in the form of a hover action or tooltip, such as my Big Bird visualisation seen in Chapter 2.5.

My main example, which is a technique I use regularly, is to use a copy of part or whole of the visualisation as a key/legend for the whole thing. In the Figure 2.8.1, I've used a larger version of the US hexagonal state map by taking a copy of the "$25,000-$49,999 earners" map and enlarging it slightly, so that I could include state labels and explanations. On the main view there is very little room to include the labelling on every tile, and any attempt to do so would heavily detract from the design. The user will hopefully understand that this more readable version acts as a template for the rest of the versions below.

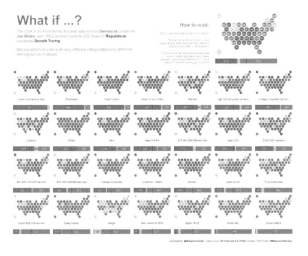

FIGURE 2.8.1   *What if …?*

This is something you've already seen me do in this book and will see me do again. Often a good way to give instructions to your readers is to take a copy of your visualisation, whether it's the whole visualisation or just a section, and recreate it again in the corner or on another page entirely. This second chart then becomes fully annotated with instructions where needed and can be as detailed as necessary without distracting from the main image.

In doing this, you have the freedom to remove labels and explanations from the main image, so you can focus more on the cleanness or the impact of your design with the story you are trying to tell.

The reader can then refer to the second copy in their own time. Although it's not the same thing, this acts in the same way that a legend would act on a simpler chart such as a bar or an area chart. Having the legend ready and available to refer to, when necessary, allows the chart designer to avoid having to label each particular colour or element on the main chart itself.

A subtle variation on this theme, although the visualisation itself is not especially subtle, can be seen in this visualisation I prepared to compare the RSPB's Big Garden Birdwatch scores of 2020 and 2021 in the UK (Figure 2.8.2).

In this example, I didn't mind that the labels for each of the individual areas of the United Kingdom were small and faint, since readers would have a good knowledge of where each region was, even in a new and unfamiliar layout. Similarly, the colour choice of the four constituent nations, plus the Isle of Man and Channel Islands, is a separation so clear it doesn't need including in any explanation. But in choosing to put diverging bars on each tile I had no way of explaining which bird was represented by which bar.

This is an example of Schneiderman's Mantra – the elements relative to data visualisation can be summed up in three steps: (a) overview first, (b) zoom and filter and (c) details on demand. Introduced in a paper titled "The eyes have it: a task by data type taxonomy for information visualizations" by Ben Schneiderman in 1996, these steps look to introduce a taxonomy of tasks to aid good communication with data. In other words, although we do want to give people the opportunity to look at the details, just as importantly we want to give them the broader story first and most prominently.

Similar to our first example, a larger, single tile performs this job nicely at the bottom right, where I am able to show which bar refers to which bird in the form of a picture. And in fact all of these pictures are labelled with further information about their overall ranking beside this graphic.

But I mentioned that this varied from our US political example – in this case the larger, separate copy of the graphic represented the UK overall figure. With no specific geographical location within the UK map, the overall figures need to be displayed separately anyway, so in this case the additional graphic is performing two jobs: that of displaying the overall data, and that of acting as an explanation or legend.

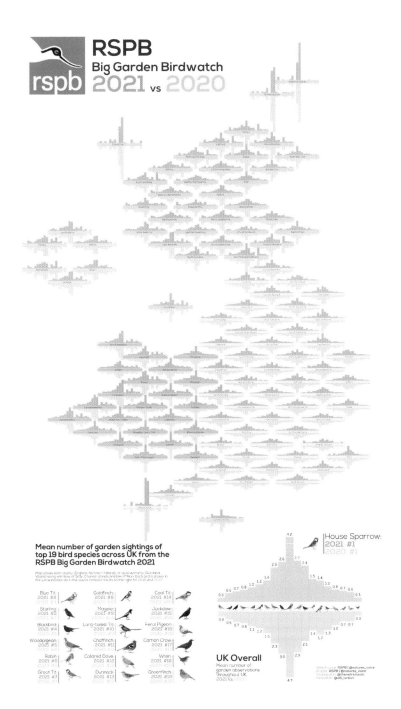

FIGURE 2.8.2 **RSPB Big Garden Birdwatch 2021 vs 2020.**

When are several visualisations better than one?

There are different answers to this question, depending on how you interpret it. It's possible that we are thinking of two or more visualisations that complement each other by visualising different elements of the same subject. A suite of charts, graphs or visualisations which allows for the overall output to be greater, more impactful or more analytical than that of any of its individual charts.

We've seen this in our discussion of "long-form" visualisations in storytelling and have alluded to it in examples such as Andy Kirk's Seinfeld Chronicles in our "unnecessary" chapter. Both of these examples add to the stories they tell and the data they display by increasing the quantity of charts output to the same project in order to give a fuller output (to paint a fuller picture, if that's not a mixed metaphor with data storytelling). And indeed, this book will finish with a similar project from myself.

But when I was recently asked what my favourite chart type was, I found it hard to come up with an answer. And then the more I thought about it, the more I realised that though I may not particularly favour one *chart type* over another, I do know that I have a real fondness for a particular *visualisation type*, namely the "small multiple" as I will refer to it. Incidentally, it might also be considered a visualisation strategy rather than a type, since the chart type of each individual element can be anything you like. But that's a moot point here. You may also know it as a trellis chart, a panel chart or a lattice chart, among other terms.

Small multiples represent a great way of comparing values across a discrete dimension which otherwise brings confusion or clutter, by showing each slice of data repeatedly in an individual chart. Here are four situations in which I like to use them.

Showing data change over time

Geographical data is notoriously difficult to show over time, since the x and y axes are, by definition, used for longitude and latitude. With your two-dimensional axes used up (and we don't discuss 3D visualisations in this book!), there's no obvious candidate for depicting time in a static visualisation. Here, small multiple charts are an ideal solution.

It doesn't just have to be a traditional map: Figure 2.8.3 is an example of mine from early in my career as I made my first explorations into the world of tile maps which is a good case allowing for easy comparison between years. Additionally, standalone copies of the same visualisation are easier to justify given that the time period between each map is not consistent from one to another – with the years very clearly labelled we get around the problem of unevenly distributed data points which might have been more of an issue in something like a bar or line chart.

It doesn't just have to be geographical data – other data types can also be sliced in the same way – if your x and y axes are already used and you don't intend to make an animated visualisation: Figure 2.8.4 is a similar non-standard example comparing identically laid out charts over time.

Showing differences across other dimensions

Figure 2.8.5 shows the 100 companies depicted in the visualisation in a pre-determined order 1–100 in overall company rating. Knowing the pre-determined order of individual visualisations allows us to "look up" our version of choice. So, the difference between this and the above example is that we can design a visualisation allowing us to compare and contrast differences from one company to another, rather than from one period of time to another, in company ranking order.

This numbered company ranking means that we can see any trends in the data should there be any from high to low overall company rating, although, in this case, we don't see any – our takeout story is that unfortunately there is very little variation among the top 100 rated companies with white males more likely to be in leadership roles across the board.

Showing differences across ordered categories

It could be that the dimension for comparison and "slicing" is a discrete categorical dimension that isn't numeric. In these cases, it makes sense to order the small multiples in an order which makes each category easier to "look up" in a different way. This will not show trends, so much, since you wouldn't expect countries arranged alphabetically to show trends but will allow for easy comparison.

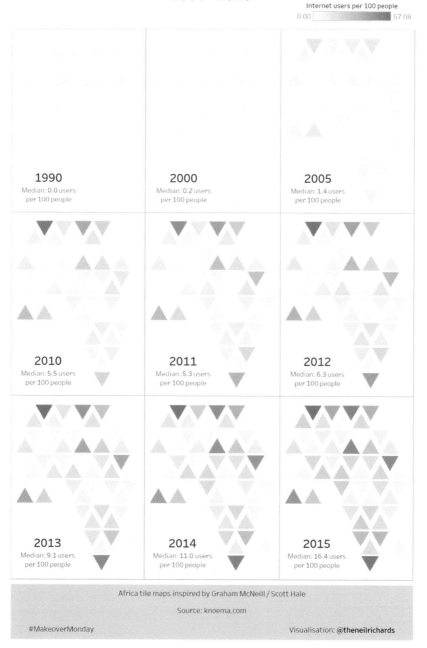

FIGURE 2.8.3   *Internet usage in Africa 1990–2015.*

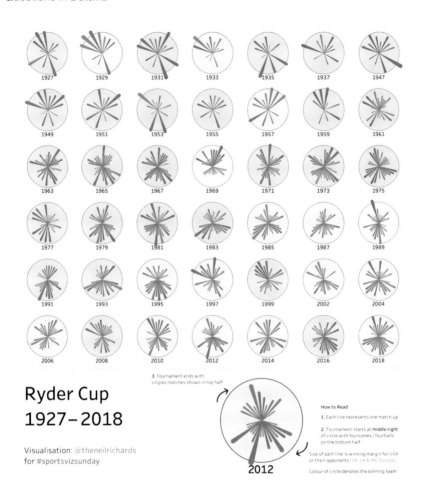

FIGURE 2.8.4   *Ryder Cup 1927–2018.*

In the example of Figure 2.8.6, where I borrow my design very much from Ed Hawkins' iconic climate stripes design to show change over time versus an established midpoint in each individual country, we show countries in alphabetical order. Ed Hawkins is a UK-based climate scientist from the University of Reading whose powerful and impactful climate-related visualisations have been widely adopted by campaigners – this specific stripe design used for the comparison of mean temperatures over time can be found in https://showyourstripes.info.

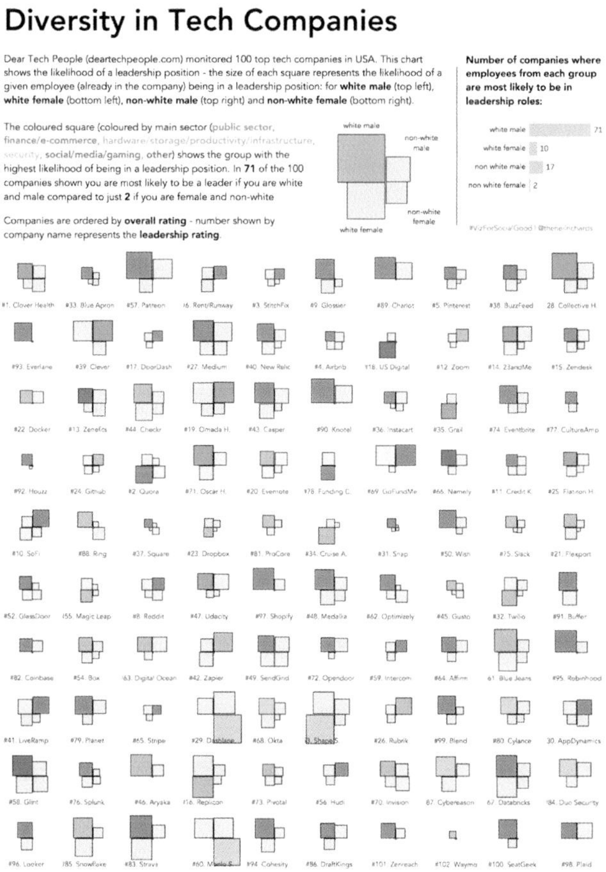

FIGURE 2.8.5   *Diversity in Tech Companies.*

Showing small, identically formatted visualisations in pleasing visual format

Finally, the links, trends or comparisons may not be obvious at all, but it can still be the case that small multiple visualisations simply look good as a simple method to see, compare and contrast every individual element in your dataset. This is something I use a lot and is really just a natural endpoint of my preference for showing disaggregated data where possible. A small multiple chart just allows the reader to spend time enjoying the visualisation – we can notice our own similarities and differences, and draw our own comparisons between whichever individual elements we choose.

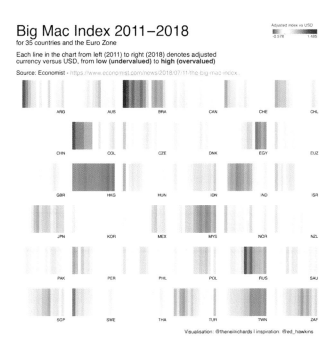

First

Challenging

Idea

FIGURE 2.8.6 *Big Mac Index 2011–2018.*

It's also my opinion that these visualisations, and the majority of small multiple visualisations in grid form, can make excellent candidates for posters. Showing elements individually, rather than as interactive filters or tooltips, removes the need for interaction such as clicks, taps or hovers, and allows for entirely static visualisations. Such poster-style visuals are then ideal for an audience who can browse, appreciate individual elements and notice different things every time they dip in.

This category is not dissimilar to the one before it (showing differences across ordered categories), but this is less about showing trends, similarities or differences, but simply making comparisons in a fun format which looks good, pleasing and geometric. To illustrate this is a somewhat "meta" square small multiple of square small multiples, where I display my recent so-called Minimalist Trilogy.

I introduced my Minimalist Mister Men visualisation in the previous chapter. In this example (Figure 2.8.7), I got great enjoyment from the process of curating the data and visualising the result, and this was enough to inspire me to make a trilogy of such visualisations. Incidentally, those who may have noticed that there are four in this trilogy will appreciate that this was not a planned trilogy from the start – the current size of the trilogy at time of writing is now six!

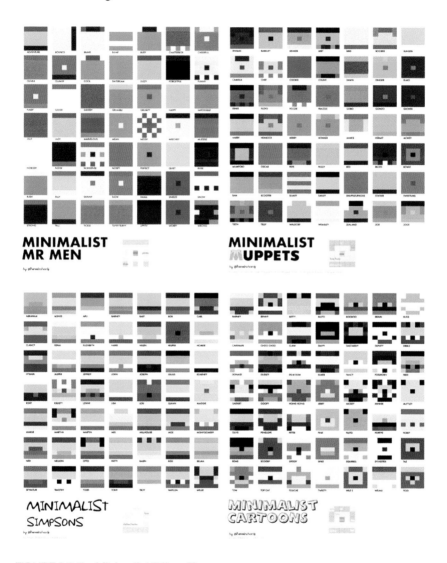

FIGURE 2.8.7   *Minimalist Trilogy(!)*

The key points that link these visualisations and all the above are the consistent design and formatting of individual visualisations within the grid, and, arguably, the use of enough white space to look appealing. Once you decide on a small multiple format, it's usually important to apply the same design decisions to each individual element that you would to a full-sized chart. Whether these are conventional design choices or the kind of choices that challenge convention that we've been discussing up to now, that's up to you.

In all cases, each individual chart needs to be readable enough on its own merits given the smaller scale in which it's displayed. But often sacrifices in detail will need to be made, such as having to omit labels and annotations, or aesthetically choosing to do so.

And this is a reason why small multiple-style visualisations are almost always a candidate for an "extra visualisation" of the kind mentioned at the top of the chapter. Indeed, of the examples of small multiple visualisations given in this chapter, the majority have an additional copy of an individual element acting as a key or a legend.

Identical visualisations with different formatting or display options

Here's a fifth use case for small multiplications that I haven't made use of myself yet, and in fact a use case which I only became aware of as I was compiling the chapters for this book. Remember Chapter 2.2 where we discussed visualisations with triangles? The creators of the triangular ternary charts (Zan Armstrong and Lusann Yang) which they used for material sciences visualisations would also use another technique using small multiple visualisations.

They presented a series of small multiple charts in a visualisation that used identical data layouts but with different scales and colour gradients. So, unusually for small multiple visualisations, it is not the data that varies across each individual chart, in this case, from left to right for each channel, but colours and parameters of scale which vary. This allows them to determine which of the individual charts, or subset of charts, show the data in the best way – which charts best presented the significant findings that would be most of interest to their expert audience (Figure 2.8.8).

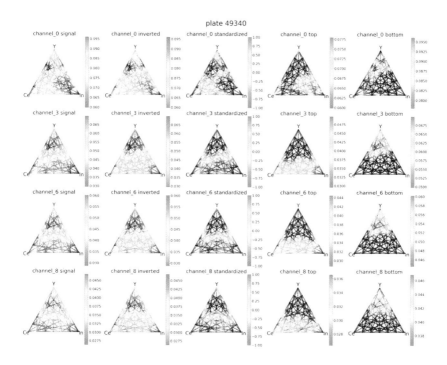

FIGURE 2.8.8 *Summary of ternary charts across channels – Zan Armstrong and Lusann Yang.*

And a few words, too, from Zan Armstrong on the colour choices:

Because rainbow color schemes are so controversial, I just wanted to add a quick note that the rainbow used in these figures was an intentional choice for the analysis. There were only a very small number of specific people using these images to analyze the results of each experiment and we knew all involved had no problem discerning red/green. And, the primary use was on a screen (not worried about printing in black & white).

Lastly, in this case perceptual differentiability was arguably the most important trait we needed in the color scheme, because we were looking for changes in color across the triangle-space. And, many popular color schemes give up a lot of perceptual differentiability while optimizing for other benefits.

I don't include the quote above as a "right to reply" or out of any feeling that the rainbow colour schemes need to be justified – from some of my colourful examples in this book, I would be a hypocrite to do so! But I quote it as a great example of questioning supposed best practice and making the design decision to go against it. In this case, the questioning process consisted of considering and choosing to ignore some of the downsides of using a "rainbow" colour palette.

In my own examples, often I am eschewing best colour practice for aesthetic reasons. However, in this case the designers are doing so for well thought out reasons with specific knowledge of both their audience and their intended use of the visualisations.

Conclusion

Perhaps to encapsulate all of the ideas where additional copies of a template chart are used in one chapter, I should have asked the question "When are $n + 1$ visualisations better than n?" But that would just be too clever for its own sake.

It should be no surprise that many visualisations satisfy more than one of the different criteria for individual discussion in this chapter, especially given that the examples in this chapter are constant examples of many other concepts introduced elsewhere in this book, such as tile maps, design-driven data, data humanism, unnecessary visualisations, etc.

Any visualisation, wherever it is shown here and whomever it is created by, has the capacity to spark a question or inspire a new idea.

First

Challenging

Idea

What can I do when data is impossible to find?

"Data" is a word that can often feel intimidating. I believe that everyone in the world is a secret data-collector, even if they don't realize it!

Stefanie Posavec

Existing sources of data

Often for personal visualisation projects, the hardest part can be getting hold of an interesting or relevant dataset. I'm not talking about the drudgery of cleaning or reshaping data for your chosen visualisation tool, which we know can also be difficult and/or time-consuming, but of actually getting hold of data in the first place.

The internet is full of excellent sources of data. Official datasets can be found on government websites or from statistical agencies. Websites such as Kaggle or data.world host community sourced data sources on a range of topics. Community projects such as makeovermonday.co.uk or vizforsocialgood.com offer datasets which are freely available and perfect for personal projects – certainly the latter two have been hugely responsible for many of

DOI: 10.1201/9781003240211-17

my own visualisations in my own development. For example, in this book, where else would I have got multi-country whiskey sales data from?

And often there are datasets that are freely available but just take a bit of work. Examples I've used in my own work include medal tables from newspaper websites, demographics data that can be pasted from Wikipedia, music chart positions that can be curated into larger datasets and many more. The list of possibilities is almost endless.

This halfway house of data will usually involve copy/pasting, a useful API, scraping skills or data manipulation. All of which involve time and patience. I would imagine that any of you reading this who are involved in data visualisation in any way, shape or form will be all too familiar with the idea of a dataset always needing extra work prior to visualisation.

Sourcing your own data

However, in asking this question, I'm referring specifically to data-sets that you know just don't exist in the form or level of detail that you want. Perhaps the question would have been better reframed as "What can I do if the data I want just doesn't exist?"

Let's use an example of one of these such datasets in a previous personal project. At one point, I knew that I wanted to do something on my favourite book: *The Hitchhiker's Guide to the Galaxy*. Initially, I couldn't find a dataset at all relating to the book online. It has to be said, I'm not sure what I was expecting to find, but whatever it was, I couldn't find it! Sometimes you have to be realistic enough to accept that not every topic has an easily accessed and analysed dataset, and this was one of those cases.

I do, however, own the book, both in old-school paperback format and as an e-book. Obviously, a book in itself could be considered a dataset – a dataset consisting of a large number of individual words which can be analysed, aggregated and visualised in many different ways.

This time, my intention was to analyse what happened in the book, in some way to visualise events, to tell the story. While I was considering the importance of data storytelling, in this case the idea was to think about data storytelling in its most literal case. I actually wanted to visualise the story. In the end I had just one option, to read the book and then create (or curate) my own dataset.

Now of course this adds a significant time element to the process, but because this was a personal project which I wanted to enjoy creating, I didn't mind that. The solution that says "Got no data? Create your own!" is not always going to be the ideal solution, but in situations where you want something particularly bespoke, sometimes you have to revisit the event or subject you plan to visualise, review it and then record and create your own data.

Remember the *Seinfeld Chronicles*? The visualisation project from Andy Kirk that I introduced in the chapter about unnecessary visualisation? Crucially, Andy includes a paragraph entitled "Notes about the data" in which he stated:

> *The data used in this study did not exist, it had to be manually captured through watching every episode and logging the times, categories and characteristics of different events within each.*

My idea was to recreate the timelines of the six main characters in the book and display them in a similar way to Kurt Vonnegut when he displayed the "shapes of stories" as described here. Vonnegut's original blackboard drawings have been recreated many times, and this particular version is from Jonathan Schwabish in his PolicyViz discussion around storytelling in data visualisation in 2017 (Figure 2.9.1).

Boy Gets Girl from Kurt Vonnegut

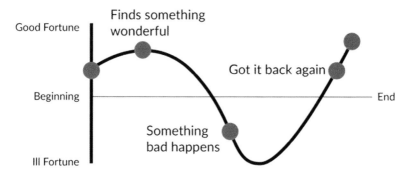

FIGURE 2.9.1   *Boy gets girl.*

So, I read the book, noted every plot point from every chapter and assigned it to the relevant character or characters and its position within the book. Eventually, this led to one brand new dataset which was perfect for my purposes. Of course, it also led to one visualisation designer who may have had to spend a little more time creating the data than initially planned for (me!), but who got to re-read and categorise his favourite book, albeit slowly, in doing so.

It's also worth remembering that every dataset has to start somewhere with a human responsible for the collection of that data. This is an integral pillar of data humanism and is also a concept that leads to an assertion that all data can be considered inherently biased. After all, in making the decision to collect data, we have already decided what data to collect, and crucially, what data not to collect.

When data is collected in such a personal way such as in this example, then there's no denying the human influence and possible bias. I've decided exactly how I want my data to be framed and structured in order to visualise it before I've begun the data collection process. And, in categorising much of the qualitative data into a quantitative form in which I can use it, I have put my own opinions, spins and biases on the resulting data.

In this case, it's an unnecessary visualisation, created purely for my own pleasure and for the enjoyment of my audience. But the consideration of self-introduced bias is always an important consideration for personally curated data.

Here's a still from my visualisation. The emotional highs and lows of each character are purely as described from my own interpretation and encoded into the data as a value from 1 to 10. Those who know the book will understand why I chose the particular twists and turns for the cast members' journeys and the resulting shape it ended up taking!

As a fan, both of the underlying book, and of Kurt Vonnegut's anecdotes as he describes the shapes of stories, this was never more than a tongue-in-cheek bit of fun. But because I had invested so much time in the data curation, I got a lot of enjoyment from the process, as well as learning and practising technical elements of visualisation (Figure 2.9.2).

First

Challenging

Idea

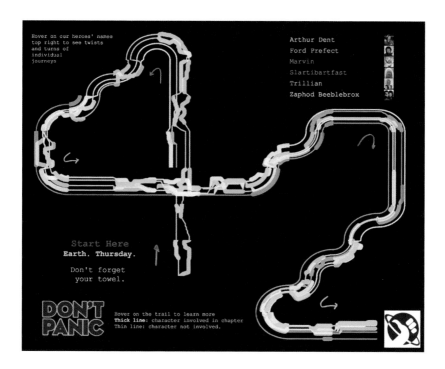

FIGURE 2.9.2 Don't panic! – visualising the story of The Hitchhiker's Guide to the Galaxy.

Sourcing sport data

It's not the only time I have done something similar in terms of collecting and curating my own data. Most detailed sports data comes from increasing amounts of human-collected data, whether from sensors on the bodies of elite football or basketball players, for example, or whether from trained observers and analysts counting, categorising and quantifying every run, kick, shot, cross or tackle; every serve, return or volley; every punch, block or dodge, or obviously whatever metrics are most relevant for the particular sport.

But this is usually done while watching or re-watching a sporting event and is much more likely to be available, given recent advances in technology and recent appetite for vast amounts of data, for recent contests rather than historic events. It's still a finite set of data and if you don't have data that you really want, you may need to curate it yourself.

Challenged by fellow Tableau expert and talented visualisation designer Simon Beaumont as part of an online "Sports Viz Sunday" community visualisation project to produce a snooker-themed visualisation, I realised that snooker data was quite scarce. This was another example where it soon became obvious that rather than look for data to visualise, having decided what it was I wanted to visualise, I would need to create the data myself.

In deciding to tell the story of every shot in the final frame from 1985, and most British people of a certain age will remember exactly what I'm referring to, I had one option. I found the match on YouTube, watched it and recorded the details and outcome of every shot. I'm not sure if shot by shot data exists with detailed metrics in the world of snooker, but I am sure that if it does, it didn't in 1985! The result, not shown here, was a visualisation walking through every shot of what was a memorable moment in British sporting history.

Personal data

Another category of visualisation that belongs squarely in this category is that of personal data. I'm not talking address or bank account details, but data about you and your actions, feeling, interactions and surroundings on a daily basis. If you're undecided on the next great dataset to use for a project, you can do much worse than recording your own personal data – data that hasn't "happened" yet. And obviously that falls into the "impossible to find" category!

In Chapter 2.4 we mentioned Dear Data – of course, each of the visualisations is beautifully designed and created, but less externally obvious is the fact that every one of the datasets used for that award-winning project was also hand curated. Giorgia Lupi and Stefanie Posavec's follow-up book encouraged readers to "Observe, Collect, Draw" in order that readers might create their own Dear Data style visualisations. The key to this is the "Collect" stage. If you need data, collect it yourself!

Conclusion

All datasets you obtain from regular sources were collected by a human at one point – either directly or indirectly via a program, device or app initially programmed and designed by a human.

Chances are the devices I mention were pencil and paper – you too can do the same thing in order to guarantee a unique, personal dataset that allows you to be as conventional or creative as you like in how you visualise your next project.

And outside of personal data, the fact remains that often the best way to get hold of data, if there's something very specific you want, is to record, curate, collate and shape it yourself. If it means you get to watch your favourite TV programs or films, or to read your favourite books, then so be it!

End of Section II

The aim of the second section was to show that although there are probably a number of ideas or principles you have learned to follow which are deemed good practice, in following these guidelines, which exist in good faith to help analysts and data visualisation practitioners to produce the clearest and most analytical outputs, it can often mean missing out on alternative outputs.

These alternatives can be more eye-catching, more aesthetically pleasing, more fun to create, or simply offer alternative visual perspectives. And it's not always as simple as whether something is suitable or not for a business client, because you may be fortunate enough to have a situation where the alternative perspectives hit the client brief, in cases when your client genuinely wants something a little bit different! Remember that asking questions reminds you to consider your intended audience, to consider your own personal preferences and goals for the project, and to consider the balance you want to strike between the two.

In Section III we'll see several examples where this leads to new ideas that can expand your data visualisation skillset while expanding your creative portfolio.

IDEA QUESTIONS

3.1

What is the third wave of data visualisation?

One thing is for sure, we have examples of those who have optimized for past best practices, now we need those who epitomize a new wave of data visualization.

Elijah Meeks

Defining waves of data visualisation

In Chapter 2.4, I introduced the concept of data humanism, following the assertion from Giorgia Lupi that data visualisation had reached the point of "peak infographics". In initial drafts of this book, this led me to title that chapter "What is the second wave of data visualisation?" and introduce the concept on those terms.

However, the "second wave" term is not as widely accepted as the concept of data humanism, and I felt it didn't really fit the description of the chapter. Indeed, google "second wave" in conjunction with data visualisation, and I can pretty much guarantee you will only find results related to COVID-19, and although that's perhaps understandable at the time of writing, as the global pandemic which

DOI: 10.1201/9781003240211-19

started in 2020 enters its second wave, it confirms that it's a less established concept than that of data humanism itself.

At the Tapestry data visualisation conference in late 2018, Elijah Meeks, who would go on to become a founding Director of the Data Visualization Society in 2020, gave a keynote speech which introduced waves of data visualisation in a different way – he said at the time that we were entering a *third* wave of data visualisation.

The first wave was summarised by **clarity**. Visualisations were generally simpler chart types (bar charts and line charts), using no colour or desaturated colour. Focus was on titles, labelling and annotations, all for additional clarity. The philosophy of the first wave was very much summarised by the teachings of Few and Tufte (Figure 3.1.1).

FIGURE 3.1.1   *Data visualisation first wave – Clarity – Elijah Meeks.*

The second wave was summarised by **systems**. The introduction of charting tools such as Tableau and libraries such as d3 and ggplot in the previous years leading up to the talk had capabilities way beyond the "first wave" outputs. Instead of the rich textual context and careful annotations, the range of output had exploded into a wide, colourful and geometric variety, described as "never meaningless" because there was always often complex data hidden within (Figure 3.1.2).

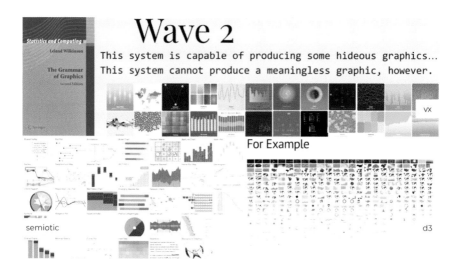

FIGURE 3.1.2   Data visualisation second wave – Systems – Elijah Meeks.

This is one of the reasons I abandoned the idea of talking about data humanism as being symbolic of a second wave of data visualisation. If anything, it's the endpoint of the second wave above which is more equivalent to the concept of "peak infographics" as introduced by Lupi. Both are acknowledging a saturation of the data visualisation field with masses of data, with an abundance of tools, and with a complexity of outputs fighting for the attention of readers. Both have witnessed this increase and are calling for a change in mentality and future direction.

The proliferation of the systems in wave two and their capabilities means that potentially anything is possible. The inclusion of more data can lead to more and more complex graphics that become unreadable or intelligible. Peak infographics, maybe?

Third wave

Where the third wave is concerned, Meeks acknowledges that many proponents still teach and espouse the first wave principles. The first section of this book references the principles built and practiced by established industry leaders such as Tufte. Best principles remain best principles, and many will continue to teach and encourage exclusively these principles and practices. So, the first wave hasn't gone away, and indeed nor has the second wave.

But the third wave focuses on **convergence**. Our behaviour has changed as a consumer, for example, in the use of faster browsers and different ways of consuming content, such as mobile versus desktop. Because the tools have greater capacities, and audiences are becoming more used to different modes and styles of visualisation, we in the current third wave are in a unique position of being able to use much more powerful and customisable systems to rein in the over-complex second phase output. Taking this further, we have the opportunity to adopt a new data humanism way of thinking that avoids overwhelming outputs from "big data".

This is why this resonates with me, and why I am framing the third wave of data visualisation as an introduction to the third section of this book. One of the effects of convergence is that BI (business intelligence) tools are growing more custom. It's easier than ever before to break out of a tool or suite of tools which once focused only on simpler "out of the box" chart types, and now people are finding ways of leveraging BI tools to produce much more custom visualisation types. And this is exactly the premise of this book.

This is intentionally a tool-agnostic book, but there's no getting away from the fact that my own visualisations are produced almost entirely using Tableau. Tableau is marketed and used as a BI tool (indeed, my business role uses Tableau exclusively for data visualisation and my role includes "BI" in its title), but outside of my professional role, I choose to stretch its capabilities to create the unconventional and the "custom" (Figure 3.1.3).

FIGURE 3.1.3 *Data visualisation third wave – Convergence – Elijah Meeks.*

And it's great personal validation to me that the example used in Meeks' slide to demonstrate this (on the right-hand side) was one of my own visualisations. A humanism-inspired visualisation in which I imitated hand-drawn disaggregated visualisations by Giorgia Lupi and recreated them in Tableau. The visual itself will feature in a little more detail later in this section.

There are many more generic examples of convergence in data visualisation, whether it's the ability to create more dashboard-like outputs with notebooks or create the illusion of more sketch-like hand-drawn visualisations in packages such as gg and R. As a result, there's not just more power to the elbow of data visualisation practitioners, but it does potentially put more emphasis on the need to design, or, perhaps more accurately, to get better at design!

Community and critique

And, of course, the nature of online communications these days, in particular, means that visualisations are open to more critique and criticism, competing for attention with so many other products, visualisations and creators. A final crucial point is one that's outside of the scope of this book but cannot be ignored is that we need to be better at giving and receiving critique in the right way. Data visualisation communities are being built at pace with sub-communities growing around tools, industries, libraries and many sub-genres.

Blogs and social media platforms mean that the scale of exposure to our outputs can be far in excess of previous levels, and so as the third wave of convergence emerges, so the data visualisation sub-communities merge into one and exposure increases even further. It is as important as ever to include all participants in a whole community – we all gain from our fellow developers' and designers' ideas.

The "third wave" isn't defined in terms of a particular point in time. We may think of ground-breaking visualisations that fit our definition that were created years ahead of any perceived boundary in time if we try and define it too discretely. But thinking in these terms gives us a tool to recognise how data and the resultant visualisations have changed over the years and a context for our visualisation tools and their capabilities.

Conclusion

The remainder of this third section will encourage you to do as I have done – embrace the third wave of data visualisation, focusing on design ideas, custom visualisations and breaking the mould of best practice and earlier styles, while also thinking with a design eye. I'll introduce you to a small, finite number of my own ideas which have arisen from the idea of converging custom visualisations and BI tools, and from my particular approach of design-driven data.

I don't expect you to use the same examples as I do, many of which might be considered unique to me. But I'm in a position where, as well as encouraging you to question principles and conventional design choices, I can also demonstrate a number of individual ideas that have arisen. For every idea that has arisen in a new visualisation or concept, there are many more still to be explored, invented and shared.

Being a data visualisation practitioner in the field means that I have two great passions: producing data visualisations and consuming visualisations produced by others. I mentioned above how we all gain from the ideas and creativity of our community, and indeed have included many examples within this book of visualisations and designers that have inspired me. Perhaps the examples in this section will do the same for new readers, and, in any case, I can't wait to see other new ideas and unique visualisations being introduced into the visualisation community!

First | Challenging | Idea

3.2

What alternative ways are there for visualising timelines?

Time is an illusion. Lunchtime doubly so.

Douglas Adams

Vertical timelines

Let's start with what might seem like the obvious observation – a standard timeline would run horizontally from left to right in a data visualisation. We read from left to right in most cultures, and we perceive time as travelling in the same direction. If we watch an Olympic running race, we always see the runners travel from left to right across our screens as they cross the finish line. And so, the majority of timelines in conventional data visualisations among cultures which write from left to right will read horizontally from left to right. But this isn't a book about conventional data visualisations.

There are various reasons why we might not wish to visualise a timeline horizontally from left to right, but they would usually be summed up in one of two ways. Either the amount of room available on the page or screen suggests that an alternative way of displaying a timeline would be a much better fit, or we make a choice based purely on aesthetics. Perhaps an alternative would look interesting, impactful or cool?

DOI: 10.1201/9781003240211-20

The most obvious alternative, logically thinking, might be a vertical timeline. We haven't mentioned constraints of space much yet in this book but it's generally accepted that the horizontal bounds of a visualisation are usually constrained by the width of your page or screen, yet vertical bounds of a visualisation are much less tightly constrained.

In the social media age, we think nothing of scrolling vertically – long-form visualisations and scrollytelling have already been discussed in this book, and let's face it, our use of many social media apps involves almost constant vertical scrolling.

In short, if the length of our timeline is likely to lead to our visualisation being "long and thin", then a vertical timeline will be a better user experience than a horizontal timeline, not least because this is the standard rule of thumb for pretty much all data visualisations and all online output.

Where do we place most recent events on a vertical timeline?

But supposing we have a vertical timeline – where does the most recent data, or more accurately the most recent date, go? Is it at the top, or at the bottom? Which is better? Of course, "better" could mean more intuitive, more aesthetic, more sensible or any number of definitions (Figure 3.2.1).

FIGURE 3.2.1   *Twitter Poll.*

I knew this was a much more contentious question, and so I put it to my Twitter followers. Crucially, I made a point of only offering a binary choice. There was no "it depends"!

Now before I give my own thoughts – my way of thinking is often to consider the options, arrive at what I might initially think is the most sensible answer, which is often the "best practice" answer, and then think again. In thinking again, I then strongly consider the counter-argument. In this case, a split of 60%/40% is far from decisive, despite a healthy sample size of 167, with thanks to everyone who voted.

Some of the comments suggested that it wasn't an easy decision to make – I've included just a selection of them below, with comments edited only for spelling and grammar:

> *I'm quite shocked at the result for this!! I read left to right, top to bottom so expected the present day to be at the bottom – from where we started down to where are we now.*
>
> *My brain totally tells me oldest top/left. Scrolling/subject/audience makes this a wild card. Personally, I would probably end up with some sort of summary section up top that spelled out whatever without needing to scroll. I voted At The Bottom!*
>
> *I regularly succumb to recency bias. I voted Top.*
>
> *It depends on the application, of course. But once you decide to go vertical, for me that breaks the "usual" direction of time, and then I want to see the most relevant (aka most recent) on top.*
>
> *It depends. Is the goal a walk through the total history of the topic? If so, I'd go oldest at the top, most recent at the bottom. If the goal is to highlight recent trends while minimizing scroll fatigue, I'd go with the most recent at the top.*
>
> *Who is the audience? Just as left/right reading direction impacts horizontal timeline design, up / down mental models of time vary by culture.*
>
> *Top, as I think of time as moving forward… also leaves space for the future.*
>
> *I think there's a case to be made for "most recent first" on its own merits, but mostly for me it's the practical consideration that most recent is likely to be most relevant, and on the web I don't want to risk people not scrolling down.*
>
> *(followed up by)*
>
> *Oh dear! I fully stand by my principle but have just realised an upcoming project goes oldest/top to newest/*

bottom and in this case that also feels like the right way round… can we have the "it depends" option please?!

In a binary choice I'm going for "At the bottom" as I'm likely reading downwards and I'd like the context of the past to frame the now/recent when I reach it.

Trying desperately to avoid another "it depends" reply. For me, the visual representation of time moves in the same way that I read things…predominately left to right, but then also top to bottom.

Like everything there are use cases for both, but I think if you're doing vertical it's because people want to see the most recent first. Horizontal everyone is accustomed to reading time oldest to newest, but I don't think that's the case for vertical.

If the question had been asked to me, I think I would have given a preference for showing the most recent data at the top, perhaps because if we are thinking of time as a y-axis for our graph, then we read from low to high, bottom to top. But I'm 100% on board with the counterarguments, and would have chosen the "It depends" option in a shot, had there been one.

From this I would conclude that if you are in the situation of wanting to try out a vertical timeline, just to think of the pros and cons – the different preconceived ways that readers would expect to read a vertical timeline. And then go with what feels right and/or looks best once everything above is taken into consideration.

So, really, the answer should be "it depends" – perhaps the story in the data or the context of the chart will determine which is better for any given example. Or perhaps we worry too much about the concept of "better" given that a well-designed chart can do the job well in either direction. The answer then becomes the informed personal choice of the designer (you!).

Lexis charts

Taking a step back, one of my first non-conventional timeline visualisations did have a simple horizontal timeline x-axis running left to right. I use the word "unconventional" because I'd chosen to create a Lexis chart. Inspired by a chart I'd recently seen in the *New York Times* looking at the longevity of European political leaders,

I chose to replicate this Lexis chart using the longevity of English Premier League football managers. Note, this chart was from 2018 – the short-term nature of football manager jobs in England means that this may now look very different now! (Figure 3.2.2).

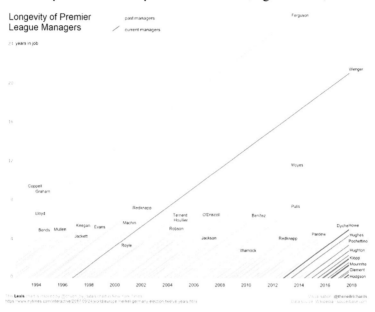

FIGURE 3.2.2   *Longevity of Premier League managers.*

In some ways, a Lexis chart could be thought to represent a number of individual timelines within one timeline. I love the aesthetic of parallel diagonal lines – every diagonal line being read, by definition, from bottom left to top right, as time passes (X-axis increases) and length of tenure increases (Y-axis increases) until it reaches its abrupt end.

And so, shortly after this I wanted to try another Lexis chart, this time looking at lifespans and presidential spans of US presidents. In this case, the time from the birth of George Washington to the then present day was only a little shy of 300 years, far in excess of the 26-year timeline I used in my Premier League football visualisation. This ruled out a horizontal design to me, there just would not have been enough room to fit everything into a standard screen size without seriously compromising readability. It seemed that the main design choice to make was to go long-form, hence using a vertical timeline, especially given that this was going to be consumed online (Figure 3.2.3).

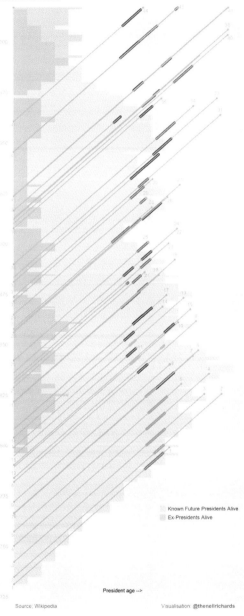

FIGURE 3.2.3   *Lifespans of US Presidents.*

This at least made my decision as to whether more recent events were at the top or bottom a little more intuitive. My choice was to travel from bottom to top in time, so that the parallel diagonals which are most reminiscent of a Lexis chart would still be shown diagonally, reading from bottom left to top right. With age being a proxy for tenure – it's the president's tenure of his own lifespan, after all – we've simply swapped both axes compared to the horizontal Lexis, which, fortunately for us, has no effect on its orientation or direction of reading.

Had we started with George Washington at the top, all of our lines would have pointed **down** and to the right. This would have been perfectly correct, of course, but I don't consider that it would've had the same aesthetic, and would have contradicted our established, albeit little-known, chart type. Age, as a continuous positive measure, would have seemed wrong descending down the screen as it increased in positive quantity.

Radial timelines

Next, I want to talk about radial timelines. The ideal thing to do at this point would be to have an example that bridges Lexis charts and radial charts. But is a radial Lexis chart even possible? As it happens, it is – and I can show you exactly that. Again, I want to emphasise that this chart came from an idea which started as a question (in fact, several questions):

- How else can I visualise a really long timeline (such as English Kings and Queens, which is about 1000 years since William the Conqueror)?

- I've used Lexis charts horizontally and vertically before – are radial Lexis Charts possible?

- If I come up with a radial Lexis solution, will it be understandable? Readable? Interesting-looking?

- What's the plural of Lexis anyway, is it Lexes?

I had to ask myself the first of those three questions throughout, and then test my answers. As for the fourth answer, it turns out the chart is not a Latin term, though it might sound like it is – instead it's named after its inventor Wilhelm Lexis. So, I guess the plural is

Lexises! This might sound like a pointless digression, and you'd be absolutely right in thinking that, except that there's always something to be learned and gained from getting a little bit more understanding of the history and origins of your chart type in order to help you use it in an appropriate context.

Below is the chart in question – the curve that each rotated Lexis line makes notwithstanding, this is a great example of where a radial timeline has allowed me to encase a full 1000-year timeline into one compact, square, space on my page rather than show it as one long horizontal or vertical timeline. Of course, the output is rather unorthodox, but it's striking and easily displays longevity information for every English monarch for those who are prepared to invest time reading the visualisation (Figure 3.2.4).

Later this decade, it will be exactly **1000 years** since the birth of William the Conqueror (King William I of England). The graphic above shows all the Kings and Queens of England from 1066 to present day.

Read round the image clockwise from the top, to travel through years 1028 to 2021. Every King or Queen is shown with a line extending from the centre which is proportional to their age – gold if they were not yet King/Queen, or **orange** when they were on the throne. Also included is the current Prince Charles, labelled as Charles III.

design:

FIGURE 3.2.4 *Kings and Queens of England 1066–2021.*

Spiral timelines

Another radial timeline which does a great job of consolidating all previous years' views into one view, from 1850 to 2016, is this visualisation from UK-based climate scientist Ed Hawkins. The visualisation is an animated build, and it was even shown to an audience of billions at the opening ceremony for the Rio de Janeiro Olympics in 2016.

The radial timeline allows for the axis to repeat every 12 months for every year in the dataset. In this case, it's a method that works well because the temperature increase, as is all too well known, is increasing over time, leading to the radial elements getting larger and larger in radius over time. Again, this is not a chart to consult when looking for detailed analysis, or for accurate reporting of any given data point over the last 166 years, but it does a phenomenal job of telling the story of increasing global temperatures in just one chart on one page (Figure 3.2.5).

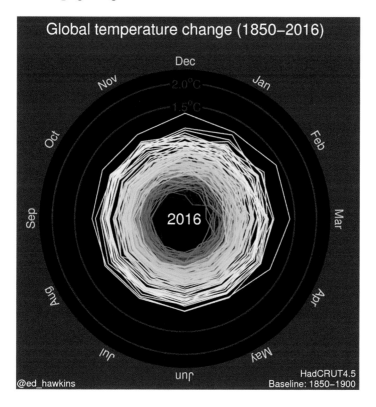

FIGURE 3.2.5   *Global temperature change 1850–2016 – Ed Hawkins.*

Mathematically, the effect of increasing radius in a radial chart leads to a spiral. And incidentally, the spiralling effect of such a radial chart can lead to an obvious metaphor. This chart, especially in its animated form, was presented often and widely as a "climate spiral" with the context, or in some cases the firm assertion, that global temperatures were "spiralling out of control".

Yes, a powerful metaphor, which perhaps really assisted in its viral nature and inclusion in the Olympic Games and beyond. But it's a metaphor added by consumers and journalists. In fact, Hawkins himself does not want to report on Earth's temperatures spiralling out of control. On the contrary, as a data visualisation practitioner who builds visualisations aiming to encourage us to notice and take action, he firmly and rightly believes that "our global emission choices control what happens next, so it is within our control". A nuanced difference, perhaps, but one that is worth noting if your visualisations are going to be published far and wide and interpreted in a crucially different manner to your own intention.

A final example – having looked at a radial timeline which led to a spiral shape due to our metric that we are measuring, i.e. temperature increase, gradually increasing over time – is to consider an intentionally spiralling timeline. A conventional radial timeline such as the one above will start and finish in exactly the same place for every repeated time period, which allows us to consider and compare differences across each time period - in this example, each year. However, an intentionally spiralling timeline will increase its radius as time progresses, so that a point's radial position will always start further away from the centre and the timeline will not overlap on itself (Figure 3.2.6).

Such a spiral can work for a small number of rotations, but note that it wouldn't be a great suggestion for the climate data above. When I looked at Twitter data from a certain Donald Trump, I could tell from the data that he already started off using Twitter a lot, but as he got more politically active, that usage just increased. I could use a much more tongue-in-cheek metaphor of "spiralling out of control", by using a literal spiral timeline, rather than a spiralling line based on a static radial timeline, thus making my literal and metaphorical interpretation a little bit more obvious!

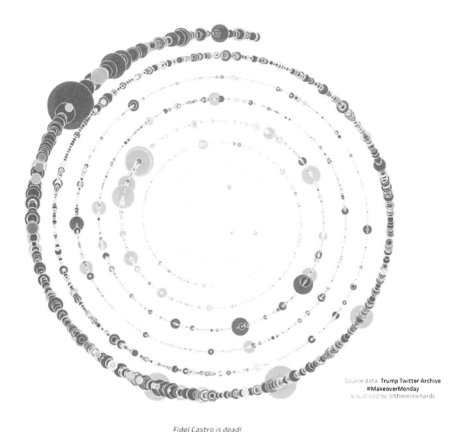

Fidel Castro is dead!

FIGURE 3.2.6   ***Are Trump's Tweets spiralling out of control?***

Conclusion

These are not the only ways of visualising timelines, but they are several of many such examples which have arisen from questioning existing standards and meeting the challenge of visualising time-based data in a creative way that allow readers to explore while enjoying a different creative visualisation type. You can improve or iterate on these, or, no doubt, find many different alternative methods that are equally engaging!

3.3

Why do I use flowers to visualise data?

Today's eccentricity is tomorrow's orthodoxy. Now go ahead: read, think, and discuss. And consider becoming a bit more of an eccentric.

Alberto Cairo, introducing Data Sketches

Introducing Premier League squads as flowers

In February 2021, I was looking for a creative way of visualising Premier League football squads. Halfway through the existing season, I noticed that there was quite a variation in squad sizes and squad numbers used, which piqued my interest for a possible visualisation. However, there's not a huge amount of analytic value to this, so it will already be of little surprise that I created what could probably be described as an unnecessary visualisation.

Of course, that doesn't usually stop me when it comes to looking at data that interests me and trying a new creative challenge. In this instance, I chose to represent each of the 20 teams using flowers (Figure 3.3.1).

DOI: 10.1201/9781003240211-21   **211**

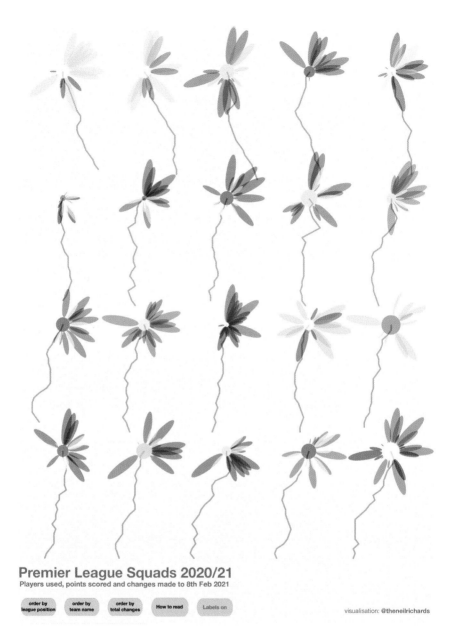

FIGURE 3.3.1 **Premier League squads 2020/2021.**

I should add that there is a second "how to read" tab to this which explains how to read and interpret each flower. But back to the question that gave this chapter its title – why flowers?

Geometry of flowers

A lot of my inspiration to create unusual visualisation forms comes from my lack of artistic ability. I can occasionally have a creative idea, whether in the form of art, music or writing, but I lack the skill to carry it out. In the case of music, my potential career as a musician petered out very quickly when I stopped practising my instruments as a surly teenager. A good theoretical understanding was not enough when I was too physically uncoordinated to become a natural and too apathetic to improve on the base level of skill I had reached.

As an artist, it's just patently clear that I have never been able to draw or paint. And where writing is concerned – well I'll let you make your mind up. So, I do get a lot of satisfaction from creating shapes, pictures and artistic versions of objects using data because in many cases it's the first time I've ever tried to undertake a creative process with any degree of success.

And if, like me, you've tried and failed to learn to draw using vector graphics packages such as Illustrator or Procreate, you'll know that very often the skill of building any image comes from building up a series of geometric dots, lines or shapes in layers, until the combination of these layers on top of each other start to resemble your intended final picture.

I'm a mathematician by training, and so the geometry needed to allow our software packages to draw the right constituent shapes and orientations doesn't put me off – in fact it's a plus point. It's this process of layering shapes that is pretty much exactly what I am doing when I create data visualisations such as flowers.

So, it's true to say that there is quite a mathematical and geometric element to flower-themed visualisations and similar outputs that evolve from the creation of layers of shapes and polygons. If you're not too daunted at the prospect of geometry underlying your final visualisations, then I hope, like me, you'll find the aesthetic reward is worth the mathematical brain workout.

A flower is an ideal example because it is both aesthetically pleasing to view, and usually a combination of many geometrical shapes and principles. After all, a flower is usually a combination of circles and radially arranged ellipses. In addition, the stalk of a flower can be a line chart either curved or stepped.

Additionally, flowers are often multi-coloured, where it's not unusual for the central part to be one colour, with petals being a second colour, or even alternating between a second and third colour. Their circular nature, the stems notwithstanding, makes them perfect for a good economical use of space within visualisations, small multiple or otherwise.

Take the bottom right flower in Figure 3.3.1, which represents Manchester United. Each petal is generated by data points. Squad numbers are encoded by position, number of matches by size, and presence in the initial team by colour. Because not all squad numbers are used, and some players play more regularly than others, all of this gives an irregularity to the flower which makes it look more natural. Overlapping petals give a more organic and realistic feel, and the different centre sizes, which are also encoded by data – the overall team score at the time of creating the visualisation, also give a nice heterogeneity to the range of flowers.

Were I to try and draw a flower, I would have neither the skill nor the nous to draw a flower that wasn't much more symmetrical, more regular in shape and generally unnatural looking. And it goes without saying that it would be much less skilfully drawn/created.

Further flower examples

Before I go further into the benefits of visualising in this format, the Premier League visualisation was by no means the first time I had tried something like this. A first example was the visualisation for the Operation Fistula charity, which has already featured in *2.4 What is data humanism?* Here the flowers' colour and position encode relevant data points, as well as the curve of the stem. This also noticeably encodes the flowers' roots as well, appearing to anchor each flower in place thus adding to the effect of a field of flowers in the breeze.

Another example where I have used the flower motif is in this visualisation of Rugby World Cup individual match results in 2019. Apart from the benefits of making something creative and geometrical, you might wonder why I chose a flower motif to represent rugby World Cup scores? In this case, I wanted to emulate the look of the cherry blossom plant, an iconic image of the host country, Japan.

Seemingly a lot more free-form, in this case, the colours, relative positions and sizes of each section of each flower represent teams and scores (Figure 3.3.2).

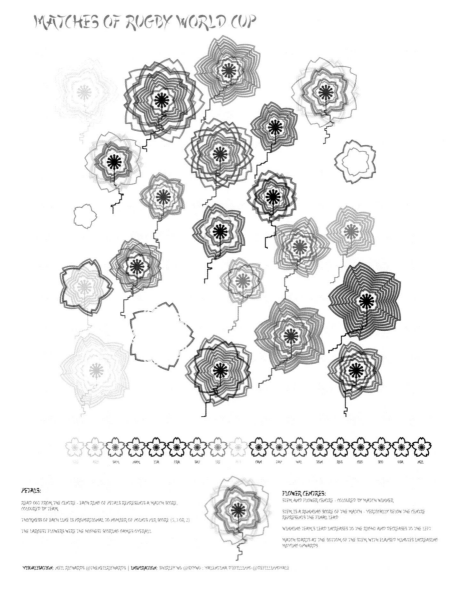

FIGURE 3.3.2   *Gender and ethnic disparities in tech companies – Ivett Kovacs & Istvan Korompai.*

Data encoding in flowers

Flowers and their stalks give the opportunity to encode many different dimensions. Petals can be different shapes, sizes, colours, in different positions, as well as being filled or empty. The central area can also be represented by different shapes, sizes or colours. That's up to eight different dimensions to encode in one flower, and that's if we include just one colour in the petals.

An additional trick I have used in each of my flower visualisations is to tell a different story with the flowers' stems. The football and rugby visualisations disguise a line chart in the form of a stem, both designed so that there is a possibility of them sloping on average to the left, right or vertically. This has the tendency to "sway" the flower to the left or right, adding a less regular and more organic look to each visualisation. The Operation Fistula visualisation also encodes slope into the stem, curving in relation to each woman's age.

The visualisation below from Ivett Kovacs and Istvan Korompai, two expert Tableau data visualisation practitioners from Starschema in Hungary, was a great inspiration to me on two levels. Ivett uses flowers (arranged simply in two layers of four petals around a central circle) to visualise gender and ethnic diversity in tech companies.

Visualising an important subject in a simple and impactful way, while comparing the 100 companies with each other in a pleasing 10 x 10 grid was an early spur to me on the aesthetic choice of flower data visualisation *and* the small multiple grid as a means for showing disaggregated data. In fact, you can see my own non-flower version using the same data in the earlier chapter on small multiples (Figure 3.3.3).

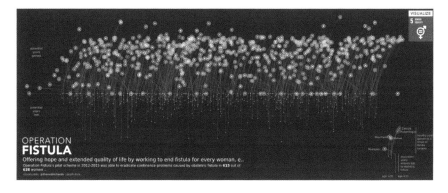

FIGURE 3.3.3   *Operation Fistula.*

First | Challenging | Idea

Aesthetics and metaphors

Flowers are sometimes emotive, but a simpler explanation for their use, on occasion, is in their aesthetics. In other words, they look pretty and attract the viewer's attention. Sometimes the flower metaphor is important, such as in the Operation Fistula example above, with growing flowers representing hope and life, and sometimes less so.

For example, there's no obvious connection with Premier League football, though you can make an argument for the organic nature of flowers with their individual differences representing the differences between the make-up of 20+ humans in each squad.

I did wonder if our cultural preconceived stereotypes mean that we're slightly more likely to consider the flower metaphor for visualisations that focus on women, rather than on men – and I must admit that I think it was a subconscious decision, or, more likely, even a conscious decision, to challenge my audience and buck that trend by using flowers to visualise men's football and men's rugby.

But ultimately, I enjoy using data visualisation software, developed with the purpose of displaying business analytics, to create something appealing to look at. And it's something I've often seen in some of the most prominent data visualisation leaders in the field.

Among these are data visualisation designers Valentina d'Efilippo and Shirley Wu, both of whom I have always cited as an influence in my flower visualisations. Valentina's visualisation at https://www.poppyfield.org is a beautiful example of the powerful metaphor of the poppy as a flower while encoding data within shape, colour, size and position of the flower, as well as in the dimensions and direction of the stalk.

The visualisation itself depicts deaths in global wars throughout the 20th and early 21st centuries, with the two largest poppies clearly denoting the two World Wars, and the size of flower representing the number of fatalities. With the poppy being a symbol used to commemorate the war dead, it's been chosen in the visualisation as a clear and tasteful symbol of commemoration (Figure 3.3.4).

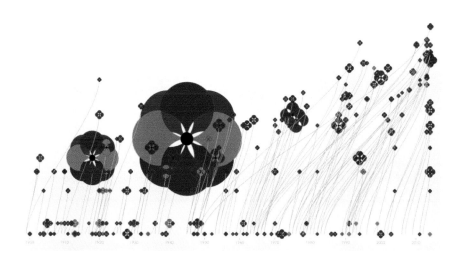

FIGURE 3.3.4   *Poppy fields – Valentina d'Efilippo.*

And Shirley Wu's Film Flowers (an excerpt of which is shown in Figure 3.3.5) was a definite influence for my Rugby Flowers viz, in particular. She uses different and more elaborate petal shapes regularly repeated to create a variety of resultant flowers.

These particular flowers were featured in the Data Sketches project from Shirley Wu and Nadieh Bremer, a series of stunning data visualisations which was recently released as the Data Sketches book. It was Alberto Cairo who summed it up best, as paraphrased here by Cole Knaflic on Twitter:

> *In visualisation, everything depends on purpose. Alberto Cairo highlights that flowers may not be right for a business report … but can be delightful in another setting.*

It's absolutely right – to re-state the obvious, flowers may not be the right choice for a business report. I would never imagine someone showing the Premier League flowers visualisation to the Newcastle United manager (at the time of creating the visualisation) Steve Bruce, in advance of their game against Aston Villa, and explaining that the different angle of the black and white flower versus the claret and blue flower explains how few changes Villa have made compared to Newcastle since the start of the season. Perhaps that

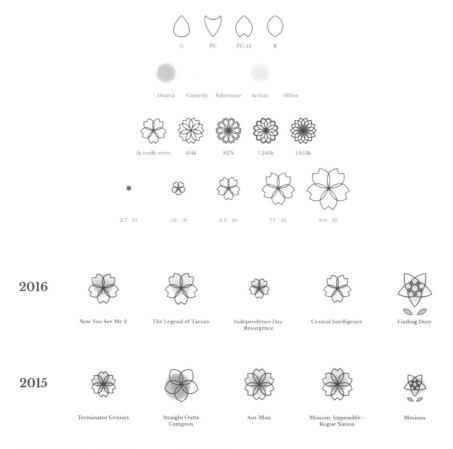

FIGURE 3.3.5   Film flowers – Shirley Wu.

would explain the different successes of the two teams so far this season as shown by the larger circular flower centre of Aston Villa's flower? Of course not.

But I do hope that flowers can be delightful in another setting. Many of those who liked my visualisation are more likely to have appreciated it than they would a simple bar or line chart, and that's for the simple reason of impact and aesthetic or artistic preference.

Conclusion

If you follow any of the examples or create your own similar examples through the same questioning and thought process, you will definitely have two kinds of people in your potential audience – unfortunately, I can't guarantee you an even 50-50 split, either. You will have a section of your audience who can see no further than the usability of your output as a business chart. Those who will use the hashtag #shouldhavebeenabarchart or similar. And that's OK.

I bear no disrespect to this section of any audience. Indeed, it's a perfectly understandable reaction to have, especially if you use what is a traditional BI tool to create untraditional output. In many ways, it's even the correct response to have, except that you are not designing with a business audience in mind. At this point, I hope you're not – you may need to go back and re-read a few chapters if you are!

Your audience consists of two cohorts of people: those who will appreciate an interesting, impactful and sometimes unconventional visualisation, and will, provided it's not intended for business consumption, generally prefer it to the bar chart that it could have been. And the second cohort of people is *yourself.* If you love your final output, take pride in it and are generally rather chuffed at the way it turned out, then that's every bit as important.

That's not to say that I want you to be your own harshest critic, although there will inevitably be designs, charts and creations that you don't publish because you don't like the end result, and that's OK. It's more to say that you will have greater success if the aim for your final design is something that you, yourself, really appreciate. Don't design your personal projects, in particular, to please others, but to please yourself. That way, you will enjoy the visualisation creation process despite times when it becomes lengthy, and get most satisfaction from reaching the end and publishing your final creation.

And speaking of Alberto Cairo, he writes about the *Data Sketches* book in an article in the Data Visualization Society's Nightingale publication entitled Orthodoxy and Eccentricity. The inclusion of the following lines is absolutely key to why we celebrate the beautiful data visualisation work of Bremer and Wu (and others like them), as well as being crucial to the ethos of this book and my way of thinking:

> *The education of visualization designers, whether it's formal or not, can't be based on memorizing rules, but on learning how to justify our own choices based on ethics, aesthetics, and the incomplete but ever-expanding body of empirical evidence coming from research and academia.*

First | Challenging | Idea

There are plenty of lengthy and detailed discussions [...] about how to balance out these considerations, and it's always useful to peek into the minds of great designers, if only to borrow ideas from them. Some of you will be persuaded by those discussions, and others will disagree and argue against them. That's fine. Conversation is what may help us determine whether certain novelties fail, and therefore should be discarded, or succeed, and therefore become convention.

I'd be first to agree on the need for so-called eccentricity for keeping data visualisation exciting, artistic and open to all. If eccentricity means encoding my data as flowers, then colour me eccentric!

What are Data Portraits?

I got a couple of my best students and put a series of facts into charts.

W.E.B. Du Bois

Data visualisation as a portrait

Sometimes there's a term that aptly summarises a particular ethos of looking at data visualisation. We've mentioned several times here the unavoidable concept of data storytelling, but we've also made clear that it's a heavily used term which leads to varying opinions on its importance and meaning.

But if we don't talk about data telling a story, what about data painting a picture? Leaving aside the obvious cliché about pictures painting a thousand words, I do like the term. Introducing the idea of a portrait emphasises the visual element of data visualisation. Throughout this book, I have tried to encourage the thought processes and creative processes to produce visualisations that appeal to the aesthetics, that might initially create impact, with the trade-off that they (intentionally) take time to be viewed, understood and consumed.

DOI: 10.1201/9781003240211-22

To take the analogy further, I've stated that my personal preference is to aim to create visualisations that would potentially look great in poster form – static pieces to take pride of place displayed on a wall somewhere. So, to me, "Data Portraits" fits rather well for creative visualisations that paint a pleasing, artistic picture of data. But it's not a term I can use to summarise this book, or my work, in general, because it's a term that's been prominently used not once, but twice that I'm aware of in data visualisation.

Data Portraits – Giorgia Lupi

First of all … Giorgia Lupi introduced the concept of personalised data-driven badges for attendees at the TED 2017 Target space in Vancouver. Attendees had answered a series of simple personal questions and she created a unique data-driven design based on these answers, which were then created into physical button badges. This was done almost instantly by generating the images, printing them, and creating the physical badges.

These were known as Data Portraits, and the intention was to consider the personal, human nature of data and to act as a talking point for attendees based on their responses – their similarities and their differences – perhaps to get to know each other in a fun, data-driven, visual way.

In November 2018, I wanted to try this for myself. These data portraits were the inspiration for me to see if I could use the same ideas and principles, but rather than being hand-drawn, or iPad drawn, I would recreate this using Tableau. So, at a Tableau User Group gathering in Manchester one evening, I asked a few questions of attendees as they joined with the intention of creating my own Data Portraits. In this case, I didn't have the wherewithal to go one step further and create physical button badges, and this was just an exercise to create the images digitally and display them at the event.

As far as I know, this hasn't been done using Tableau before. Introducing this to the group would fulfil three criteria: demonstrating a new skill in my chosen visualisation package, talking about the concept of data humanism and introducing this new audience of data visualisation practitioners to Giorgia's work and concepts. Of course, it was clear that the concept itself absolutely wasn't my original idea, other than to recreate it in Tableau (that was my original take as far as I was aware).

My version was a fairly faithful recreation of the original work, albeit tailored slightly to my audience. Giorgia introduces the concept here where she documents not just the badges and their interpretation but shows the finalised finished physical products. Below is her schematic and some resulting images (Figure 3.4.1).

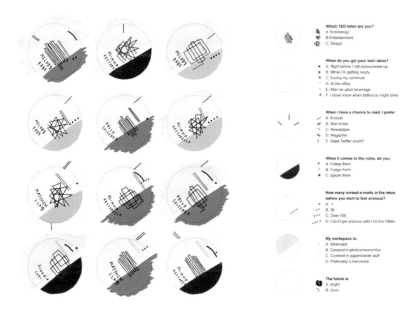

FIGURE 3.4.1   *Data Portraits – Giorgia Lupi.*

Now moving on to my version: first I invited the attendees to fill in the below simple survey on Google – you can see from here that the questions are simple and don't give away too much information about each attendee (Figure 3.4.2).

A quick data manipulation and Tableau workbook later, and my badges were ready in a small multiple visualisation on screen. Fortunately for me and my love of square small multiples, in particular, there was an exact square number of attendees who replied to the survey questions: sometimes a plan just falls together in the nicest way! (Figure 3.4.3).

My "how to read" section is shown in Figure 3.4.4.

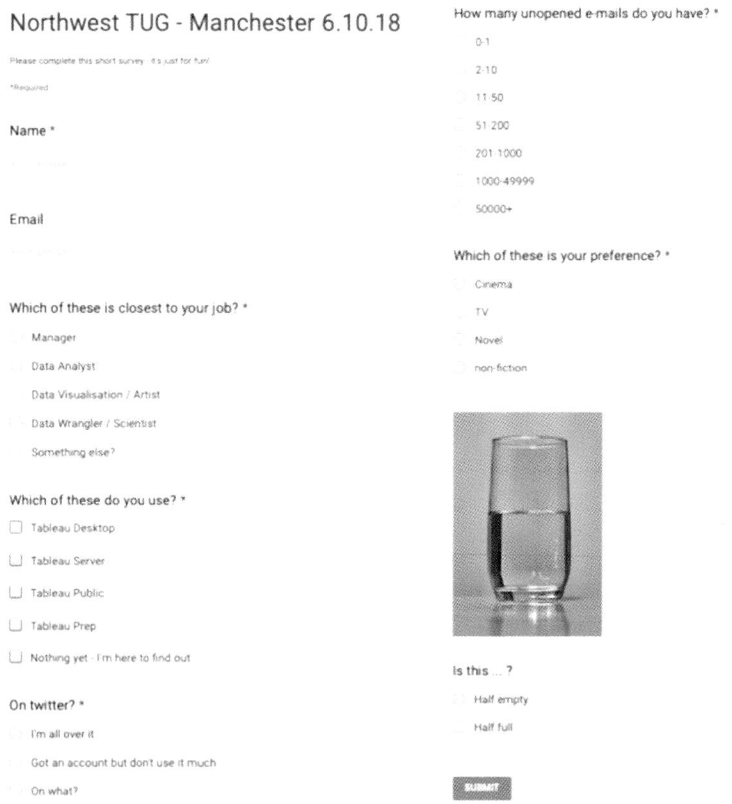

First | Challenging

Idea

Northwest TUG - Manchester 6.10.18

Please complete this short survey - it's just for fun!

*Required

Name *

Email

Which of these is closest to your job? *

Manager

Data Analyst

Data Visualisation / Artist

Data Wrangler / Scientist

Something else?

Which of these do you use? *

☐ Tableau Desktop

☐ Tableau Server

☐ Tableau Public

☐ Tableau Prep

☐ Nothing yet - I'm here to find out

On twitter? *

I'm all over it

Got an account but don't use it much

On what?

How many unopened e-mails do you have? *

0-1

2-10

11-50

51-200

201-1000

1000-49999

50000+

Which of these is your preference? *

Cinema

TV

Novel

non-fiction

Is this ... ?

Half empty

Half full

SUBMIT

FIGURE 3.4.2   *User group attendee survey for use in Data Portraits.*

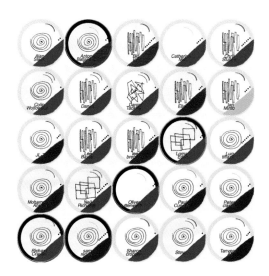

FIGURE 3.4.3   **Data Portraits.**

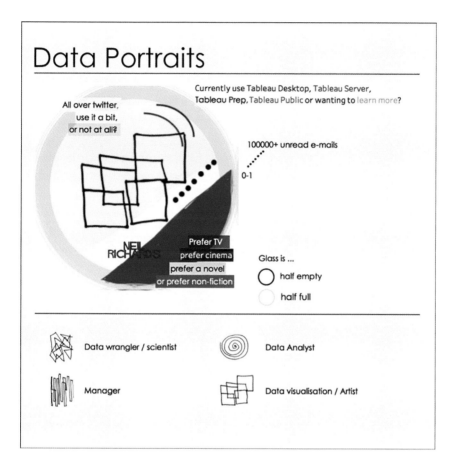

FIGURE 3.4.4 **Data Portraits – How to read.**

And although I'm reporting on just a small gathering where just 25 people were in attendance and completed the survey, it did seem to work as a talking point. When people talked to me afterwards, some would introduce themselves first as their name, but second by describing their badge as their position on the screen. "Hi, I really enjoyed that – I'm XXX, the blue one, second row near the left hand side!".

In terms of the final output, I take no design credit for anything other than being inspired to recreate and introduce to a Tableau audience. It's this first chart, featuring the 25 data portraits, which was featured in Elijah Meeks' third wave talk I referred to in Chapter 3.1 where he asserts that BI tools are developing greater capabilities for displaying data visualisation types more commonly associated with custom visualisations.

Data Portraits – W.E.B Du Bois

I came across another different use of the term Data Portraits almost immediately after I completed my online badges for the User Group and wrote my initial blog post. As I searched for the term, I came across a book of the same name written by Britt Russert and Silas Munro which highlighted the work of W.E.B. Du Bois at the turn of the century. Du Bois composed a series of powerful and unorthodox visualisations shown at the Great Exhibition in Paris in 1900 depicting black Americans in the US, with many focusing on Georgia, in particular.

I was inspired to buy the book and was further inspired as soon as I read through it, both by the story of Du Bois and his exhibition and by the full catalogue of the visualisations from Du Bois and his students. The book itself does a great job of introducing Du Bois and documenting his life and works culminating in the exhibition in Paris – consisting of a series of hand-coloured visualisations created by a team of student designers led by Dr. Du Bois. Commentary can be found on every one of the visualisations.

I would love to feature, analyse and discuss at length each of the visualisations. But I couldn't possibly do justice to the commentary on them that already exists in more detailed articles, blogs and books. So instead, I'd like to focus on just two images, in which it's important to caveat the use of the word "negro" from time to time

– it's not a word that would usually be used today of course but was used in context by Du Bois and his team; hence a word I will only repeat in context of the charts in which it is used.

First, "Assessed value of Household and Kitchen Furniture Owned by Georgia Negroes" (Figure 3.4.5).

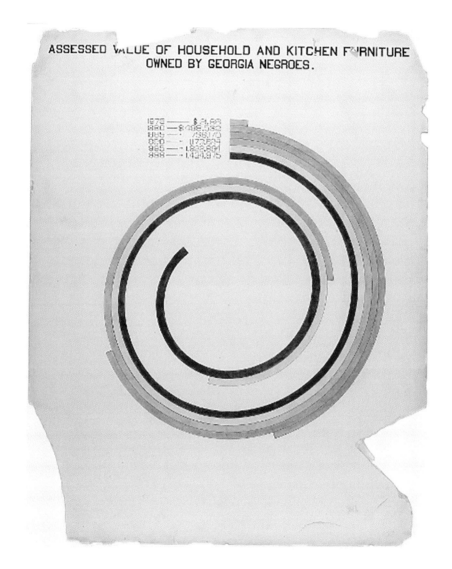

FIGURE 3.4.5 *Assessed value of household and kitchen furniture owned by Georgia Negroes – W.E.B. Du Bois.*

Du Bois will have been aware of bar charts and their uses, but this chart stands out as very obviously flouting those rules. Each bar is steadily longer than the bar for the preceding date but instead of a stepped bar chart, Du Bois emphasises this by spiralling each bar inwards towards the centre of the page. He would have had enough understanding of bar chart theory to know that his conscious decision to display in this alternative way was in contradiction to the orthodox bar charts first devised by William Playfair over a century earlier.

It's my belief that Du Bois considered two things: first, that this chart was for an exhibition. Spirals stand out and are noticed – they intrigue the viewer, and we are likely to engage with something we find intriguing, even if our speed of initial understanding is not so great. Du Bois did have space to display these charts at the Paris Exhibition, but it would not have been the prime, most accessible area of all the displays on show – space will have been more limited than would have been ideal.

His images were assembled in a sort of shutter-like exhibit, not like a modern poster-like exhibit, so may not have received the attention they deserved. But within this constraint, once the audience is engaged, the design of the full collection of his charts screams to the potential audience to notice, view and engage with the charts better than any standard bar chart would do, especially in an exhibition open to the general public.

Second, this chart choice added variety – Du Bois knew the importance of engaging the reader with different chart types, particularly in a large group of diagrams. The analytical shortcomings of spiralling bars are negated by the clearly defined and aligned labels, allowing the visuals to have the striking and engaging effect desired.

Russert and Munro describe the chart as "Simultaneously easy to read and hypnotic". Even I, in my love of the unorthodox, might accept that the chart isn't immediately easy to read, but the description of the chart as hypnotic is perfect. I'm we can all associate with the hypnotic nature of spirals and their ability to draw in our gaze as a reader – and there's no better way to intrigue and engage your audience than with a chart hypnotic in nature!

My second chart to consider from Du Bois is "City and Rural Population 1890". We won't reproduce this chart in full size here since it's already included in the Introduction chapter to this book where I cite the originality of Du Bois as an inspiration for my work, but the chart certainly bears further discussion (Figure 3.4.6).

FIGURE 3.4.6 *City and rural population 1890 – W.E.B Du Bois.*

The most obvious observation is that there is nothing conventional at all about this chart. We see bars heading in all different directions, including a ridiculously oversized spiral. Perhaps Du Bois was at an advantage because the population at the time was less data or graphic literate than they are now. There was less of a conventional mainstream to move away from, so that may have allowed him more creative freedom than he would have faced in today's times.

But in any case, I believe that's exactly the point Du Bois was trying to make: there is no way to show the red bar, representing by far the largest category, as a traditional straight line. Du Bois didn't have the ability to scroll horizontally or vertically, so he needed to be innovative to illustrate the point.

You don't need to know how much bigger the red line is than the yellow, blue or green lines (though the expertise shown in other charts leads you to believe that the proportions are correct). You just need to know the red figure is *much* larger than the other three. The negro population of the time was almost entirely in rural village communities. For exact numbers, you can read them from the chart. But for impression and effect, go experimental and impactful!

Indeed, Russert and Munro describe this chart as "memorable, and experimental" – and for those aware of Du Bois' work, the likelihood is that this work (sometimes described eponymously as a Du Bois spiral) is one of the best known from the collection. Given my penchant for being experimental and encouraging you to question established methods and be experimental yourself, it's important to mention that it doesn't necessarily follow that experimental means memorable, but, if done well, I believe experimentation is one of the best ways for a more memorable visualisation.

Inspired by what I had seen, studied and learned from Du Bois, I wanted to recreate my own Du Bois-inspired visualisation. But how can I represent an oppressed minority or a struggle against supremacy? I'm a privileged white male from the UK and it would be wrong of me to represent myself as anything else. In the end I tried not to over-think it and widened my scope from humans to fellow primates: I went for the representation of a commodity across four geographies that is crucial to the survival of a very much oppressed primate, the orangutan.

My own Du Bois spiral representation is below. I made the decision to scale the top green line to the second highest value and depict the straight amount of the long red line to the same amount, so that the remainder – as in Du Bois' case, the vast majority – of the red line formed the hanging large, red spiral. In showing the vastness of palm oil production being down to just two countries, I want to highlight in an explanatory context that these are the only two countries which house orangutans, with palm oil–related deforestation a devastating factor in habitat loss and population decline (Figure 3.4.7).

I did briefly consider whether to modify this, given the capabilities of the tools at my disposal which Du Bois didn't have. Could I take the metaphor further? Doesn't the large hanging weight look like a durian fruit hanging from a tree, the orangutan's favourite fruit? Or a large, red ape itself holding on to a tree branch for security? But such modifications or alternative considerations of meanings behind my new visualisation would almost have been accidental and taken away from my original plan, which was to be inspired by the Du Bois spiral and recreate the original simple and powerful visualisation as best I could within my BI software tool.

FIGURE 3.4.7   *Annual palm oil production – inspired by W.E.B Du Bois.*

In researching and emulating W.E.B. Du Bois, I had found a new influence, 118 years after his work gained prevalence. Du Bois believed that experimentation and unorthodox methods got results. The intrigue and the interest shown in a visualisation would then lead to insight. He may not have lived in the social media age with the "data viz police", but if he had, I suspect he would have asserted that they are not always correct, or to be listened to!

If you are willing to expand your initial learnings and question your textbook data visualisation influences, there are a wide variety of influences past and present who can shape and expand your own portfolio of creative ideas. W.E.B. Du Bois is never likely to be one of the first pioneers you come across in your data visualisation journey, indeed I learned about him in 2018, after approximately three years of immersing myself into data visualisation learning, personal projects and the online community.

Earlier this year, at the start of 2021, I felt a great feeling of warmth as many other visualisation practitioners relatively early in their careers also learned of him and his work for the first time, through diversity initiatives launched by Tableau and others, and highlighted by Allen Hillary who ran his own Du Bois challenge to encourage people to find out more about his work and recreate their own versions of many of his classic originals, ensuring that many more in our field continue to learn and be inspired by his story and ground-breaking visual representations of data.

Conclusion

Both of my own Data Portrait–inspired examples here are examples where I looked outside of the traditional data visualisation sphere, both in terms of chart type and in terms of tool use. My aims in each case were to be faithful to the original, and to replicate the designs using my chart design tool of choice, fully citing and crediting my obvious inspirations.

Such examples are perfect opportunities to push yourself creatively and technically while learning from some of the most influential and instructional examples within our field. In these cases, as so many others, the principles of the designers will inspire me to diverge further from their original creations to push the boundaries of creativity and unorthodoxy further.

Chapter 3.5

How can I take inspiration from album covers?

There's a strand of the data viz world that argues that every-thing could be a bar chart. That's possibly true but also possibly a world without joy.

Amanda Cox

Album covers as inspiration

In an earlier chapter I introduced the ridgeline plot, which was directly influenced by recreating an iconic album cover from Joy Division. And while I'm always looking for sources of inspiration for design, I soon realised that there was now a whole new, huge, source of such inspiration available to me. Album covers, which themselves cover so many genres of photography, imagery and art, are bound to lend themselves to potential design inspiration.

Now don't get me wrong, the vast majority of these album covers might be of no use at all – a moody looking band photo isn't going to lead to an obvious data visualisation. But with tens of thousands of albums released every year (exact numbers are hard to come by, and, for the sake of this chapter, not important), even the small percent-age of images that are useful might lead to an image that, with a bit

DOI: 10.1201/9781003240211-23

of imagination, could be the next Unknown Pleasures as potential for a data visualisation.

I'm well aware that you can't just pick an album cover and visualise it. Most of us know iconic images from classic albums such as, for example, Abbey Road by the Beatles or Born in the USA by Bruce Springsteen. Although album covers that are photographic in nature, and/or album covers depicting people, might not really be to be suitable, what about stand-out covers which are geometric in nature, usually hand-drawn or computer-drawn? Something that looks like it *could* be a data visualisation if you squinted hard enough or used a bit of "artistic license"?

Screamadelica

Below is the album cover for "Screamadelica" by Primal Scream, released in 1991 (Figure 3.5.1).

FIGURE 3.5.1 Screamadelica – *Primal Scream, designed by Paul Cannell.*

In choosing an album cover as a contender for inspiration, there are two things I'm not really considering. First, is the image a great piece of art? Second, is the music album itself any good? In the first instance I think it's important to use an image you like though. In the same way that if you're doing a personal data visualisation project it's important to enjoy the overall subject and enjoy the data, since you're going to be spending a lot of time with it, I would say it's also important that you appreciate the image. Not only is it potentially one you will be spending a fair amount of time trying to emulate, but it's something you are going to be potentially associated with.

So, for that reason, who's to say if any music is "good"? Of course, it really doesn't matter, but, because of prior preference, musical taste and association, in my case, it's unlikely I'm going to make an album cover derived visualisation from a Justin Bieber album. A cheap shot, with apologies to all you Beliebers, but you get my point.

The Screamadelica album cover is very well known, derived from a design by Paul Cannell of Creation Records. According to Wikipedia, though it looks like a bright sun, it was inspired by a damp water spot Cannell saw on the ceiling of the Creation Records, after taking LSD. And I know this album cover ticks all the boxes: it's geometric, it's visually impactful, it's hand-created, and the overall shape is formed of plenty of geometric elements that could be used in data visualisation such as lines and circles. The meaning, influence or artistic merit of the original – that doesn't matter, because I'm going to regenerate something similar. And I'm going to use data pertaining to an entirely different subject to generate it.

I'd had this album cover in mind for a while. Having always enjoyed including circles and radials within visualisation, this had great potential to recreate as a design-driven data project. Could the twelve radial lines represent twelve months of the year? Maybe this could represent climate change data spiralling out of control again? And two roughly circular internal elements, which might look a little like the sun's "eyes". Perhaps they could tell something else? Maxima/minima? Rainfall figures?

Although I first looked at climate-related data, in order to find data to recreate an album cover there's no obligation to tie in the end image with the data subject. In many ways, it's often more fun to include a certain amount of wit in having no association at all between image and subject.

Take another look at the image, and it could be considered to have eleven arms/spokes rather than twelve since the twelfth is much smaller and streakier. Now, with eleven ordered data points of different sizes, a potential additional two data points in the centre and an overall image featuring what looks like the summer sun, even if, as mentioned above, that was never the artist's intention, my idea was born: I chose to generate the image using cricket data.

Before you roll your eyes at the topic of cricket and move to the next chapter, the topic of cricket is really just incidental to the exercise. Of course, this wouldn't be an obvious leap of faith to most people, but that's not important. Much of the fun and interest in creating visualisations from album covers can come from the unconnected and seemingly random nature of the visualisation's subject.

The key thing was to recognise the potential of the image for dimensions and measures to visualise. We could equally well use measures associated with movies, record sales, country or city demographics, whiskey sales and so on. In any such instance, the process relies on considering the constituent elements of the album cover image as elements of a more conventional data visualisation.

Once I could see it as a radial with eleven spokes, most of the work was done and the possibilities were many and varied. Cricket was just my personal choice – it's a great source of numeric data and it came to mind because there are eleven players in a team. But there are very many great alternatives. And if you didn't know there were eleven people in a cricket team, well that's OK, there are many other alternative ideas for visualising that are more likely to fit with your own level of interest, knowledge or expertise.

Using the principle of design-driven data, I now had my idea. I could use data which fits into the idea of eleven line lengths for batsman scores, eleven line widths for batsman strike rates, one large circle size for team score and two smaller circle thicknesses and areas which could be used to represent bowling figures: wickets and runs against.

In other words, I can visualise a cricket scorecard. And this makes this particular example scalable - I can visually compare any one innings against another, regardless of whether they were from the same match or not.

To be clear, the thing I don't want to do is recreate a piece simply as art. My visualisation, using the first innings of the first Test of the

England versus Australia Test Match (from late 2017, when I created it), is below. As is always required, full reading instructions and tooltip information were also provided (Figure 3.5.2).

FIGURE 3.5.2 *England vs Australia 2017 – based on Screamadelica album cover.*

My thinking behind creating each individual sun was that this is basically a large yellow circle with spokes radiating from it, a dark blue circle overlaid on top and two smaller circles created in a similar way – the white "circles" with black on top. The yellow and blue circles would need to be centrally aligned, and the black/white ones offset.

My circles are created by drawing spokes from a central point before thickening these lines which then "colours in" all of the shapes. It doesn't result in a perfectly smooth set of circles, the thick round edges of each original spoke leading to more of a wavy effect, but that's a bonus because it inadvertently recreates the rough brush stroke nature of the original. As I write, four years later, I can think of more sophisticated ways I might have created this to approximate the original a little closer. But it's not my aim in this book to demonstrate technical brilliance. My aim is to show examples of questioning regular data visualisation to generate interesting creative ideas.

I mentioned above that I wanted to make this process scalable to reflect any cricket innings. Fortunately, this is relatively easy. With no need to rewrite any code or change any part of the visualisation structure, it becomes a matter of pasting in batsman, bowler and team scores only, and updating the descriptive dimensions.

One important thing to add is that I really enjoyed making this! It's an odd project to undertake if it's not something you enjoy, and I wouldn't recommend recreating a design with data visualisation if you're not going to really enjoy every part of the challenge and creative process. Though I challenge the more custom use of BI tools, the trade-off is that to create something more unconventional and custom without such tools will inevitably take longer.

More album cover projects

These kinds of projects are only ever likely to be personal projects for your own benefit, and for the benefit of those of a similar mindset who may eventually read and enjoy your final image. Having the final design firmly in mind as I worked through the data visualisation elements was a little like completing a jigsaw or colouring something in. It was almost like painting by numbers. Maybe it's a combination of these childlike fun creativity stages along with visualisation principles and software tool skills which are new and relevant to me as a grown person, but it's a combination I really enjoyed this time around.

Following my forays into album covers as data visualisation inspiration – a very specific example of design-driven data – I had a lot of fun finding more candidate images to generate visualisations. I've used album covers by Pet Shop Boys, James, Lightning Seeds, Talking Heads, Depeche Mode, Pink Floyd, and more.

And data subjects have included city sustainability records, life expectancies, FIFA World Cup teams, UK University rating scores, football again and Pride marches across the world. But I want to include two more examples in this chapter to further demonstrate the possibilities from album cover inspired visualisations and design-driven data in general.

Lemon Jelly

The first was inspired by the below cover art from Fred Deakin, designer for the album lemonjelly.ky by the band Lemon Jelly. I don't know the album or band, but when I saw this image being referred to by a friend in my Facebook feed one day, I knew I had to bookmark it for a future album cover inspired data visualisation. Once again, the geometric elements and bright colour schemes were perfect (Figure 3.5.3).

FIGURE 3.5.3   *lemonjelly.ky – Fred Deakin.*

The encoding took some thought – the overall shapes are mostly one large circle attached to a smaller circle or just one circle. The majority of circular elements have a number of concentric elements, using a palette of six colours. And what about the positioning of each shape and the direction they point? Could that mean something?

The important thing is not to overthink. There's no way I can find data that exactly encodes or matches the above. It's likely the horizontal and vertical positioning can only ever really be arbitrary, so I chose to place each element where it fitted best to ensure that there weren't too many gaps. In terms of everything else, I wanted each of my data points to be split into two categories, so they could either be encoded by two connected circles or just one, with the latter case coming into effect if they only had data in one of the categories. And I needed a way of using multiple colours in some cases, and just one colour in others. Here's my visualisation below – the interactive version online has a tooltip of explanation of the actor's career nominations for every object (Figure 3.5.4).

By choosing Oscars data, I have a collection where many of my actors have been nominated in both the leading and supporting roles, but some have been nominated just for lead/supporting role only. That solves my issue of some having two circular elements and some having just one. Note that I include actors of both sexes, which have been traditionally known by the Academy as actors/actresses.

For my six ways of using colour to categorise each actor, which by design and definition will sometimes result in one classification, and sometimes result in several, I use the age in decades at which the actor was nominated for each individual award. It turns out that just one actor was nominated in their eighties, so I needed one more additional colour added to my palette that was not in the original colour palette of six colours, that's your fault, Robert Goddard!

In the same way that I was able to think in terms of geometrical shapes and traditional data visualisation elements to simplify the Screamadelica image to a radial image with eleven spokes, I've simplified the Lemon Jelly image to a collection of hand-placed dumbbell charts at 45° from the horizontal. That then defines the core data visualisation, the rest of the image just consists of additional design elements.

FIGURE 3.5.4 *Actors with six or more acting Academy Award nominations.*

The reason for including this example is to emphasise that we are not trying to recreate every individual design quirk of the original, or to encode everything that it's potentially possible to encode. For example, we're not encoding horizontal and vertical position, nor one or two examples of additional blobs within some of the larger shapes. The original image is impossible to recreate with data in its original form without completely making up data, so the image is best achieved by underlying the visualisation with accurately encoded real life data where possible. It's the differences between the original and the final product which what makes it clear that there is real and interesting data behind it.

Stefan Bernacinski

Here's a final album cover inspired example for this chapter (Figure 3.5.5).

FIGURE 3.5.5   *Premier League profiles.*

I won't analyse this in detail in the same way as the examples above. The inspiration for this is a design from Polish designer Stefan Bernacinski from the 1960s. The data in this case came from individual football games in the Premier League in one week of the season. In this case, finding a scale to match the colour palette was possible by looking at score differences over the individual minutes of each game. Once again, we have no more than an approximation to the original, but with 100% of the inspiration.

First | Challenging | Idea

But sometimes it's an unexpected inspiration that gives you the incentive to do something different – in this case, these are essentially just 20 colourful stacked offset Gantt charts. Gantt charts are usually used in project timelines and consist of filled horizontal bars representing start and finish times of different project elements.

That in itself might have made for an interesting visualisation, but the fact that I was using a specific image as the template for my output meant that I rotated those Gantt charts 45 degrees anti-clockwise. There's probably no other thought process that would have inspired me to make that change, but the fact that the constraint of the original inspiration piece has led me to make that rotation for no other reason has really added to the unique nature of the output in data visualisation terms. In doing this, I hope it also adds to its visual individuality, its appeal and its impact.

This exercise is wonderful for allowing you to explore a whole genre of album cover art in areas you would never previously have discovered. Data visualisation design inspiration can be cyclical – through looking for design inspiration in one form, such as album covers, I have learned how much I personally appreciate European geometric design style from the 1960s and 1970s. I could never have created anything approaching the original in any art media or software package. But data has allowed me, and allows anyone, to create artistic output inspired by whatever your personal preference is.

Conclusion

As we asked in Chapter 2.5, we could consider at this point whether these qualify as data art. Personally, I think so, yes, but I don't think that's an important question here, even as a footnote. My justification for thinking so is that the output resembles the original inspirations which I don't think people would argue with the description "art" since they have nothing to do with data. Replace the term "album cover" throughout this chapter with the more accurate "cover art", especially in the age of downloads, and it's a simple justification.

Most importantly to me, data must be the primary medium for creating the output. Anything created with an artistic aesthetic, whatever your interpretation of that might be, using data as the medium, should qualify as data art, in the same way as if the medium were paint, or clay, or anything else. In the end, the definition doesn't matter, but I am more than happy for many of my design-driven data pieces to be called data art by those who wish to do so.

And it's this perception that allows me to appreciate the creative side of data visualisation and of this style of visualisations in particular. If you are interested in creating your own data art, you can do a lot worse than finding your own design influence from an existing source, and taking that as the inspiration for your work. Album cover art is just one such example.

First — Challenging — Idea

Chapter **3.6**

How many ways can you tile the United States?

Human nature is to need a map. If you're brave enough to draw one, people will follow.

Seth Godin

Defining tile maps

This chapter is one of two devoted to tile maps – a visualisation form I've taken a lot of enjoyment from in recent years. I've chosen the United States to focus on since US tile maps will probably be most familiar to the majority of readers, whether or not you hail from the United States yourself.

I use the term tile maps – they are often termed hex maps, but I want to consider the wider options available, with tiles not just restricted to hexagonal tiles. A tile map is a map representation that shows every contingent territory of the map as an identically shaped tile, regardless of its actual shape and size. In the case of the United States, each tile represents a state. Often District of Columbia is shown separately if there is a separate data point for DC, usually as part of the main tile map, but sometimes separately. The best well-known forms are square tiles or hexagonal tiles (Figures 3.6.1 and 3.6.2).

DOI: 10.1201/9781003240211-24

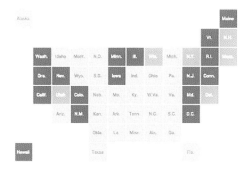

FIGURE 3.6.1 *Square US tile map example - with DC included in main tile map.*

FIGURE 3.6.2 *Hexagonal US tile map example - without DC included in main tile map.*

First of all, since the title question is asking "how many ways?" I should point out that neither of these two examples is set in stone. There may be different positionings of AK and HI, and there may be slightly different arrangements, particularly around the Northeast, or the angle of Florida, or perhaps where the tile map designer decides to place DC having chosen to include it. There isn't a "right" or "wrong" tile arrangement for USA or any other tile map.

What would be wrong would be not to label each tile in some way, either on the tile or using another method such as an interactive tooltip or separate legend. However good your representation, it is, by definition, not geographically accurate and unlikely to be familiar to all of your audience, so will need explanation.

If you are interested in creating tile maps for any territory at all, the possibilities are almost endless. But first, we should look into why we might want to use a tile map. What are the advantages and disadvantages, and in which situations might they work better than others?

There are always questions to ask around your choices so that you're aware of issues your audience might encounter. Now you should know by now that I would never discourage any design choice if you've already questioned the principles behind it, and in terms of tile maps, these are the main criteria I would be aware of that might make you consider them a wise choice or otherwise. I'll use the term *country* for the whole and *regions* for the constituent areas below, but for the constituent areas we could of course be talking about states, counties, territories, prefectures, countries themselves (if the whole map is a continent, for example) or any geographical area.

Equal prominence to unequal regions

Since every tile is (usually) the same size, equal prominence will be given to every region within the country, regardless of size, from the tiniest to the largest.

This is perhaps the easiest to question and to counter. A tile map is a good map to consider in exactly these circumstances, when you have information about every region you want to display, regardless of each region's size or shape. In other words, if all your data values are equally important, regardless of the geographic size of each region, then the tile map becomes an excellent choice. However, if you don't want to give equal prominence to the data from each individual region, then the tile map is not such a good choice.

Skewed or unrecognisable overall shape

Again, if the individual regions vary a lot in size, the overall shape of the tile map as a whole might look very skewed or unrecognisable versus the overall country outline which will be much more familiar to your audience. This can represent both the challenge and the charm of tile maps. As someone who loves to create these manually I can attest that, it's a matter of minimising this effect as best you can whilst acknowledging that it does exist. Every tile map with distorted areas is simply a function of that particular country's demographics and geography.

For example, the US tile maps are known for having a much more exaggerated North-eastern area since the states in that area of the country are generally smaller than those in the Midwest and West. But the standard tile maps allow for that as best as possible, while still keeping within a simplified recognisable USA shape.

Geographical anomalies

There will almost certainly be regions where you have to take fairly extreme geographical liberties. Unlike the above two considerations, regions which will have new neighbours or find themselves in unfamiliar territory significantly to the north (or east/south/west) of where they should normally be on the conventional map.

For example, New York State in the USA reaches from the Great Lakes to the Atlantic coast. It's simply not possible to look at a tile map and expect to see Niagara Falls and New York City both in exactly the right place in relation to the ocean, to Canada or to the neighbouring states. Something has to give!

Of course, there are other considerations, for example, you would always consider your audience and be clear whether there might be issues introducing an unfamiliar map. But a recurring theme I have tried to encourage is to explain and annotate and I work under the assumption you are now prepared for your readers to spend time consuming and understanding your charts.

Mapping further afield

But why limit these maps to the United States? Whichever country you are from, the chances are you have seen more such tile maps for the United States than you have any other country, region or continent. If you're prepared to study maps and convert them into squares and hexagons, then you can see many areas of the world in a whole new light. You might have the programming skills to generate tile maps – however, in my case I have pencils, coloured pens and both square and hexagonal graph paper.

Let's show some examples of my own – starting with one of the first countries I attempted. France is divided into several regions called departments (or départements in French) and overall there is not too much variation in size in each of these regions. It is also a country that fits neatly into a square format, so was a great first non-US tile grid to try.

Below is a detail from an election graphic I created of the France 2017 first-round presidential election voting. Each candidate was represented by a different colour, the overall colour of the highest vote for each department forming the tile's background. As shown by the "real" map alongside it, we can see that the France tile map is quite an accurate depiction. There are much smaller departments in and around Paris (centre North), but our map can allow for that and we would imagine that the familiarity of most French readers would allow for the fact that they would expect a concentration of regions around the densely populated capital (Figures 3.6.3 and 3.6.4).

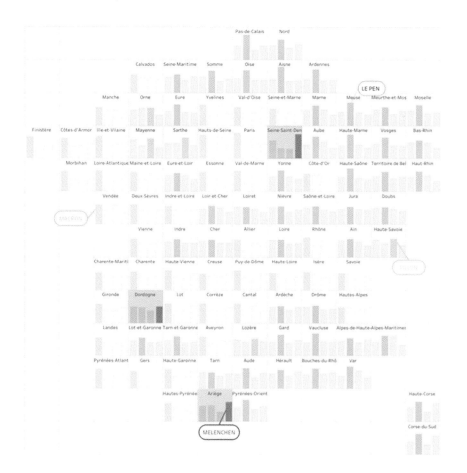

FIGURE 3.6.3   *France election results.*

FIGURE 3.6.4   *France standard geographical map.*

I can't give an instructive suggestion as to when hexagon tiles might work better than squares, or vice versa, except to say that hexagons might work better where there are fewer straight borders or coastlines. This is probably the case in the majority of maps – if in doubt, try both and go with what feels best, but remember that hexagons have two possible orientations, namely each hexagon resting on its "point", or on its side.

An example is a tile map I used in small multiple format for Papua New Guinea. Key geographical information, such as the province name, was included in the tooltips of both the regulation map and the tile maps, allowing for understanding between the familiar and less familiar. And the tile map allowed me to give equal standing to the smaller island regions versus the larger mainland regions. The irregular shape of the country and coastline intuitively suggested that a hexagon tile map would be a better fit (Figure 3.6.5).

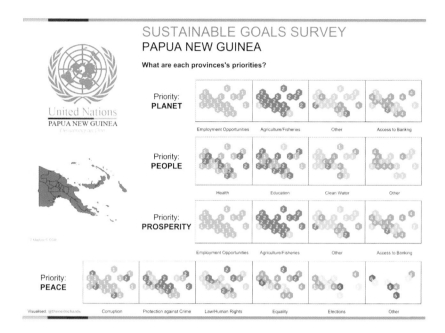

FIGURE 3.6.5   *Sustainable goals survey – Papua New Guinea.*

Triangles as map tiles

As well as hexagons and squares, the third regular polygon suitable for a tile map is an equilateral triangle. Triangles will tessellate if used with two different alignments, alternating between a triangle on its base and a triangle on its point. Below is an example for the continent of Africa, initially introduced in "2.8 When are several visualisations better than one?" This, or other triangular tiled maps like it, would also be an excellent candidate for "2.2 Why do we visualise using triangles?"

There are two reasons why I think a triangle tile map works well in this instance. One is the way that the southern part of Africa tapers to a point, so the lower part of the continent nicely tiles to this point. The second is the way the brown wavy lines from alternating triangle outlines emulate traditional African patterns such as the example below from the Kuba people of Democratic Republic of Congo (sourced from Wikipedia).

This particular design nuance was really appreciated and got a lot of visibility to my Africa tile map while still early in my career, yet I have to admit there was a lot of luck involved. Sometimes, experimentation that results in a new, unconventional visualisation style will result in a really pleasing result that you didn't originally foresee. They say you make your own luck – you won't stumble across a really pleasing design effect within data visualisation itself if you don't make the decision to try the new technique that leads to it in the first place! (Figures 3.6.6 and 3.6.7).

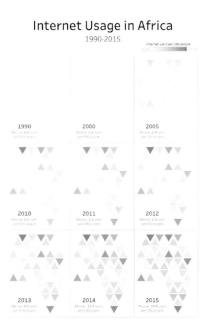

FIGURE 3.6.6   *Internet usage in Africa 1990–2015.*

FIGURE 3.6.7   *Traditional African design pattern – Kuba people of Congo.*

My catalogue of tile maps using squares, hexagons or triangles includes the UK, Scotland, New Zealand, Japan, Germany and more, and I'm always delighted to see other examples, however much of a geographical challenge they might face (Canada, for example!)

Trapezia

From a mathematical point of view, the reason I focus on squares, hexagons and triangles is because these are the three regular shapes whose internal angles divide regularly into 360°, allowing them to meet in packed form. Regular equilateral triangles have 60° angles, squares and rectangles have 90° angles, and hexagons have 120° angles.

However, any irregular shapes that tessellate in the same way can also be used as tile maps. So, if you have shapes with angles that can tessellate in the same way as a triangle, square or hexagon by adding 360° at each intersection, you can have plenty of fun.

For example, you can use trapezia. Below is a snip from a visualisation from Klaus Schulte. Klaus's inspiration for this was from a tetrahedron tile map for Germany created by Heidi Kalbe, also below. Because the tetrahedron's angles are always either 60° or a multiple of 60° (some are 120° and the straight edges are 180°), they will still tessellate perfectly in certain combinations. I don't think it solves a lot of geographical difficulties, for example we can see Scandinavia somewhat jumbled compared to its recognisable shape, but personally, I really like how tetrahedra bring a bit of visual unconventionality to the map, while still keeping every tile to a uniform shape and size (Figures 3.6.8 and 3.6.9).

As an addendum to Klaus' map, you will undoubtedly find that no two Europe tile maps are the same, because Europe contains so many small countries and city states, such as Andorra, San Marino, Vatican City, Liechtenstein and Luxembourg, that it's unlikely that any dataset has every country included. If these aren't included it makes sense to exclude them from your map and not try and tile in the tiniest of states, but when they are included, it can really make your design challenging. We'll come across this issue when we discuss tiling the world.

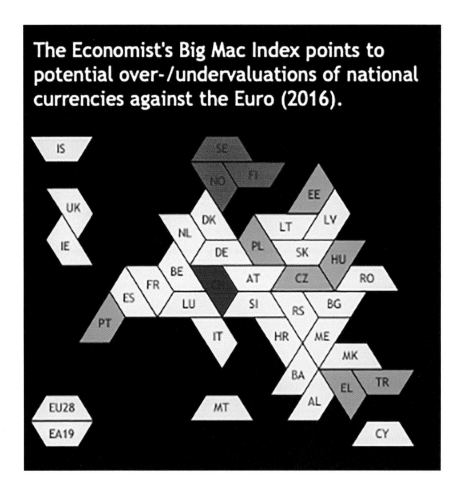

FIGURE 3.6.8   *Big Mac Index – Klaus Schulte.*

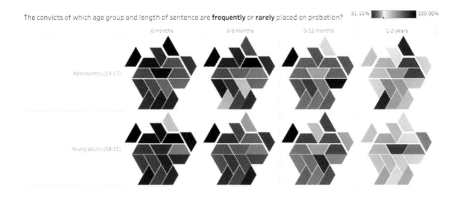

FIGURE 3.6.9   *Crime in Germany – Heidi Kalbe.*

Unconventional tile shapes

We can take the idea of unusual shapes even further, as seen in the below example of tessellating wind turbine shapes. It doesn't add to the analytic value, but it adds to the fun aesthetic, although arguably the shape works quite nicely for FL and TX at the bottom. Really these are stylised triangles, tiling in such a way that they align top and bottom (as we saw in the more regularly aligned Africa triangle tile map above) (Figure 3.6.10).

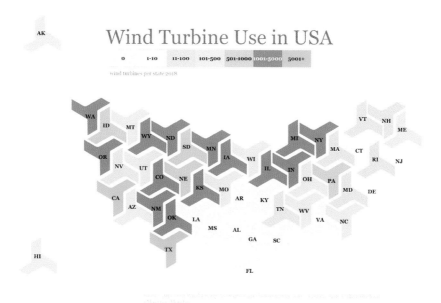

FIGURE 3.6.10   *Wind turbine use in USA.*

The previous examples using trapezia show that you can align and tile more irregular-shaped polygons by rotating them to fit your overall region geography. On one occasion, this got me thinking – since any shape that allows for interlocking pieces, that is to say shapes with external angles that are divisors of 360°, could conceivably be used, we can use combinations of different tile shapes that fit these criteria instead. Because we're not generally trying to pack our tiles into a regular shaped square, rectangle or triangle, since countries themselves are not regularly shaped, this allows for much more irregular tiling within the "interior" of a tile map. The only stipulation, which we haven't yet deviated from, is that tile areas are all the same.

Inspired by this idea, I stayed with the familiar geography of the USA to try something new. As mentioned above, there's no getting around the fact in the USA that you'd have to have Rhode Island, California and Alaska all using tiles of the same size. I started off trying to tesselate using L-shapes. This was all very well for Florida and part of the west coast of the map, but so many of the larger US states are very square, meaning that the shape isn't really that great in this case. But what if I could use different shapes – L-shapes and squares, and maybe other shapes too if I could be sure all tiles were still equal in terms of area?

Thankfully a Russian game company has had similar thoughts on tiling equal-sized shapes before. What if we tiled the US using Tetris shapes? Fun to do, this worked out nicely. L-shapes for Florida and Idaho, T-shape for Texas and lots of 2 × 2 squares for the more regular shaped states like Colorado and Utah. It's impossible to do, whichever tile shapes you use, without bulging the eastern side of the States disproportionately. But you get the same issue with squares or hexagons too (Figure 3.6.11).

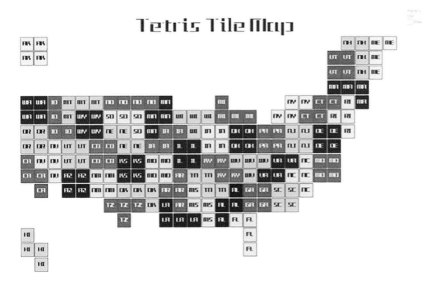

FIGURE 3.6.11   US Tetris-inspired tile map.

I don't know what this proves – it's unlikely you'll ever want to use a Tetris tile map as the basis of a serious visualisation unless perhaps you're visualising computer game sales or the metaphor is otherwise equally relevant. But this example, as well the example of the trapezium tile maps, does show that if you want to tile using non-regular shapes, in other words, shapes that don't have all their sides the same length that enable you to place tiles at different orientations, there are a lot more options that might make tile maps more achievable, or at least more fun.

Tiling USA by county

So far we've discussed the question of different ways of tiling the United States with one tile per state, with or without the District of Columbia. But is it possible to create a tile map for the United States which includes every **county**? The answer is yes, it is possible, I've done it – at least I've done it for the lower 48 states.

Of course, the better questions to consider are "Should you …?", or maybe "What are the pros and cons of such a map type". Or perhaps "How on earth did you do it?" and the related "Why?". Most of these questions we have covered above. US counties can vary significantly in size, but even more so in population. It's important to be aware that each individual hex tile can represent over ten million people, in the example of Los Angeles County, California, to just 169 people at last count in Loving County, Texas.

For my first US county tile map, I didn't worry about population figures – it was purely a celebration of pride and colour, and an exercise in tiling over 3000 counties. This map shows the number of same-sex couples in the US at county level. There are some notable trends in terms of colours – the reds and oranges, representing fewer same-sex couples by percentage, are concentrated around the Midwest areas; with pinks and purples, representing higher percentage same-sex couples, showing closer to the coasts and major urban areas (Figure 3.6.12).

FIGURE 3.6.12   *Same-sex couples in United States.*

But the key element here is the small grey map colouring counties by state – it's this that shows the distortion. In general, easternmost states are more likely to have more counties – states such as Georgia and Illinois are exaggerated in size, with the likes of Nevada and California shrunk to a shadow of their usual selves. My representation does at least keep all of the states just about in the correct positions in relation to their adjacent states while keeping the US in a recognisable shape. The downside of this is some artistic license required in the shape of some states, in particular Texas which is distorted almost unrecognisably.

The whole process of creating a tile map is always one of compromise. Choosing a hexagon tile map allows for six neighbours for every non-coastal county, whereas square tiles allow for four neighbours with four more touching just at the corners. Aesthetically I prefer hexagons, but not only do they allow for six neighbours, they allow for exactly six neighbours, no more, no less. Of course, this won't always be the case.

The most extreme example of this is San Juan County, Utah, with 14 neighbouring counties: three touching at corners and 11 with borders in four separate states. This is as close to unmappable as it gets in tile map terms, a clear indication that tile maps can never be seen as entirely accurate. I'm not sure exactly where in my tile map San Juan County, Utah, ended up, but we can be sure that no more than six of its actual neighbours adjoined it on the map, with at least eight left stranded more than a county away. However, in this case, the State integrity has been maintained as much as possible.

Returning to the issue above around the problem of even representation of American population, our tile map does not achieve this any more than a regular US county map does. A regular US county map gives the following misleading representation of a sea of red votes in the 2020 presidential Election, despite a clear victory, in terms of overall number of voters as well as using the electoral college system, for the Democrats as represented in blue (Figure 3.6.13).

FIGURE 3.6.13 *US presidential election results by county 2020 (vividmaps. com).*

Here's the more recent county tile map I've created, showing the same results from the 2020 US presidential election by county (Figure 3.6.14).

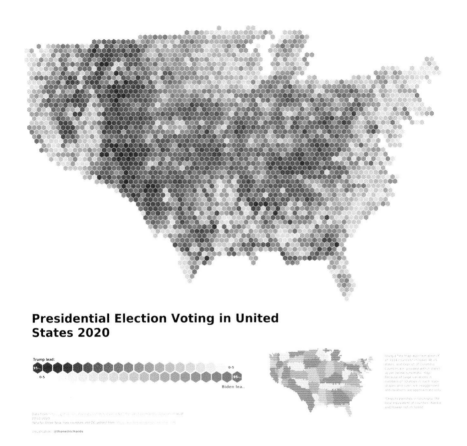

FIGURE 3.6.14   *Presidential election voting in US 2020.*

We know that in a geographically representative map, voting patterns will tend to show a sea of red in the USA, almost regardless of which party is voting higher. Midwestern and rural areas, sparsely populated and traditionally Republican, represented in shades of red, will swamp the map.

Realistically, our tile map doesn't really do much of a better job, given the issue of low population in so many of the red counties. One option we do have, albeit which goes against the idea of tiles packing tightly together with each other, is to size the tile in proportion with the number of voters. Now, the point is made so much better – we can see the huge counties in terms of populations such as Los Angeles and Cook County, Illinois, and how they, along with almost all of the other larger population counties, contribute to the blue vote (Figure 3.6.15).

Presidential Election Voting in United States 2020

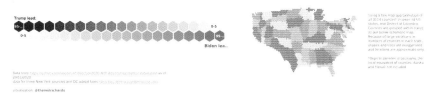

FIGURE 3.6.15 Presidential election voting in US 2020 - counties sized by voter population.

So, I would certainly recommend only using the US level county map, with equally sized hexagons, with caution. It can show geographic trends and could be an interesting talking point, but it's unlikely to tell the true story of US distribution, whether in same-sex relationship tolerance, 2020 voting trends or anything else.

Some words on creating the hex map: this was a monumental task that was frustrating and fun in equal measures. An individual state or collection of one or two of them is not too tricky, but the challenge of knitting them together is very complex, trying to balance the twin tasks of creating individual states that approximate their own individual outlines and the overall US shape.

I soon realised it was very difficult to get everything stitched together if I just considered one state at a time since some states are so much more densely packed with counties than others. Texas was the biggest problem – with so many counties in Texas coming at just the point in the USA where there are more counties per square mile to the East than to the West keeping the true shape and size just wasn't possible (you can see the effect it's having on North Texas and the Oklahoma panhandle!

Conclusion

The best advice is to ignore the limitations, enjoy the fun nature of the challenge and celebrate the results when you're able to create an output tile map. Appreciate the strengths of the tile map format, consider whether the weaknesses are an issue and tell the data story as best you can in a visually impactful way within the constraints of the format. Whatever your decision, the answer to the chapter's question is quite possibly a larger number than you might have thought!

3.7

Is it possible to tile the world?

And look at Russia. It spreads all around and everywhere, and yet ain't no more important in this world than Rhode Island is, and hasn't got half as much in it that's worth saving.

Tom Sawyer Abroad (**Mark Twain**)

Considerations for world tile maps

Moving on from our introduction to tile maps, the logical next step might be to wonder whether it's possible to tile the world. Is it practical, or sensible? We've seen tile maps for countries, regions and continents now, but what about a tile map for the whole world?

Before I go too far into this, this chapter is less a debate on the pros and cons of using tile maps, or world tile maps in particular. We can certainly answer the chapter's question quite easily – since we know and have demonstrated that tile maps can be created to represent all manner of countries, regions and continents, it must surely be possible to extend tile maps to cover the world. I can answer the question without much in the way of spoiler by asserting that the answer is indeed "yes".

DOI: 10.1201/9781003240211-25

This chapter instead assumes that we've already decided to consider displaying our global map-style visualisation as a tile map. We know the pros and cons of tile maps in general, and we might be particularly wary that they are likely to be large factors when it comes to including every nation of the world in a global tile map, such as the issues of geographical recognition and large varieties in area of different countries, but we've made the decision. We're tiling the world!

As you can imagine, including every world nation in a tile map comes with a number of challenges. In this chapter, we suggest three methods you might want to consider.

Traditional tile map

When I came up with my first couple of projects where I wanted to visualise global data in tile map format, I initially didn't consider a traditional tile map. The huge variation in nation size seemed too much of an obstacle to overcome, even for me and my love of creating my own tile maps. However, when Jonathan Schwabish, with the help of his blog readers at policyviz.com, circulated a proposed grid via Twitter for use as a world tile map, I couldn't resist trying it out. Accepting that the grid itself was a prototype, I knew it would be fun to recreate using Tableau and had a dataset to try it out with, looking at public holidays around the world (Figure 3.7.1).

Some of the limitations are clear: first of all, that the overall outline of the land masses and continents has become so unrecognisable, and it's particularly hard to locate individual countries. For that reason, I've intentionally included colour encoding for continent to assist in geographical recognition, as well as using intensity for my chosen metric, which is the number of public/national holidays per country.

We can see that North America has shrivelled into one corner, and Asia is distorted through the great variety of country sizes, most notably Russia, and the island areas such as Oceania and the Caribbean show more like land masses because there are so many small countries that need to be shown together.

The continent colouring is, I think, a nice visual aid. But the feedback I got from this first version was understandable. How can you compare the number of holidays across continents? You can't

Which countries have the most Bank/Public Holidays?

The deeper the colour, the more national public holidays the country has.
Hover over the **?** for more information on how these are defined

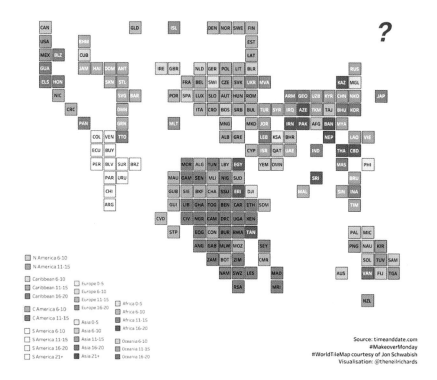

Source: timeanddate.com
#MakeoverMonday
#WorldTileMap courtesy of Jon Schwabish
Visualisation: @theneilrichards

FIGURE 3.7.1 *Which countries have the most bank/public holidays?*

tell if a particular shade of green is equivalent in darkness to red, blue, grey or yellow. The legend is of use but only a limited use, and cross-continental comparison is impossible. Bearing that in mind, I reproduced the chart in one single colour, with the following result (Figure 3.7.2).

I think this is analytically better. It's still hard to tell steps in gradient, but at least is consistent across continents. But I don't think it's as aesthetically pleasing, and it's a harder to find where one continent ends and one begins. Without colour coding, then, for example, the makeup of North/Central America and the Caribbean are not intuitively obvious.

I still think we can do better. Every tile has a maximum of four neighbours in a square tile map, whereas in reality Russia borders 14 countries. Brazil borders 10, France and the Demographic

Which countries have the most Bank/Public Holidays?

The deeper the colour, the more national public holidays the country has.
Hover over the **?** for more information on how these are defined

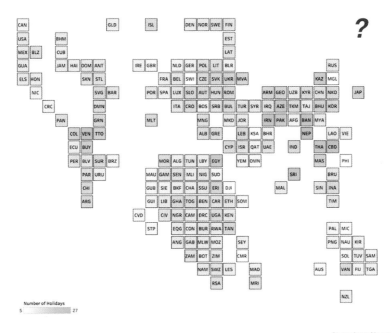

FIGURE 3.7.2   Which countries have the most bank/public holidays? (alternate).

Republic of Congo border nine – this is a problem similar to that of San Juan County mentioned in the last chapter. Using hexagonal tiles instead of square tiles increases the number of borders between tiles so that a surrounded country borders six others instead of four, so instinctively it feels that it might be a better fit.

Here's my version of the map above using hexagonal tiles (Figure 3.7.3).

I think this, perhaps including continental colouring if possible, depending on your intended visualisation, is geographically, if not analytically, about as good as we can get using a traditional tile map. But the sheer country size difference, which is amplified across continents, is a huge hindrance. For example, there are many small nations in Central America, Europe and Oceania, but just three large nations across all of North America.

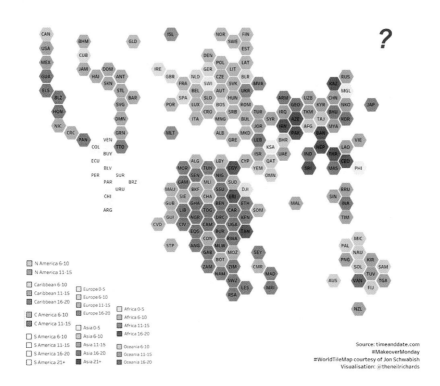

Which countries have the most Bank/Public Holidays?

The deeper the colour, the more national public holidays the country has.

FIGURE 3.7.3   Which countries have the most bank/public holidays? (hexagonal).

In addition, it's likely that datasets are inconsistent as to whether they contain some of the tiny nations. Our map above is missing San Marino, Vatican City, Andorra and Liechtenstein, for example. Because they were excluded, but also so small in area, it makes sense to design our map as if they weren't there. But with no gap for them, if our next dataset used all of those tiny states, where on earth would they go (pun intended)?

Hybrid examples

If you consider the issues of the traditional world map style are too much to overcome, chances are that you might decide that a one tile per country tile map, with all tiles equal shape and size, is just a step too far. What on earth do you do with Russia when it's just a matter of miles from Alaska on the east and borders Norway on its west? A country that's literally millions of times larger than many of the smaller countries on the map? When tiling the world, sometimes the need to normalise every country to a tile of identical size just obscures the geography too far.

With that in mind, I devised a compromise. It's a global tile map system I've used several times now, and the example below shows a version I used to visualise access to global sanitation around the world (Figure 3.7.4). This was referenced earlier in Chapter 1.5 (Figure 3.7.4).

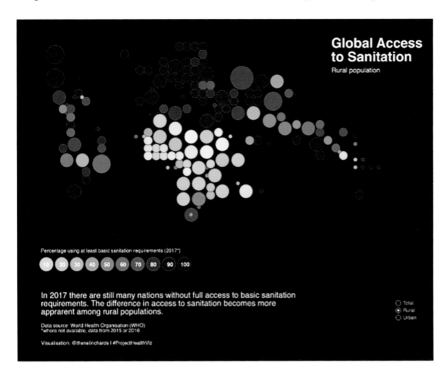

FIGURE 3.7.4 *Global access to sanitation.*

The first thing to mention is that I've chosen circles here – circles can easily replace either squares or hexagons in any tile map without loss of accuracy. They don't tile edge to edge, but they will still have the same properties, whether in terms of proximity, or number of adjacent regions, as the squares or hexagons they are replacing in the template tile map you're using. In this example, I feel like the circles give a more organic feel to the map which seems to work well, though my hybrid tile map was initially designed using squares.

First | Challenging | Idea

This has five different tile sizes: tiny, size 0×0 (e.g. Andorra); small, size 1×1 (e.g. Ireland); large, size 2×2 (e.g. Mexico); very large, size 3×3: (e.g. Australia); and huge, size 5×5 (for Russia only). This has enabled me to create grids of country sizes from 1×1 to 5×5, with the "tiny" countries showing as a dot rather than a circle, and sitting on intersections of grid lines.

Using just these five categories feels like a nice compromise, since if we sized every circle, square or hexagon exactly to match the country area, which is also perfectly possible to do, it would look a lot less uniform and more chaotic. But more to the point we would be back to a stylised version of a more traditional map, where every country has the same prominence as its area. This system sits somewhere between the two, with only a minimal number of tile sizes so as to be able to compare across countries more easily, but enough size differences to aid with familiarity and layout.

The system works nicely for the "tiny" countries like Luxembourg or Burundi, since they can sit on corner points between territories without taking up any assigned grid space, and it allows small island countries not to mass together too. An additional advantage is that countries such as Lesotho which are entirely surrounded by other countries can sit within the larger countries, such as South Africa in the case of Lesotho, instead of next to them.

There are some pleasing additional design benefits to this in comparison with the traditional world tile map in addition to those we've already described – first that the largest nations are now more visible and show as good placeholders (e.g., Brazil, China and Russia help us anchor our place in the world), and second the continents are much more recognisable now. Central America/Caribbean and the Oceania islands are more recognisable as islands instead of appearing as a connected land mass. Crucially, because the world map is more recognisable in shape underneath, we don't need to rely so much on additional encoding for continents.

A further advantage of the setup with "tiny" countries only occupying vertices on the grid is that if a country is not included in the dataset, chances are it's a "tiny" country in size, so it is less likely to affect the overall look of the graphic. You can see in Europe that Andorra and Luxembourg have been squeezed into gaps, but San Marino and Liechtenstein are not included in the dataset. But had they been included, there is room for them to pack in the corners between the regular-sized circles.

Does it do the job? I have three encodings for each country.

Position: Here I think each country is much easier to find than on a standard tile map. Countries are closer to geographical positioning on a true map, though not perfect. It does particularly well for Africa and South America, which are often the most important continents when visualising data where more significant or outlying results are found in developing countries.

Colour: Colour is used as my main encoding for the quantity visualised, in this case access to sanitation. I've chosen the Viridis scale for two reasons – first because the extremes of the scale (from green to yellow) are most pronounced, highlighting the issue I want to focus on. And second because the low values stand out clearly, but the high values, against a dark background, do not. That's just what I want. Of course, analytically we can't compare colours quantitatively, but I hope it does a good job comparing nation to nation and highlighting areas of concern. I've been sure to include a legend with scale and make sure to include country names and exact metric values on a hover tooltip for each country.

Size: As mentioned above – size is just a proxy for the size of the country and therefore doesn't represent the value we're trying to highlight. Is this a downside to the visualisation, particularly because the form is unfamiliar? I think what you gain in country/map recognition more than makes up for any confusion, but I accept that it's an interesting trade-off that not all will agree with. It's particularly important when the map is being shown as a kind of "minimalist" representation.

The visualisation set off an interesting discussion with Steve Wexler. Steve is a Tableau Zen Master Hall of Famer and co-author of *Big Book of Dashboards*. He's certainly a person I look up to in the industry and I value his opinion greatly – it's important to me to consider these points of discussion:

> *I think you have something that is less misleading than a choropleth but still suffers from some of the problems. VERY easy for me to critique, but I've not offered an improvement. Circles of the same size with the map showing underneath will kill some of the soul.*
>
> Steve Wexler (@DataRevelations) March 3, 2020

First — Challenging — Idea

In a stubborn way, I take this as a compliment. There is no under-lying geographic map underneath it, but the suggestion that there is an underlying map means that my design has worked well in terms of initial shape recognition! And I'm glad there's an acknowledge-ment that I have to make certain design decisions in order to incor-porate soul – ultimately that's what the above paragraphs try and consider. It's a thought that permeates through most of the later chapters of this book too.

Mitigating the downsides of two approaches can result in a compromise which is unlikely to entirely solve either approach's issues. The decision then becomes down to the designer, who must consider his/her audience and design wishes, as to whether a compromise is even an option for the particular scenario. I'll continue to use my hybrid world map as a tool for representing metrics by country, but always in circumstances where I think its advantages make it a good candidate for the particular visualisa-tion, since it may not be the best option in every case.

Dorling Cartogram unit chart

Here's my third global tile map example. It's arbitrary whether you would call it a global tile map, but I include it here because it's a map of the world and it's got tiles in, so there's no need to over-think the categorisation! It's never essential to be con-strained by exact chart definitions and taxonomies because you may then miss out on exactly the visualisation you're trying to create, whether that's because your inspiration is something that doesn't confirm to a pre-set chart type in the first place, or whether that's because your idea is not quite the same as more conventional existing types.

A Dorling Cartogram is a type of cartogram or tile map, usually consisting of circles or squares, where the tile for each district is pro-portional to the metric you wish to visualise. I've taken this a step further, so that instead of one proportionally sized tile, I've chosen to use several tiles per country, as might be done in a unit chart, hence my decision to name this a Dorling Cartogram Unit Chart (Figure 3.7.5).

FIGURE 3.7.5 *How global is the Olympic Games?*

Here, it works so well because the exaggerated sizes of some nations, whether large or small, are down to a quantifiable metric, in this case Olympic medals won. By happy coincidence, in this case, it solves the problem of Russia. It was never going to be possible for Russia to adjoin Norway, Eastern Europe, Central Asia, China and Korea, but the specifics of Olympic representation in 2020, with Russia competing as the independent "Russian Olympic Committee", gave me a valid editorial reason for leaving Russia floating seemingly as a distinct, distant island.

Conclusion

My favourite unsolicited feedback to the above Olympics chart was "I love this chart – it's so *you*!". If you've experimented with enough unconventional methods which question traditional designs and principles to generate a portfolio of visualisations that are recognisable as your own style, and that are appreciated by at least some of your audience, then that's a great feeling of validation and incentive to keep doing what you do!

If that feeling extends into world tile maps, then the obvious caveats can be considered alongside the appropriate choice of any of the methods above. The practice of world tile maps is uncommon, for good reason, but sufficiently so to allow for more work and more experimentation on a method or format that improves on the examples publicly available. As with every example discussed in this book, they represent an enjoyable distraction and excellent learning opportunity.

3.8

Can you create visualisations using only numbers?

Do you know why they call me the Count? Because I love to count! Ah-hah-hah!

Count von Count, *Sesame Street*

A love of numbers and patterns

My love of data visualisation may be fairly recent, but it evolved from a love of data and all things analytical. And the love of data stems from an early love of numbers. At the basic level, growing up as children, I suspect all of us would be able to categorise ourselves as loving words, numbers, both or neither; and it's the pedantic analyst in me that makes sure every possible combination is covered with one categorisation. With me, it was numbers.

One of the reasons I loved numbers was because I loved seeing patterns in numbers – it was these patterns that made numbers make sense. And so many mathematical formulas, numbers and concepts can be "explained", or at least shown visually using these patterns, that I have chosen to create data visualisations, or, if you choose to describe them as such, data art, based on numbers and their patterns.

DOI: 10.1201/9781003240211-26   **277**

I could state the obvious here and say that the possibilities are literally infinite. It's something we might glibly say in normal conversation in circumstances where we want to encourage people to expand their imagination, but if ever there were a definition of an infinite dataset, it's the set of numbers, whether they are whole numbers, real numbers (such as fractions) or irrational numbers.

Don't worry about the exact definitions of these types of numbers if you can't remember these from back in your school or college days. Rather, just think of the possibilities of visualising patterns in numbers. Thinking beyond the conventional idea of our numbers representing a measure, or a quantity, here we can take a step back and visualise them purely as numbers, nothing more. This chapter can look at a small selection of examples to inspire you or give you further ideas for visualising numbers.

Whole number sequences (integers)

Let's start by looking at number sequences, typically integers. These might well be infinite, in which case you'd just need to decide how many numbers you want to visualise. Some such sequences might already be well known in public usage – for example, the Fibonacci sequence, which starts 0, 1, 1, 2, 3, 5, 8, 13, 21, 34, 55, … with each number being calculated as the sum of the previous two. We can visualise the Fibonacci sequence just by considering it as a dataset with as many rows as we want and just one column.

If we visualise each number in our data as a square with a quarter-circle connecting opposite vertices, we can generate something like this – which is known as a Fibonacci spiral, demonstrating how any two numbers add to the next number while generating a renowned geometrical shape in the process. Already we have an annotated data visualisation, which we can further use to illustrate or explain the golden ratio if we wanted to take it further (Figure 3.8.1).

But what if we just want to look at every whole number, or at least every number 1–100? If we choose to visualise properties of each of these numbers, we have a ready-made potential 10 × 10 small multiple grid arrangement. You should already know that I get aesthetic pleasure from such grid arrangements in my visualisations!

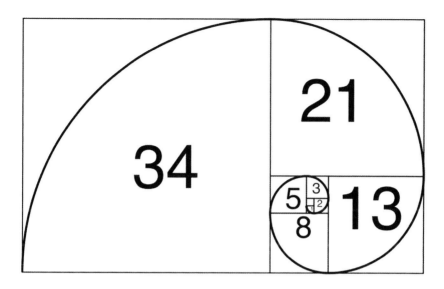

FIGURE 3.8.1   *Fibonacci spiral.*

Let's consider prime factors (excluding 1 and the number itself) –
now we have a potential dataset consisting of 100 rows (1–100) and
a column for each prime factor. Our first rows in the data will be:

1: (1)
2: 2
3: 3
4: 2, 2
5: 5
6: 2, 3
7: 7
8: 2, 2, 2
9: 3, 3
10: 2, 5

Using pure numbers as datasets will give you patterns to show and
stories to tell, however you choose to visualise them. My own ideas
were very often based on recreating awesome ideas generated in
other media. The following comes from an original from Sondra
Eklund, who has produced this design not only in poster format but
even knitted, and on T-shirts! (Figure 3.8.2).

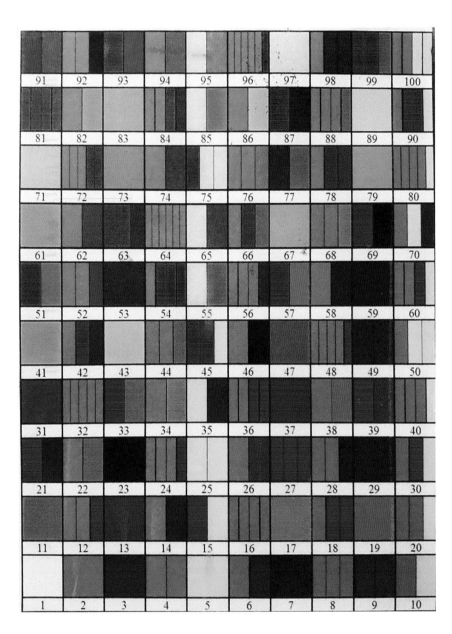

FIGURE 3.8.2 *Prime factors – Sondra Eklund.*

I chose first to recreate faithfully in Tableau, then to make a simple change to add my own slant and show the data in a different geometrical way, using circles. You might of course choose something completely different (Figures 3.8.3 and 3.8.4).

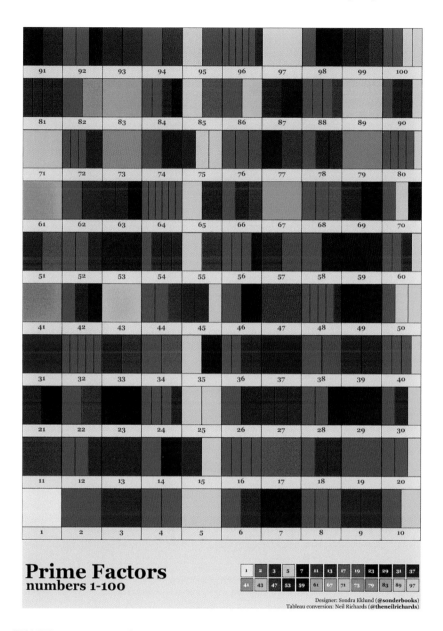

FIGURE 3.8.3 **Prime factors – blocks.**

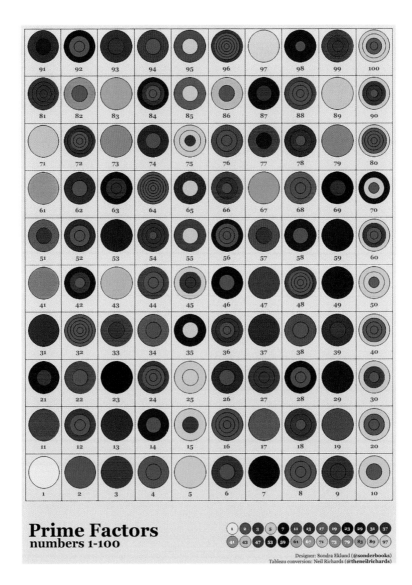

FIGURE 3.8.4 *Prime factors – circles.*

Rational numbers (fractions)

In layman's terms, rational numbers include not just integers (whole numbers) but any number that can be expressed as a fraction, for example 1/4 or 0.9275323.

If I cast my mind back to being a precocious numbers-obsessed child, I remember being fascinated by the number 142857 and what happens when you multiply it. It always cycles through the same numbers in the same order, until you multiply it by 7 when it just turns into nines. This always seemed amazing to me.

$$142857 \times 1 = 142857$$
$$142857 \times 2 = 285714$$
$$142857 \times 3 = 428571$$
$$142857 \times 4 = 571428$$
$$142857 \times 5 = 714285$$
$$142857 \times 6 = 857142$$
$$142857 \times 7 = 999999$$

And then, not long after, I learned that 1/7 (one-seventh) was 0.142857 *recurring* when described as a decimal, there was that same sequence of numbers again! And so it was that a few decades later, while searching for data visualisation ideas and having hit on the idea of visualising something number related, I wondered whether there might be some interesting opportunities for visualising fractions that can be expressed as recurring decimals. If fascinating things, in my eyes, anyway, happen with sevenths, what happens with other fractions?

Once again, to cater for my preference for small multiples and grids, I set about looking at the first 100 digits of the first 100 fractions (1/1, 1/2 through to 1/100). The result follows in Figure 3.8.5 – true to my preference, I wanted to design an eye-catching "poster style" visualisation and I was pleased with this result. So pleased, in fact, that this visualisation is now adorning posters in a home office in the United Kingdom and a mathematics classroom in Oregon (as you may have seen already in *2.1. Why do we visualise data?*).

In fact, this was just a precursor to looking at a more sophisticated data visualisation, or at least a more complex one, anyway. Because patterns were bursting out of the visualisation above – look at the diagonal stripes in 81, or the rotating colours in 7, 14, and the multiples of 7, for example, I was already wondering if I could show these fractions in a different way.

Over the course of working on the visualisation I'd learned, or at least I'd confirmed what I knew, that all fractions that don't abruptly end will recur, meaning they repeat their decimal sequence of numbers again ad infinitum, after a certain number of digits. What I didn't know, but researched during the course of creating the visualisation, was that this property of every recurring fraction is called the *repetend*. For example, for 1/3 the repetend is 1, because just one digit

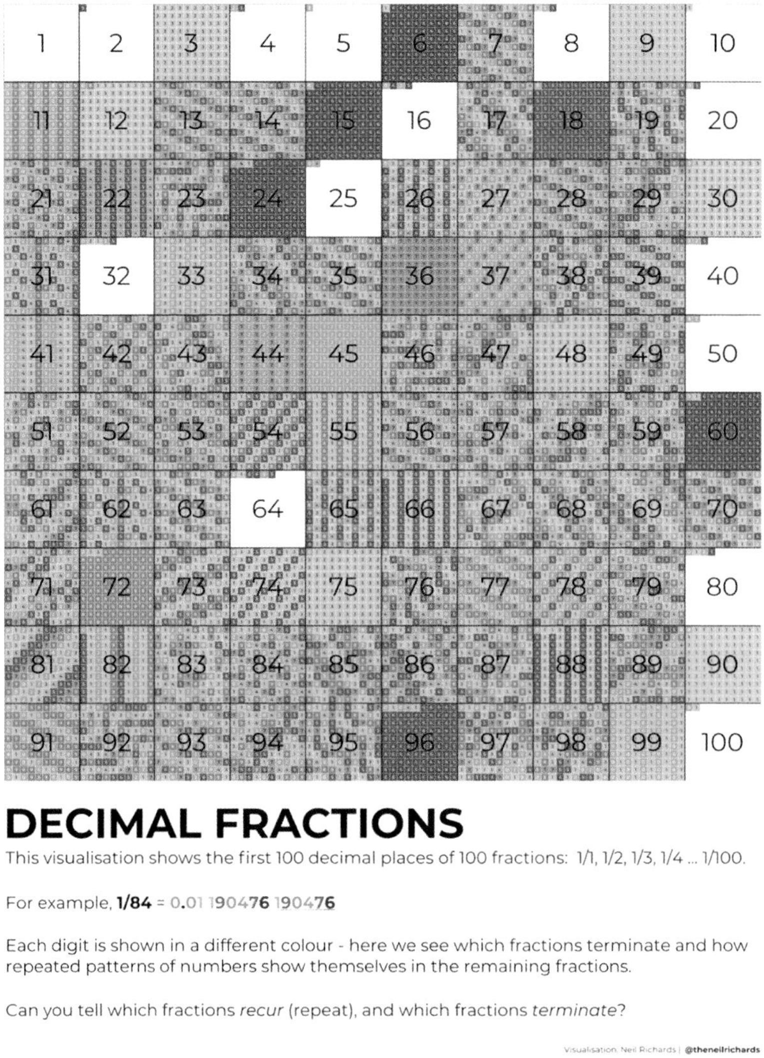

DECIMAL FRACTIONS

This visualisation shows the first 100 decimal places of 100 fractions: 1/1, 1/2, 1/3, 1/4 ... 1/100.

For example, **1/84** = 0.01 190476 190476

Each digit is shown in a different colour - here we see which fractions terminate and how repeated patterns of numbers show themselves in the remaining fractions.

Can you tell which fractions *recur* (repeat), and which fractions *terminate*?

Visualisation: Neil Richards | @theneilrichards

FIGURE 3.8.5 **Decimal fractions.**

recurs, the number three. For 1/7 or 1/14, the repetend is 6 because a sequence of six digits recurs before constantly repeating itself.

My resulting visualisation was a series of decimal "walks" for every fraction 1/1, 1/2, ... 1/100. With much experimentation, I figured out that if you "walked" the distance of each digit and then made a clockwise turn just the right amount so that you made exactly (*repetend* + 1) turns before you were facing the same direction, you would create a beautiful symmetrical flower-like shape and always return to your start. Also credited as a collaborator in this visualisation is Michelle Gaudette, who assisted me in some of the more technical elements and shared design advice, while I was indulging in much of the creative idea process and iteration of versions (Figure 3.8.6).

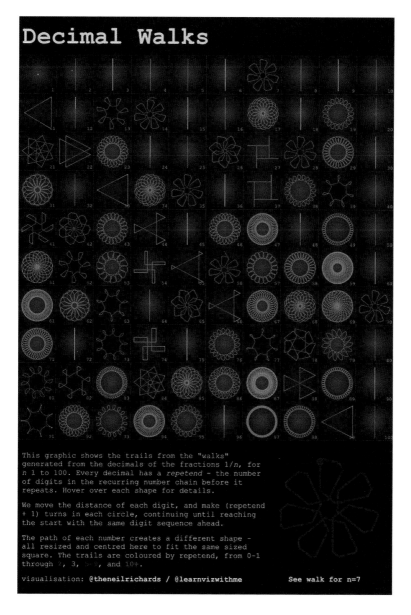

FIGURE 3.8.6   *Decimal walks.*

I won't explain all of the mathematics behind this, because I'm not sure that I can! But I can explain the data visualisation process behind it, which is no different from the creative process behind many more conventional data visualisations. In this case, my dataset was simply 100 rows again, with columns consisting solely of the repetend value and repeating digits for every associated fraction.

- Find a dataset that you find interesting
- Play and iterate with the data to see if any interesting developments occur
- Find what you consider the most interesting or engaging visual story or pattern, even if that relies on a stroke of luck
- Add any necessary design polish, include explanations where necessary, share, publish and present

Irrational numbers

My layman's definition for an irrational number would be any real number not already defined in the two categories above (integers or rational numbers). In other words, numbers that are not definable as fractions. And since any number with a decimal that terminates can be described as a fraction, we are basically looking at numbers whose decimals go on ad infinitum.

The most well-known of these is almost certainly π (or *pi*). Defined as the ratio of circumference to diameter of any circle, it is always the exact number 3.14159265 ... and so on. In its simplest form, this then becomes the perfect one-column dataset, with the number of rows being the number of digits we care to process, we're simply visualising digits and can do so in any way that takes our fancy, and there is literally no limit on the number of digits we want to include. There are many visualisations of π which lead to spectacular art-style visualisations – typically each digit 0–9 will be represented by a different colour and bright, colourful visualisations will ensue.

One data visualiser who regularly visualises π (on the North American version of Pi Day, which is March 14th, or 3/14,) is Martin Krzywinksi, a data visualization expert based at the Genome Sciences Centre in British Columbia, Canada. Figure 3.8.7 shows a visualisation of his from 2014, showing frequency distribution of digits for the first 768 digits of π in groupings of 3, and for each grouping of three the number of times a digit was seen is proportional to the width of the ring.

However frivolous purely visualising a number might seem, especially an irrational (or *transcendental*) number such as π, there is always the opportunity to tell stories and learn – it wasn't until researching and selecting this image for the chapter that I first learned of the Feynman point.

The Feynman point is a point relatively early in the infinite number of decimals in π where there are six nines in a row starting at the 762nd decimal place – a famous mathematical coincidence that might suggest, if you could memorise and recite the numbers, that you could end with "nine nine nine nine nine nine and so on", which would seem to suggest, incorrectly, that π is rational.

This shows us the final two purple blobs in the bottom right of the image below. The design choice to end at the Feynman point was undoubtedly deliberate, with the number of digits chosen and their arrangement designed to highlight this. It certainly had that effect on me when I encountered it for the first time.

Another advantage of visualising π, or any other irrational number you choose to visualise, is that its digits are essentially an infinite source of random numbers, with all numbers 0–9 equally likely to occur. So if you have any kind of random-looking data art you are interested in creating, then it's a great place to start. You can take it further, too – if you want to reduce your colour palette you can choose to visualise π in a different base instead of base 10. That idea might sound somewhat daunting, but you can easily find websites online that will calculate it, at least for a manageable number of digits.

Two examples of this follow – first of all an online replication of a physical artwork in the University of Cambridge by James Holleyhead where the numbers of π in base seven are represented in a hexagonal grid by seven distinct colours (Figure 3.8.8).

And it was the combination of the above: representing π in a different, non-decimal base and the concept of using the digits of π for a random-seeming source of numbers that gave me the idea to replicate another classic design. A very simple in nature design-driven data piece follows below that uses π as its source data and emulates the original Bridget Riley artwork *Cool Edge* in form and palette (Figure 3.8.9).

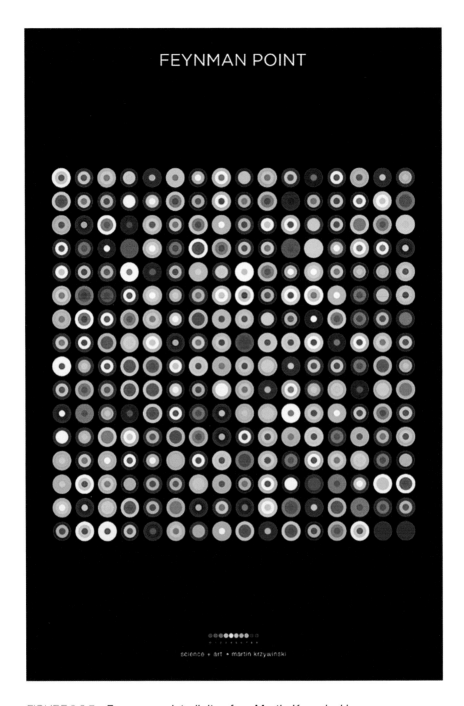

FIGURE 3.8.7 *Feynman point: digits of π – Martin Krzywinski.*

Visualising π in Base 7

Π =

3.0663651432036134110263402244652226643520650240155443215426431025
...5161154565220002622436103301443233631011304100550041024125 3521

This visualisation recreates an artwork by **James Holleyhead** from 2003 on display at the School of Mathematical Sciences in the University of Cambridge. The original painting was to represent the value of π in mod 7 to 127 digits. The central hexagon represents the initial 3 and subsequent digits spiral colockwise.

127 is the seventh *centred hexagonal number* and the seventh *Mersenne number* ((2^7) -1). The artwork uses the seven colours comprising of the six primary and secondary colours plus black for zero.

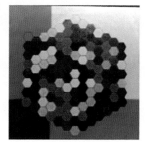

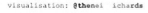

visualisation: @thenei ichards

FIGURE 3.8.8   *Visualising π in base 7.*

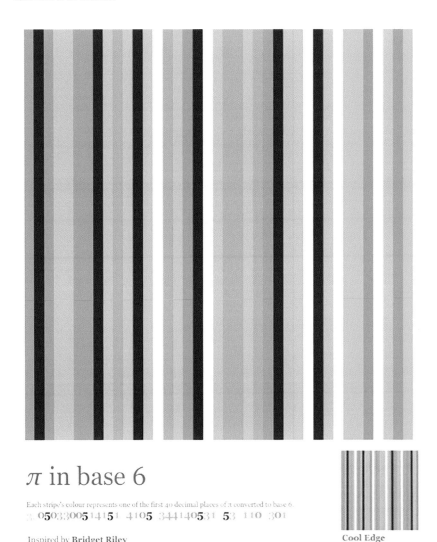

π in base 6

Each stripe's colour represents one of the first 40 decimal places of π converted to base 6.
3. 050330051415140534414053315311030

Inspired by **Bridget Riley**
visualisation: **@theneilrichards**

Cool Edge
Bridget Riley, 1982

FIGURE 3.8.9 *π in base 6.*

Conclusion

Just purely considering numbers and digits for data sources can be a rich source of inspiration for data visualisation – either to search for the patterns within them to visualise in an engaging, often impactful and artistic way, or as an ideal simple data source to generate a series of digits to align with colours or metrics in a pre-planned visualisation. Either way, numbers, whether simple or not so simple, might provide exactly what you're looking for in your next project.

How do you visualise music?

I try to apply colours like words that shape poems, like notes that shape music.

Joan Miro

Musical notation

Visualising music is a topic that feels like it could occupy an entire book, or volume, rather than just a chapter. But if you've never considered music as a data source, or how music might be visualised, this chapter should give you an introduction to the concept and leave you with a number of influences and ideas to adopt, adapt and improve.

As an aside, my first successful attempt at a project to visualise music began, as so many ideas do, by thinking about something entirely different and then thinking tangentially. I was considering an entry to the Tableau Iron Viz feeder competition, a data visualisation competition where each feeder contest – the qualifying contest to determine finalists – is always based around a pre-determined theme. The theme in this instance was "water", meaning that my brief was to build a visualisation that focuses on the theme of water.

DOI: 10.1201/9781003240211-27

I knew that a more traditional and predictable infographic and fact-based visualisation about water wouldn't really play to my strengths, and the temporary creative block I had as a result meant that for a while I didn't consider entering this particular feeder competition. But as I thought more tangentially about my options and what I could do that aligned better to my own strengths and design preferences, this gave me the opportunity to take the word "water" and allow me to indulge myself in a completely different, and still yet loosely water-themed, way. I decided to visualise Handel's *Water Music.*

Spoiler alert – I didn't win the qualifying contest or qualify for the final. I wasn't going to hit the brief of storytelling, design and analysis that could be better achieved by more traditional visualisation, but that was never my aim. After all, it's hard to argue "analysis" when looking at musical notes. I'd stumbled across a new angle on visualisation, and I loved it!

In terms of visualising music, I've since been privileged enough to give presentations around the subject, and I usually then make the distinction between visualising the actual music, for example, the notes: their pitch, volume, tempo, duration, octave, positioning, sequencing and the instruments that played them, and visualising "everything else", which could be any metadata around the music that's not specific to individual notes: the performers, chart position, name, "danceability", valence, words, album title and so on. The combination of measurable metrics around notes and metadata around pieces of music is what leads to such a rich topic for visualisation.

In this chapter, I'm going to be focusing just on the first of the two options: how do we visualise music?

Visualising music is nothing new. In much the same way that we use a small finite number of symbols to visualise language and communication, for example in English, we would use an alphabet of 26 letters, a group of ten digits and a finite collection of punctuation marks, we use a small finite number of symbols to visualise music.

To understand written communication, we order and space the symbols in a manner that they will be understood, due to the way we have learned and been taught to understand them. To understand music, the same principles apply. We might use a subset of the following symbols, arranged and spaced in a way that those who have been taught to read music will understand, and those who have learned to play an instrument can recreate the intended musical output the composer originally intended.

After all, a musical score is just another example of an alphabet: a complex visual encoding message to visualise and record the sounds, tones and patterns of individual languages. If a concept such as language, or music, is so detailed, varied, complex and beautiful to the extent of being almost infinite in its possibilities, then why shouldn't our methods of visually encoding be simple but not so simple that they are instantly understandable without skill or practice?

In fact, I'd argue that music *is* infinite – there are an infinite number of places you can put your finger on a violin string between the positions of C and D, for example, and you can play that note for an infinite amount of time – so that's infinity squared already! (Figure 3.9.1).

FIGURE 3.9.1   *Symbols used in standard musical notation.*

Music as data

Essentially, visualising music is a very "data visualisation" thing to do. Traditionally, we are arranging data points on a series of timelines, positioning them according to pitch, placing them according to other dimensions such as musical instrument and choosing the mark type to encode the data according to the duration of a note. Taking this analogy further, then all of the creative, non-standard questioning we can apply to regular data visualisation, we can apply to music visualisation.

Some questions off the top of our head might be: can I introduce/encode colour? What would be the best or most innovative timeline I can use – horizontal, vertical, radial or something else? And if vertical, then travelling upwards or downwards? Is there a story I can or should tell? How much annotation do I need, if any? These are all questions we've asked about data visualisation in this book already, and all would apply to visualising music.

And as for the concept I mentioned above: that our methods of visually encoding might be simple but not so simple that they are instantly understandable without skill or practice – in other words that it may take time to interpret, digest and appreciate visual encoding of music – well, if you'll excuse the terrible pun, that's music to my ears.

It encapsulates the ethos that I've mentioned a few times now in this book, that if you are questioning conventional methods and practices in data visualisation and going against such methods and practices as a result, it's not your aim to give instant gratification at the expense of impact and creativity, and have a simple chart understood in a matter of seconds.

A final consideration with visualising music that's both an inspiration and a caveat – there is probably no better visualisation better suited to animation than visualising music. After all, if your visualisation moves, changes or animates along with the music, it's a perfect way to tell the story of the music you are visualising, or to engage your reader, who in this case might also be your listener, with the visualisation so that the experience is enhanced and every element of the visualisation is obviously linked, highlighted and connected to the relevant note. The downside is the fact that it's impossible to consider that in a book, unfortunately.

Handel's *Water Music*

Back to Handel's *Water Music*. Having decided that I wanted to visualise the score, I soon decided I wanted to show the music radially. This can be quite an obvious design decision to make when visualising music, but that doesn't make it a bad or wrong decision in my opinion.

Two reasons stand out for this choice – first, musical scores can be lengthy, and visualising around the diameter of a circle is one of the most efficient and compact ways of showing data on a timeline. After all, if we have 1000 units of width on our screen, and we assume that each second of music will occupy 10 units, then we can show 100 seconds worth of music. But if we assume we have 1000 units of height available too, and we can curve this timeline into a circle, then we can increase our maximum amount of visible score to $(1000 \times \pi) = 3142$ units, or 314 seconds.

And second, and perhaps more obviously, records and CDs are circular. We don't think twice about that association, music is traditionally played by rotating discs, whether vinyl, CD or even via traditional music box, so it's aesthetically pleasing to us to see visualisations shown in that way.

Off the Staff

My first influence was Chicago-based information designer Nicholas Rougeux and his project "Off the Staff" where he radially visualises a number of well-loved classical tunes. Figure 3.9.2 is his visualisation of Pachelbel's *Canon* – a piece for four-stringed instruments, each instrument shown in a different colour. The piece runs clockwise from the top – the pleasing thing about visualising the Pachelbel piece in particular is the metronomic regularity of the dark blue cello part – its low pitch means it doesn't overlap with the three melody colours of the violin parts, and it results in a perfectly regular symmetrical pattern throughout.

Rougeux's website, at *https://c82.net*, draws the animation in time to the music, in much the same way that I wanted to do, and also gives one excellent method of converting midi data files to data of a format that most data visualisation software packages or libraries will understand.

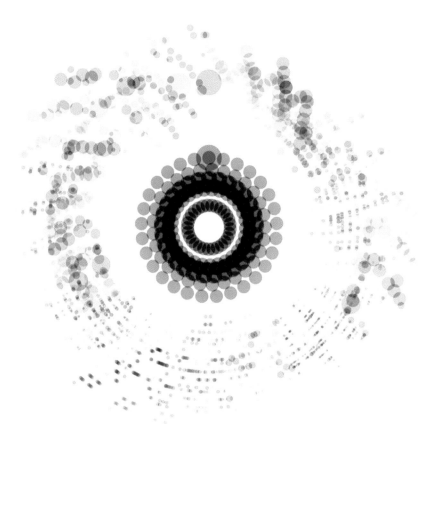

Canon in D
Johann Pachelbel

FIGURE 3.9.2 **Off the Staff – Canon in D/***Johann Pachelbel – Nicholas Rougeux.*

Radial score

My own version of *Water Music* had an alternative approach, where the circular score shows in its entirety throughout, with each group of notes moving into highlight focus at the top of the visualisation when played. In other words, my disc was rotating in real time with the music instead of being drawn in real time with the music. A little like the metaphor of traditional rotating musical boxes, where a set of pins are placed on a revolving disc or cylinder, with the raised musical notes plucking the teeth of a fixed steel comb to play the notes at the correct time.

However, my static image is somewhat simpler – the main difference in comparison with Rougeux's *Off the Staff* visualisation being that length of note is encoded by length of arc rather than size of circle (Figure 3.9.3).

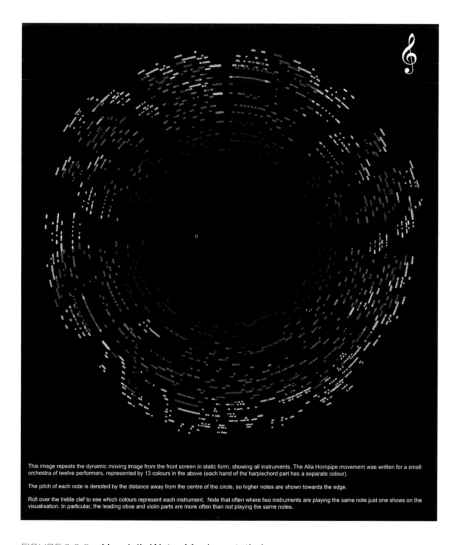

This image repeats the dynamic moving image from the front screen in static form, showing all instruments. The Alla Hornpipe movement was written for a small orchestra of twelve performers, represented by 13 colours in the above (each hand of the harpsichord part has a separate colour).

The pitch of each note is denoted by the distance away from the centre of the circle, so higher notes are shown towards the edge.

Roll over the treble clef to see which colours represent each instrument. Note that often where two instruments are playing the same note just one shows on the visualisation. In particular, the leading oboe and violin parts are more often than not playing the same notes.

FIGURE 3.9.3 *Handel's* Water Music – *static image.*

I wondered what insights and patterns Handel's *Water Music* might show. After all, I wasn't very familiar with the piece and hadn't picked it with a musical reasoning in mind. I picked it for no other reason than wordplay based on a word in its title.

Fortunately, I knew I was choosing a Baroque classic. I did know that Baroque music was more systematic and melodic than its classical and romantic descendants. Masters of Baroque music loved to demonstrate and repeat a theme, often with variations – in other words, there is more mathematics in Baroque music, and more regularity of patterns to be discerned. Pachelbel certainly falls into that category, but so does Handel.

Handel was born in the same year (1685) as Johann Sebastian Bach, and so was an exact contemporary of his. And the seminal book, *Gödel, Escher, Bach: An Eternal Golden Braid* by Douglas Hofstadter links the themes of regularity and recursion as found in the works of mathematician Gödel, artist Escher and baroque musician Bach. It uses this as a basis for talking about cognition and intelligence in computing, which was pretty forward-thinking for a 1979 book. But getting back on track, from my point of view, as a mathematician who adores the tessellating patterns of Escher, it's enough of a signpost to confirm to me that I'm looking in the right sphere of music.

The way to read Rougeux's piece and mine is essentially the same, whether static or moving. We are looking at a timeline, but showing the timeline in circular form rather than straight, and then showing the pitch of each individual note on the axis. What would be the y-axis on a normal horizontal timeline graph becomes the radius, or distance from the circle's centre, on a radial timeline graph.

We're actually not restricted to traditional horizontal timelines either – does anyone remember the video game Guitar Hero? Presenting a vertical moving 3D timeline … this game visualised notes of different pitches moving towards you, to be played when the note reached the "front" of the screen. But leaving Guitar Hero to one side, most ways of visualising music seem to be either horizontal or circular timelines.

Visualising musical themes

I wanted to add some more visual analysis to my *Water Music* animation, so I was able to add some static circular timelines. The following tried to highlight repeated patterns across sections of the
music as well as across different instrumental parts. I think it does
this reasonably at best but needs a certain amount of instruction
to the reader to understand the significance of highlighted sections
they are referring to (Figure 3.9.4).

FIGURE 3.9.4   *Handel's* Water Music – *"call and answer" themes.*

Orchestra sections

Another option was to make comparisons along the radius of the circle by looking at what different instruments were playing at different times, which could be done in a striking manner in this visualisation. This splits the visualisation into four copies, one for each section of the orchestra (woodwind, brass, violins, harpsichord), and displays the distances in pitch between "first" and "second" parts (first/second oboe; trumpet and horn; first/second violin and harpsichord right/left hand, respectively) (Figure 3.9.5).

FIGURE 3.9.5 *Handel's* Water Music *– orchestra sections.*

As mentioned above, there's little doubt that the attraction of a circular depiction comes from the iconic shape and image of a vinyl record. Without even realising it, I think that was also one of the reasons behind my all-black background choice. But the vinyl album metaphor can be used to visualise many more elements in music than just the pitch.

OddityViz

In 2017, UK-based information designers Valentina D'Efilippo and Miriam Quick created OddityViz – a series of vinyl record-themed static visualisations about David Bowie's *Space Oddity* track, which was to win a silver award at that year's Information is Beautiful Awards. Here are two of their works below, focusing on "structure" and "emotion". The full suite of ten records (originally displayed together as an art exhibition piece) can be found at oddityviz.com (Figure 3.9.6)

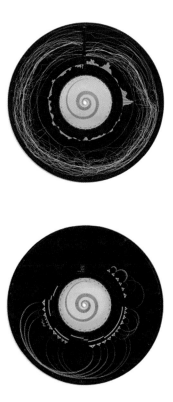

FIGURE 3.9.6 *Oddityviz: 10. Emotions and 6. Structure – Valentina d'Efilippo and Miriam Quick.*

This inspired me to think that when it comes to visualising music, it's possible to visualise so much more than just the notes, parts and pitches. If I took pitch out of the equation, I could depict a lot more other dimensions using length, shape and colour.

The image below looks at all of the instrumental parts, with each instrument in a different colour. The marks indicate note duration, whether a trill was played, and whether the note was not in the original key of D major. Although the image resolution isn't perfect, I was able to see a lot more about the melody's structure and reliance on triplicates of three *staccato* notes, which show up as unconnected dots, as well as the middle third being played in a different key, indicated by much more white areas (Figure 3.9.7).

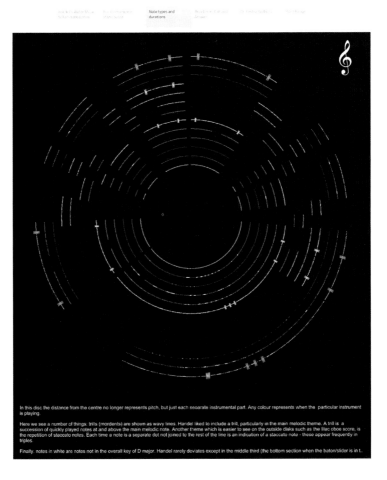

FIGURE 3.9.7 Handel's Water Music – note types and durations.

Encoding pitch in portrait form

But I felt that I hadn't answered all the questions I was looking for. I could see some of the repetitions between the first and third sections, but that's because I knew they were there and could point them out to the reader. It's not at all easy to see this within the context of a circular timeline – we like to see similar things next to each other or at the very least aligned at the same angle. This would mean breaking out of the circular visualisation structures for the first time in this project.

As I looked for more inspiration, I came across the following image by Maria Tsirodimitri, Head of Design at the Mo Ibrahim Foundation in London. Maria visualised the different parts of a piece of music by assigning a colour to each note, in a horizontal timeline form. Crucially, the legend element used a colourful but cyclical palette.

Since music scales repeat every thirteen notes (for piano players, that's seven white and five black in every octave, with the thirteenth note repeating the first, an octave higher), this shows us the flow of the melodies regardless of octave and allows us to compare parts playing the same notes at different octaves. So, for example, a melody played on the oboe and the bassoon an octave apart will show the same. Similarly, the colour hue difference between any two notes a semitone apart will be consistent even if you have gone up from one octave to another (Figure 3.9.8).

Maria's work is cut into sections, partly, I think, to allow a portrait-style artwork to fit on one page, but I was able to use this idea to do something similar, looking at three sections of music, to see how similar Sections 1 and 3 were. Now that they are aligned and depicted by discrete colour bands, the comparisons come alive in a better way than we could manage in circular form (Figure 3.9.9).

The look is a little different – there are more sustained gaps where instruments don't play, and there are more short gaps between notes, due to the short, staccato notes I mentioned above. But this shows the "A/B/A" nature of the piece better than I'd hoped. I knew from listening repeatedly, that after the bit in the middle, the same themes returned. Until I visualised it this way, I didn't know it was *exactly* the same, note for note, part for part!

First | Challenging

Idea

WHERE 'ER YOU WALK

FIGURE 3.9.8   *Visualising music – Maria Tsirodimitri.*

Visualising the data showed me something I hadn't picked up on even though I'd repeatedly listened to the music. This left me really pleased how the simplest of all the visualisations showed this so well, and finally did a good job of visualising some of the structural themes that Handel used in the music.

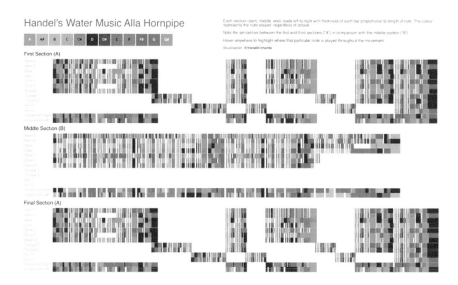

FIGURE 3.9.9 *Handel's* Water Music *– visualised by section.*

Individual parts

I wasn't finished yet – I wondered if there was a more appealing visual way I could display this in a circular fashion. Now that I had the idea of "normalising for pitch", in other words playing the note D will show in bright red, whatever the octave and whatever the instrument, the visual look of what I was able to produce opened up different ideas. Below is the main violin part visualised, alongside the rest of the string section for comparison – note how a small multiple allows us to compare between parts (Figure 3.9.10).

This has just scratched the surface of what is possible analytically and artistically – in converting music into data then the possibilities are endless. I don't intend to demonstrate much beyond the *Water Music* examples, since although I've taken the ideas introduced in this chapter and used them to visualise several more musical pieces, there are enough concepts here to demonstrate many ways of encoding music without exploring many further pieces. I'll leave that up to you!

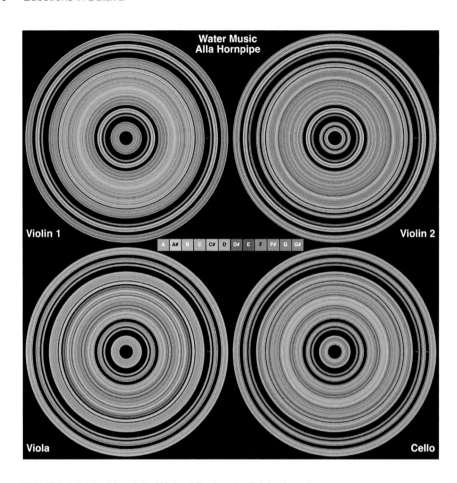

FIGURE 3.9.10 *Handel's* Water Music *– individual parts.*

Revisiting Pachelbel's *Canon*

But I couldn't resist revisiting Pachelbel's *Canon*, the first Baroque piece that inspired me to dig into visualising music. Again, an animated version of this which rotates in accompaniment to the actual music exists, but below is a still poster-style version which visually demonstrates the progression of melodic themes through all the repeating sections of the piece. You might recognise the inner black rotation as being remarkably similar across every section, and that might be either because you know the music or you're familiar with Rougeux's visualisation earlier in the chapter (Figure 3.9.11).

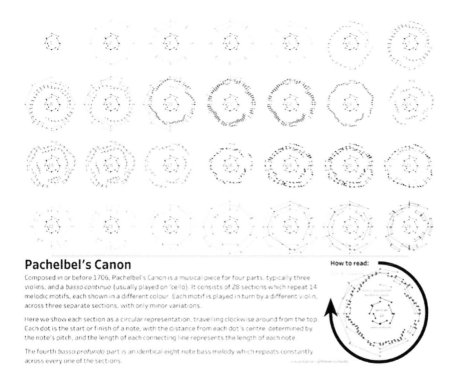

FIGURE 3.9.11 **Pachelbel's** Canon.

Conclusion

If you want to visualise music, there are so many options across tone, pitch, tempo, structure, volume and notation that there are few better sources for static visualisations. Then, add in real-time animation and accompanying music, and the possibilities just increase further. With very little consistent data visualisation by way of rules and convention, apart from conventional musical staves, this gives so much potential to the data visualisation designer to create something unique. I certainly recommend it.

Chapter **3.10**

What are Truchet tiles?

Everything starts from a dot.

Wassily Kandinsky

Generative art

The thinking behind this chapter and this question arises from the theme of generative art. Generative art is growing noticeably in popularity – many notable data visualisation practitioners and data artists are beginning to produce striking and often highly artistic creations.

With my own preference for data art, creative visualisations and poster-style static output that would look great on display, I had been wondering if generative art would represent a natural progression for me. It could certainly be something that would be the next stage in my own personal development, or a means to creating something new to add to my increasingly eclectic data visualisation portfolio.

At the start of 2021, the hashtag #genuary2021 began to proliferate on Twitter, full of examples of generative art, with each day having a different "rule" to guide participants. It wasn't a new concept by any means, but this was the first time it had really come to my

DOI: 10.1201/9781003240211-28

own attention. Though I am not in any way a coder, it did make me wonder if there was a way that I could participate in the initiative using my own skills and software tools in data visualisation.

But to further investigate this concept, or to understand what was being shared, I needed to understand a bit more what generative art is. Wikipedia defines it as "art that in whole or in part has been created with the use of an autonomous system" – the implication being that it is created by something non-human, and that this process in itself determines features of the artwork without human intervention.

In other words, in the context of generative art shown on Twitter, we are talking computer-generated and random/algorithm-driven art. Crucially, one word that doesn't get mentioned as the input or medium for generative art is "data".

It's important to understand that at the time of writing the field of generative art is very much linked with the fields of non-fungible tokens (NFT). Digital art, and generative art in particular, has been an early use case for NFTs, because of the ability of blockchain technology to assure the unique signature and ownership of NFTs. So, the concept of ownership of such digital art pieces can be crucial, and potentially also means that the field could become quite lucrative. And it's a reason why I can't just take any example of generative art I might see online and include it in this publication!

One data visualisation expert who is moving into the field of generative art is Nadieh Bremer. Already the holder of many Information is Beautiful Awards and co-participant in the *Data Sketches* project and book (with Shirley Wu), Nadieh has begun to create generative art pieces. One such piece, named Genesis, from the Wanderlust collection, is shown in Figure 3.10.1.

As Nadieh explains, technically the image isn't 100% pure generative art either because she is using the data of an Ethereum block, where each shape represents a transaction that happened in a specific Ethereum block, and the shapes are sized and given shape according to their value transferred/type of transaction.

However, the colours applied and positions are totally random, which forms the pure generative part of the image. And even though I may, personally, have very little understanding of what an Ethereum block is, I appreciate the wit of including it as an integral part of the image to understand the "meta" nature of that particular design choice.

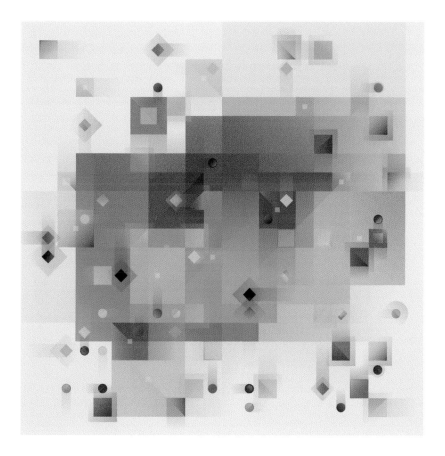

FIGURE 3.10.1 Genesis *(Wanderlust Collection) – Nadieh Bremer.*

I've certainly been inspired by generative art before – the work of Saskia Freeke inspired my *Hitchhiker's Guide* visualisation, as detailed in Chapter 2.7 (on unnecessary visualisations) but however abstract-looking or random-looking my data art style visualisations have been, I've always preferred to stay true to my data visualisation roots and generate output using data, however trivial or tenuous the source might be. However, if Nadieh Bremer still also uses an element of data for part of the generative art above, then perhaps crossover creations aren't as unusual as I might think.

Truchet tiles

With these ideas in mind, two data visualisation practitioners and friends had independently started conversations with me about

Truchet tiles – they had both recently discovered them, and both knew me well enough to know that it would be a subject that would pique my interest. These people both saw Truchet tiles and thought of me and the possibilities for future visualisations. But what are Truchet tiles and how could I use them for my next data visualisation idea?

Truchet tiles are tiles that are not fully rotationally symmetric and are designed so that when placed squarely in a grid they generate interconnecting patterns. If the tiles are placed systematically, then the new design may look equally regular, but when placed seemingly randomly then new random patterns emerge.

The most famous and simple Truchet tiles are known as Smith tiles – two diametrically opposed quarter-circles as shown below (Figure 3.10.2).

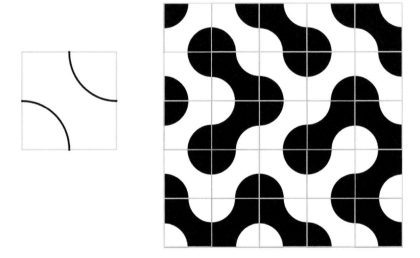

FIGURE 3.10.2   *Tessellating Truchet tiles – using Smith tiles.*

By this point I have decided that Truchet tiles are going to be my entry into a generative art style visualisation. I maintain that it doesn't qualify as generative art per se, since it will still be designed by me and generated by data, but my graphic generated from Truchet tiles will definitely be inspired by it. And ideally for me, I can create these tiles in exactly the same way that I love to create other types of visualisations, essentially as a small multiple grid of squares, and by designing, creating and positioning my own polygons.

I know now that I have the idea on how to go about this technically – but I wanted to look for something with more variety than the Smith tiles, since Smith tiles can be placed in two different orientations only. When I came across a blog page from Christopher Carlson, a US-based designer specialising in geometric design, that looked into more complex examples, then I knew I had my source of inspiration. Carlson designs his tiles to use multiple sizes in multi-scale Truchet patterns.

A multi-scale Truchet pattern, so that some tiles were 1×1 size, some were 2×2 and some 3×3, for example, was my initial first idea and could certainly be a more advanced project to try in the future! But even within the constraints of using tiles of the same shape and size as each other, he designs 15 separate overlapping tiles which tile together in grid form, which allows for much more variety in resulting pattern than the two simple Smith tiles. These individual tiles will be shown further on in this chapter as part of my final output.

I mentioned above that my visualisation would remain data-driven, however random or generative it would appear in nature. So, my final question was around the underlying data – what could generate its own Truchet tile grid? And then could we see similarities, differences and patterns in tile grids generated using different data from the same category?

I could have chosen any manner of things – in the end, I decided on opening passages from famous books, poems and songs, with the idea of somehow encoding each of the first 64 words into a number 1–15 to select one of the Truchet tiles. The best, and, to my mind anyway, most fun way I could think of to assign a value to a given word in true almost-random style was to use the Scrabble score of each word to choose the tile. I would then have a pseudo-random generated tile for each work of literature. Inspired by Shakespeare, Orwell, Dr. Seuss, and the Beatles, among others, I then had the data I needed.

Below is my final version – starting with the "how to read" page in order to explain the 15 different Truchet tiles designed by Carlson and explained above (Figure 3.10.3).

This is followed by an example of one of my generated tiles, in both black on white and white on black, since I couldn't decide which I liked best! This particular tile uses the first 64 words of Lewis Carroll's *Jabberwocky* (Figure 3.10.4).

Truchet tiles

are square two-coloured tiles, not generally fully symmetric, designed to tessellate and generate more shapes as they tile together. The simplest examples were devised by Smith (1987) shown right.

The below tiles, using three possible join locations on each side, are more complex examples as designed by Christopher Carlson. Each design on the main page is set out as an 8x8 grid, with each of 64 squares using one of the fifteen tile designs below. The tiles align and overlap at the dotted lines. The pattern on each tile is generated by the first 64 words from a number of classic novels, poems or songs (hover to see), and each word's Scrabble score generates the following pattern:

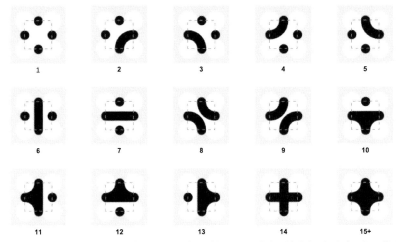

Also shown is the reverse (white pattern / black background) overall design alongside the original, since they look pretty good too!

FIGURE 3.10.3   *Truchet tiles – 15 tiles used in Truchet tiles for literature visualization.*

Truchet Tiles from Literature

Jabberwocky
Lewis Carroll

Uses single tiled "winged" tile design from Christopher Carlson
https://christophercarlson.com/portfolio/multi-scale-truchet-patterns/
visualisation: @theneilrichards

Choose Tile   Jabberwocky - Lewis Carroll

FIGURE 3.10.4   Jabberwocky – *Truchet tiles from literature.*

First | Challenging | Idea

Conclusion

As always, the process towards my final visualisation was a journey of questions and discovery, this time learning more about generative art and finding a very specific tile pattern that can be used, before settling on a data-driven solution. Truchet tiles for me became a very specific destination to one of those particular journeys, but my hope is that in touching on both of these avenues that it inspires readers to explore their own ideas – either for true generative art, for data-driven generative art-style pieces, or perhaps both.

3.11

How do you create 31 visualisations in a month?

I think as an artist you have to reinvent yourself every day.

Damien Hurst

Setting the challenge

It seems appropriate to end with this chapter, in relation to a challenge I gave myself, during a month in 2020. I chose a music album and wondered if I could visualise it in a different way every day for a month. But in addition to the "how" it makes sense to look at lessons learned, in relation to questions we've discussed in different chapters in the book.

We can even briefly cover the question "Why?". It would be easy to dismiss it as madness, of course, and you'd probably be right. But I found it was a great, ambitious target to set myself to force me into really getting immersed into a subject and its associated datasets, and to impose my own tight deadlines on visualising my way out of a bit of a creative slump.

Producing and publishing one visualisation a day meandered from being a fun project to sometimes a bit of a millstone, and there were certainly times when I regretted choosing a 31 day month such

DOI: 10.1201/9781003240211-29

as May instead of a shorter month such as February, but the satisfaction of the completed project proved, as it so often does in challenges like this, well worth it.

My self-imposed project came from an idea of wanting to visualise an album. In "How do you visualise music?" I introduced the idea of visualising the actual music within a tune and divided everything between "music" and "everything else". This was more of an attempt to look more into the possibilities of the "everything else" to create a visual record (no pun intended) around an album.

Straight away, the lessons from two more chapters come to mind. First, I asked "Why create unnecessary visualisations?" This is, absolutely, an unnecessary project. It's a challenge for me, and a passion project for me. I did expect some of my readers to appreciate it, and many of them did, but that was almost secondary.

It almost goes without saying that the work needed to create 31 visualisations, not least the work to find, prepare and clean the data, means that the project needs to be something that represents enjoyment for the creator. And anything that goes into this much detail on one subject fits our definition of an unnecessary visualisation perfectly.

At this point, I haven't mentioned the subject of my visualisation yet – I chose the album *Flood* by They Might Be Giants. A favourite of mine from 1990, it wasn't an attempt to convert others to my musical taste from three decades ago, it was simply chosen because the topic of most of the songs was light-hearted and fun, almost frivolous, so it didn't seem disrespectful or out of place to convert it into 31 sets of colourful, geometric images based around words, syllables and letters.

The other reason for choosing it was because I knew that one song had just two words and another song was less than thirty seconds long. The quirky album had quirky metadata to accompany it which I hoped would be seen in the various outputs – I knew I'd see some unusual findings and noticeable differences from track to track.

Second, I asked "What can I do when data is impossible to find?" Here we discussed that if data isn't out there on a particular topic, you'll probably need to record and create it yourself. In this case, most was available, having been fan sourced and published on the internet, but the process of converting song lyrics and their sentences, words, syllables and letters into several different Excel data files was a largely manual task. This had taken place over a few weeks before I launched into the visualising month of May before I took the plunge to create the first of 31 images. It certainly requires having your data ready up-front.

If you want to undertake such a project, I recommend having the vast majority of your data and at least 12 or so ideas ready before you start. Other ideas will evolve from these 12 as you get more immersed in the project, and your self-imposed deadline requires you to continue coming up with ideas on the fly, but you want to make a running start!

I knew that I wanted to focus on words, lines, syllables and letters, though I knew at the start that I may need to expand the scope to make it to day 31. I didn't want to visualise anything musical per se, although I think just one visualisation broke this rule slightly as I introduced chords used in each track. And because I was looking at music, with lots of data per track, I knew that there would be a lot of compact radial visualisations, and quite likely there would be a lot of small multiple visualisations, one for each song. Both of these scenarios suited my design preferences and visualisation style.

Prior inspiration

The idea wasn't entirely new. Stefanie Posavec, a UK-based designer and artist who we have already mentioned as co-collaborator in the Dear Data project with Giorgia Lupi, had previously visualised *Of the Blue Color of the Sky* by OK Go! – her visualisations were commissioned to form the artwork for the album cover. In Figures 3.11.1 and 3.11.2 we see two of the visualisations and the full "How to Read" section.

This proved to be a great spur to get started and an influence on the style of the overall look. My visualisations were going to be mostly black background with a bright colour for each song. And my track listing explanation with tracks written in each relevant colour took a very similar look to Stefanie's. Although at this point the need for one colour per song meant that I was already ruing my decision to choose an album with 19 tracks!

FIGURE 3.11.1   Of the Blue Color of the Sky *(visualisation) – Stefanie Posavec.*

FIGURE 3.11.2   Of the Blue Color of the Sky *(explanation) – Stefanie Posavec.*

31 Days of *Flood*

My project took place throughout May 2020, and I was pleased to hit my goal of producing a visualisation for each day. Figure 3.11.3 shows a collage of a selection of the visualisations (there were, of course, 31 in total) – the full project can be seen online at https:// public.tableau.com/app/profile/neil.richards/viz/flood7/floodintro.

First | Challenging | Idea

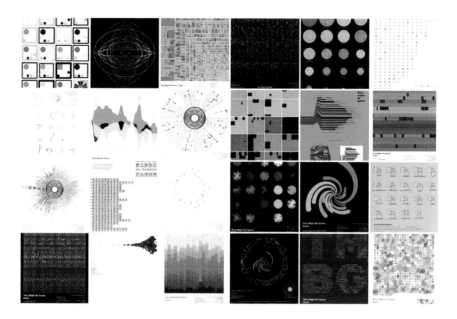

FIGURE 3.11.3 **31 days of** Flood.

In addition to the inspiration quoted above and the lessons relevant to the questions in this book already quoted for the preparation of the project, I'll summarise some more of the questions below which had relevance.

When are two visualisations better than one?

As mentioned above, the overall project's topic was an obvious candidate for small multiple visualisations. A handful of days fitted 19 songs nicely into a 5×4 grid, with the twentieth slot free for titles/credits or instructions. The example below, from day 16, also looks at each song individually, but using a 10×2 grid instead. A very simple visualisation that looks at the length of words in each song shows that many of the visualisations are stylised versions of quite simple charts. Probably a necessity in a project like this!

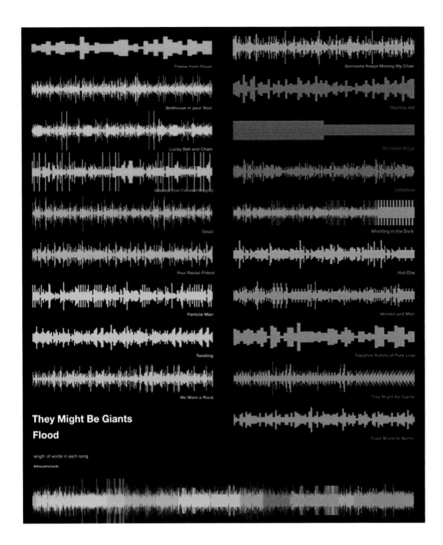

FIGURE 3.11.4   *31 days of* Flood – *day 16.*

Is white space always your friend?

It's probably quite clear from the majority of the images that the "data-ink ratio" is something that I eschew in favour of colour and impact. Figure 3.11.4, from day 16, is a perfect example of this. So, in many ways, Day 3, a step graph looking at cumulative word use over time, is the exception to the rule.

For many of the other charts, I was happy to fill the page with more data, and more colour, but here I've chosen minimal annotation and very little data ink with the exception of the title and lower panel. Not that that matters in the context of data ink, but it's also one of the few on white background rather than black, to accentuate the minimalist feel to this particular chart (Figure 3.11.5).

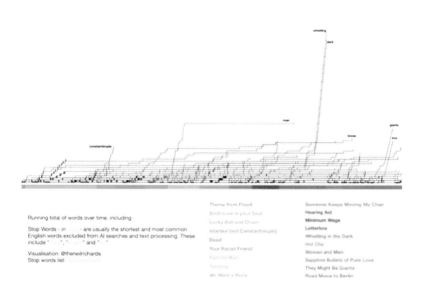

FIGURE 3.11.5   31 days of Flood – day 3.

Do we take data visualisation too seriously?

Here is the visualisation from day six. It's probably safe to say that almost nobody in the data visualisation world likes bubble charts. How can you read or take anything analytical from this? They say "whistling" and "dark" rather a lot, don't they, that's about it? Maybe that's true – and you can notice the above fact in rather a lot of the charts. There's a good reason for that – they sing "whistling in the dark" on repeat at the end of the song. But this breaks the rules on considering Gestalt principles, it breaks the white space rules, and there are probably a handful of other rules it breaks too.

This chart got a lot of positive reaction though, from fans of the band as well as the band themselves. It's fun to explore, it's colourful, it's impactful, and in some people's eyes at least, it would look great as a poster if the subject interested you. So, I'm delighted with my choice of a best practice-busting bubble chart here (Figure 3.11.6)!

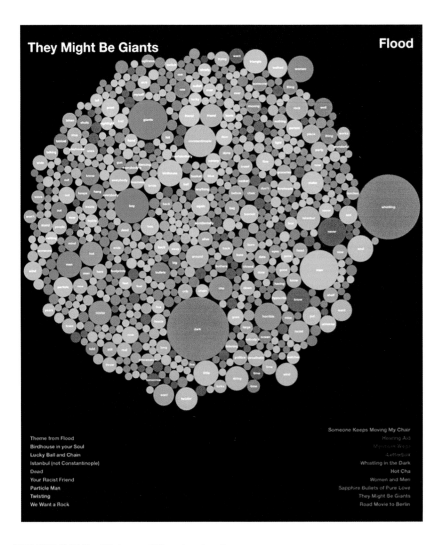

FIGURE 3.11.6   *31 days of* Flood – *day 6.*

What is design-driven data?

It was always likely that given 31 visualisations, I would want to recreate at least one to recreate a prior design. With the amount of data to hand, I was fortunate not to have to source additional data. Day 8 was a simple radial chart looking at length of words by syllable travelling around a radial timeline of the album.

I wanted to recreate the visualisation by Tiziana Alocci, a London-based information designer and lecturer, who created an album cover for German dance EP *Sum Over Histories* by visualising the musical elements of the tracks (Figure 3.11.7). This was a great cross-over opportunity – a chance to recreate a visualisation of physical music, which I could easily have included in "How do you

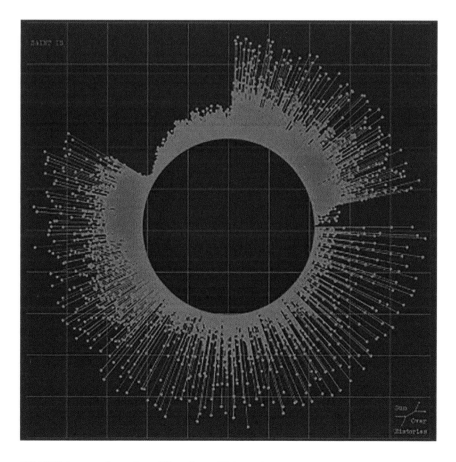

FIGURE 3.11.7 *Sum Over Histories – Tiziana Alocci.*

FIGURE 3.11.8   *31 days of* Flood *– day 8.*

visualise music?" but with music metadata rather than data on the actual musical notes. In this case, I used word length (Figure 3.11.8).

Does it matter if shapes overlap?

Figure 3.11.9 is the visualisation from day 29. We discussed overlapping shapes in the chapter of the same name – with so many disaggregated visualisations looking at words and syllables, there was always the opportunity for overlapping shapes to soften the "grid" style of the visualisation and draw the eye to the larger blocks. And, in this case too, to emulate the original visualisation which partially inspired it – namely "Plane Stupid" by Information is Beautiful, referenced in the visualisation itself.

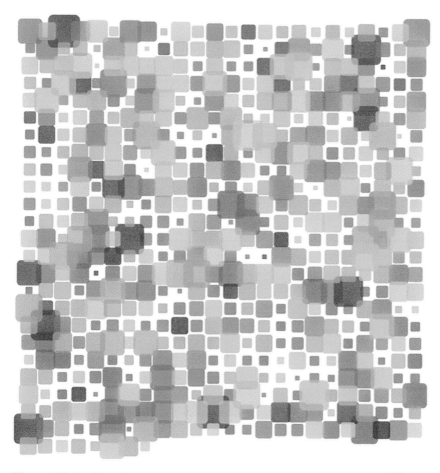

They Might Be Giants
Flood

All the lines from every song
Squares sizes by line length

visualisation: @thenedrichards

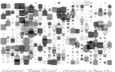

inspiration: "Plane Stupid" - Information is Beautiful

FIGURE 3.11.9   31 days of Flood – day 29.

Why do I use flowers to visualise data?

In the chapter where we discussed using flowers to visualise data I shared my love for that particular visualisation shape and metaphor. There's no doubt (to me) that it's a real opportunity to explore geometrical and radial visualisations to present them in a visually appealing manner, whatever the visualisation topic.

It's arguable whether you'd describe the resulting shapes from day 13's visualisation as flowers, but they evolved from the idea of radial display of songs' sections with lyric lines branching off them, in the knowledge that every track would give quite an individual-looking organic shape, but without knowing what those particular end shapes would look like (Figure 3.11.10).

First | Challenging | Idea

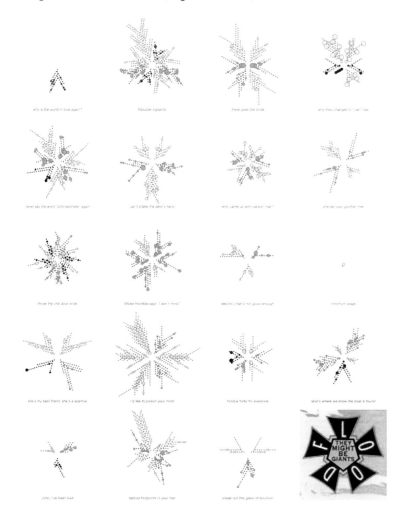

They Might Be Giants - Flood

Each song by sections with alternating lines
Words sized by number of syllables
intro, verse, **bridge**, chorus, outro
Visualisation: @theneilrichards

FIGURE 3.11.10   *31 days of* Flood *– day 13.*

What is the third wave of data visualisation?

I've partly structured the chapters of this book around the concept of waves of data visualisation, and the idea that in the current perceived "third wave", business intelligence tools can be much more custom. It's that mindset which is behind most, if not all, of the visualisations I create (certainly those that feature in this book), and hence each of the visualisations in the *Flood* project too.

I'm keen that this book is tool agnostic – there are unavoidable mentions of Tableau which is the tool I've learned, use professionally, and the tool that I take great enjoyment in creating the unconventional with. Twenty-six of the 31 visualisations used Tableau, either exclusively or predominantly, and the wide variety of outputs show that the ability of a tool to be "more custom" comes not just from the capability of the tool itself, but just as importantly from the design mentality of the user and their willingness to stretch creatively and technically.

And that said, it's important to emphasise during the course of this project, to fulfil some of my ideas and ensure that the full complement of 31 visualisations were hit, there were several occasions where I used a different tool to get the end result. A suite of visualisations showcasing a variety of outputs across the same data is a perfect opportunity to take advantage of the capabilities of different tools, and there will always be examples where a different tool has better, faster capabilities for the specific output that you're interested in. Day 14's stream graph was generated using RAWGraphs (Figure 3.11.11).

There were other potential examples for inclusion in this section linking different images to different chapter questions: day 18 represented another example of using an album cover as inspiration for data visualisation, with a nod to *How can I take inspiration from album covers?* It felt right to choose an album cover from the same band, albeit not the album cover of the album I was visualising which would have been a design step too far and was another standout fun project to include within the suite.

And day 5 was an attempt to recreate the idea introduced in "What are Data Portraits?" representing each track as a Data Portraits style data badge. I wasn't overly happy with the end result in this instance but I enjoyed the challenge and creative process of using the metadata I had to produce a data portrait style output with one "badge" for each song.

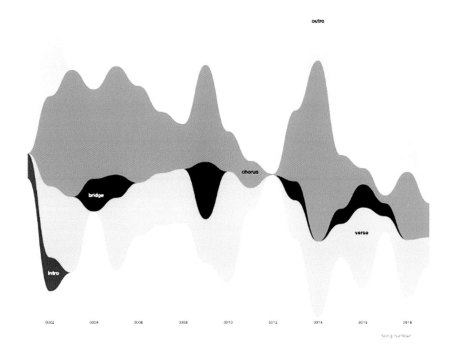

**They Might Be Giants
Flood**

FIGURE 3.11.11 *31 days of* Flood *– day 14.*

In summary, I needed three things for this project before I started in order to give it a chance of success and/or completion:

1. Several large, curated, datasets
2. Several pre-formed design ideas
3. An open, enquiring mind to find inspiration and develop new ideas on the fly
4. Time

I know that time (4) is very often the limiting factor. In my case, this was an ideal project during times of pandemic-induced lockdown, and the self-imposed time limit focused me to keep working and get to the end of the challenge. But if you haven't timestamped your project, then time is no longer a crucial factor.

First | Challenging | Idea

It's my belief that by continually questioning the principles you learn and developing your own new design questions that you have the inspiration to find and create the first of these things (1), as well as the confidence, the learned thought processes and eventual experience to have the second of these things in your data visualisation portfolio (2).

And you're very unlikely to make it this far into a project without the enquiring mind, experimental nature and most of all the enjoyment to make it to the end with new ideas that you can put into practice (3).

Conclusion

A month-long challenge focuses the mind to experiment, be creative and commit to ideas. Thirty-one visualisations is a chance to challenge every one of the chapters in this book and more – after all, if there is an advantage gained and lesson learned from each chapter, there are 31 times the opportunity to experience that in projects such as this.

And if you are pleased with the results of even one of your visualisations, having had the opportunity to learn from the process of creating many others, you can count it a success – a success hard-earned is even more of a success.

End of Section III

Right from the start of the book, we've walked through a wide range of questions eventually leading to many of the ideas and projects that have influenced my own data visualisation projects.

Your own journey will be different - you will have different ideas and different inspirations. It hasn't been my aim to provide you with a specific list of exactly the right questions to ask in order to start a creative project, far from it. But my hope is that the book has encouraged you challenge the status quo, to consider the consequences of bending, breaking or ignoring usual practices, to be inspired by designs and practitioners in data visualisation and further afield, or to simply take your own curiosity further by trying ideas in visualisation you haven't seen before.

If your experience is anything like mine, your skills and creativity will improve, and you will enjoy every step of the way.

Index